W9-ASJ-577

THE EARLY SPANISH BALLAD

by David William Foster

Along with Golden Age comedy, the ballad tradition of Spain has been undoubtedly the literary
form of greatest vitality within Hispanic culture
and of greatest recognition by scholars and writers
outside the Peninsula. As a result, academic study
of the Spanish ballad is a particularly prestigious
activity; omission of a consideration of this body
of traditional literature would be to misrepresent
seriously the totality of the Spanish literary
heritage.

This present volume, therefore, is included in the
Spanish Section of the Twayne World Authors
Series, despite the fact that the ballads to be considered (the seminal production of the fourteenth
and fifteenth centuries) are all anonymous and
unattributable in nature to any known artist.
Nevertheless, the quality of these untitled and unsigned compositions is so great, and the growth of
a ballad tradition by known poets during and after
the Renaissance, unparalleled in other European
countries, so extraordinarily rich in results as to
make a discussion of the beginnings of the ballad
tradition an imperative in a series that is committed to giving a balanced panorama of Spanish
literature.

This study focusés on the general characteristics
of the compositions involved and their thematic
and stylistic classification as well as the competing
theories on origin and authorship of the late
medieval ballads. Central attention is given an
examination of those texts that represent a modern
canon of the traditional Spanish ballad. Our
assumption is that each text has come to constitute
a literary monument and that it is possible to
discuss the anonymous medieval ballad in the
esthetic terms of contemporary critical modes. In
approaching in this way a corpus of texts that have
attracted more interest for the erratic nature of

(continued on back flap)

their origins and spread, the hope is to justify in critical terms the often expressed intuition that the ballads are in fact the best poetry of the pre-Renaissance in Spain.

ABOUT THE AUTHOR

David William Foster, a native of Seattle, born in 1940, studied at the University of Washington, where he received the Ph.D. in Romance Languages and Literature in 1964. Currently Professor of Spanish at Arizona State University, Professor Foster has taught also at the University of Washington, Fresno State College, Vanderbilt University, and the University of Missouri. During the Fall 1967 Semester, Professor Foster was a Fulbright Lecturer in Linguistics at the National Institute for Foreign Languages in Buenos Aires and the National University in La Plata, Argentina. Professor Foster's research interests include, in addition to medieval Spanish poetry, Spanish bibliography, Spanish linguistics and the contemporary novel of Spain and Argentina. Support for research has come from the U.S. Office of Education, the Fulbright Program, the Research Councils of the University of Missouri and Arizona State University, the American Philosophical Society and the National Endowment for the Humanities. Scholarly papers include over seventy titles published or scheduled for publication and books and monographs with the university presses of the Universities of Washington, Missouri, Kentucky, and North Carolina. Professor Foster also writes frequent reviews on contemporary River Plate literature for *Books Abroad* and is a member of the Bibliography Committee for Spanish 6 and 7 sections of the Modern Language Association.

Professor Foster is also the author of the Twayne World Authors Series study on The Marqués de Santillana.

TWAYNE'S WORLD AUTHORS SERIES

A Survey of the World's Literature

Sylvia E. Bowman, Indiana University

GENERAL EDITOR

SPAIN

Gerald E. Wade, Vanderbilt University

EDITOR

The Early Spanish Ballad

(TWAS 185)

TWAYNE'S WORLD AUTHORS SERIES (TWAS)

The purpose of TWAS is to survey the major writers—novelists, dramatists, historians, poets, philosophers, and critics—of the nations of the world. Among the national literatures covered are those of Australia, Canada, China, Eastern Europe, France, Germany, Greece, India, Italy, Japan, Latin America, the Netherlands, New Zealand, Poland, Russia, Scandinavia, Spain, and the African nations, as well as Hebrew, Yiddish, and Latin Classical literatures. This survey is complemented by Twayne's United States Authors Series and English Authors Series.

The intent of each volume in these series is to present a critical-analytical study of the works of the writer; to include biographical and historical material that may be necessary for understanding, appreciation, and critical appraisal of the writer; and to present all material in clear, concise English—but not to vitiate the scholarly content of the work by doing so.

The Early Spanish Ballad

By DAVID WILLIAM FOSTER
Arizona State University

Twayne Publishers, Inc. :: New York

CARNEGIE LIBRARY
LIVINGSTONE COLLEGE
SALISBURY, N. C. 2814

Copyright © 1971 by Twayne Publishers, Inc.

All Rights Reserved

LIBRARY OF CONGRESS CATALOG CARD NUMBER: 79–152012

MANUFACTURED IN THE UNITED STATES OF AMERICA

861.04
F 754

SD. 4.76

1/24/73

85867

Sino yo, triste, cuitado
que vivo en esta prisión,
que ni sé cuándo es de día
ni cuándo las noches son
sino por la Marusiña
que me descuita en su amor.

Preface

Along with the Golden Age comedy, the ballad tradition of Spain
has been undoubtedly the literary form of greatest vitality within
Hispanic culture and of greatest recognition by scholars and writers
outside the Peninsula. By the same token, the Spanish ballads have
evoked a large body of criticism, largely theoretical in nature and
devoted to the debate on ballad origins, diffusion of texts, and the
interpretive problems associated with the dominant scholarly position. As a result, and unlike other countries, where ballad research
is quasi-anthropological rather than literary, academic study of the
Spanish *romances,* as the native ballads are called, is a particularly
prestigious activity; omission of a consideration of this body of
traditional literature would be to misrepresent seriously the totality
of the Spanish literary heritage.

This present volume, therefore, is included in the Spanish Section
of the Twayne World Author Series, despite the fact that the ballads
to be considered (the seminal production of the fourteenth and
fifteenth centuries) are all anonymous and unattributable in nature
to any known artist. Indeed, one basic set is made up of little more
than fragments of the longer—and equally anonymous—medieval
epics. Nevertheless, the quality of these untitled and unsigned
compositions is so great, and the growth of a ballad tradition by
known poets during and after the Renaissance, unparalleled in
other European countries, so extraordinarily rich in results, as to
make a discussion of the beginnings of the ballad tradition an
imperative in a series that is committed to giving a balanced panorama
of Spanish literature.

Our procedure in this presentation will be to review the enormous
interest the ballads of the fourteenth and fifteenth centuries have
attracted from literary scholarship. Discussion will focus not only
on the general characteristics of the compositions involved and
their thematic and stylistic classification; we will also consider the
competing theories on origin and authorship of the late medieval
ballads. The vast majority of criticism written to date has ap-

proached the ballads from the "genetic" point of view, stressing how a ballad comes into being and survives. The bulk of our study, in contrast, will center on an examination of those texts that represent a modern canon of the traditional Spanish ballad. Our assumption will be that each text has come to constitute a literary monument and that, despite the highly questionable authority of its authorship as a finished poetic composition, it is nevertheless possible to discuss the unquestionably excellent piece of art that is the medieval ballad in the aesthetic terms of contemporary critical modes. Although the genesis of the ballad may differ from that of, say, a sonnet, both are poetic compositions that admit the full range of analytical textual analysis. In approaching in this way a corpus of texts that have attracted more interest for the erratic nature of their origins, we hope to justify in critical terms the often expressed intuition that the ballads are in fact the best poetry of the pre-Renaissance period in Spain.

Contents

Chronology

711   Moslem conquest of Spain.

1140   *Poema de Mio Cid (Poem of the Cid)*, only epic poem surviving virtually intact.

1421   A Majorcan student in Italy copies a ballad into his notebook, which becomes the earliest surviving text.

c 1440   Earliest known version of "Infante Arnaldos," one of the best-known ballads.

1449   The Marqués de Santillana uses the word *romance* with scorn in the famous *Prohemio é carta (Prologue)* to his works.

c 1471   A British Museum MS contains glosses of several important novelesque and Carolingian ballads.

1492   Conquest of Granada.

1492   Antonio de Nebrija (or Lebrija) quotes generously from the early ballads in his *Gramática castellana (Castilian Grammar)*.

c 1505   Several early ballads are included in the *Cancionero musical de los siglos XV y XVI (Musical Songbook of the XVth and XVIth Centuries)*, the "Palace Songbook."

1535   Juan de Valdés defines the word *romance* in his *Diálogo de la lengua (Dialogue on Language)*.

c 1548   The first printed collection of ballads, Martin Nucio's *Cancionero sin año (Undated Songbook)* or *Cancionero de romances de Ámberes (Songbook of Ballads)*, is published in Antwerp (then part of the Spanish Empire).

1595   Ginés Pérez de Hita's *Guerras civiles de Granada (The Granada Civil Wars)* reproduces many frontier ballads.

1600–   *Romancero general (The General Book of Ballads)*, composed
1605   entirely of pieces by "professional" court poets, marks the first major artistic departure from the framework of the early, medieval ballad and introduces the flowering of the form in subsequent centuries.

1815   Jakob Grimm's *Silva de romances viejos (Flower of Old Ballads)* is the first example of Romantic interest in the Spanish ballad.

1896   Ramón Menéndez Pidal publishes his study on the Infantes de Lara, the first major traditionalist document.

CHAPTER 1

Literary and Cultural Backgrounds

I Basic Concepts

A NY definition of the European ballad is only partially adequate in describing the similar production of Spain. For example, the following characterization, taken from the *Encyclopedia of Poetry and Poetics*[1] is indicative of the problems of orientation immediately presented: "The 'folk,' 'popular,' or 'traditional' ballad is a short narrative song preserved and transmitted orally among illiterate or semiliterate people" (p. 62). Accurate enough, this description points out appropriately the short, narrative, and musical nature of the traditional European ballad. However, what Hispanic scholars would find most needed modification here is the emphasis on the folk nature of the compositions involved. Like the vast majority of ballads in other European countries, the Spanish ballad is noted for its preservation among "illiterate or semiliterate" segments of the population; in contrast, however, in the Peninsula the ballads uncovered and discussed so widely during the last hundred years are in themselves only marginally to be considered folk literature. While many possess characteristics associated with folk poetry—such as formulistic diction[2]—the overwhelming evidence would indicate that the actual composition lay in the hands of skilled minstrels who satisfied the certain "aesthetic demands" of their popular audience. Preservation and transmission, while often carried out by illiterate minstrels during our present age, are thought to have rested, during the formative period, with performers who, while not themselves poets in any sophisticated sense of the word, were able to select and to modify the items of their repertoire and to have established in this way the major and important variants, from an artistic point of view, that constitute the basis of modern anthologies of the Spanish ballad.

The major thrust, then, of any modification of a characterization of the European ballad in order to make it fit current opinion on the Spanish ballad would be in the direction of stressing acceptance by a popular audience of a type of composition that itself was not of folk origin. In the following paragraphs, we will extend this modification toward sketching more accurately the intermediary role of the ballad in Spain between the folk song, of interest to the anthropologist, and formal poetry, of interest to a cultivated elite and their literary scholars.

To begin with, it is well to recall the origin of the Spanish word for ballad: *romance*.[3] *Balada,* a loan-word from French, is used to refer to the autochthonous production of non-Hispanic areas. Indeed, the fact that Spanish has imported a separate word for these works is indicative of the desire to highlight the uniqueness in European balladry of the more traditional and longer-lived *romance*. *Romance* is the reflex of a Latin adverb, *romanice,* which, used in an expression like *loqui romanice* ("to speak in the Roman manner"), differentiated between the Roman speech, habits, traditions, and those that began to spring up in the colonized areas of the Roman conquest (in Spain, 219–19 B.C.). Curiously enough, the former is referred to by the adverb *latine,* derived from the noun used to refer to the cultivated language of the Roman artistic and governing aristocracy. *Romanice* referred to the relatively uncouth and untutored versions of the popular Italic dialects carried by the lower-class soldiers and their leaders to the areas of colonization. While the later administration of these areas resulted in the importation of individuals and the development of a regional culture whose speech was the refined dialect of the upper class, in the areas of colonization, the popular dialects prevailed among the majority of the population. Over the period of the Roman dominion and as a result of the normal communication gaps of the period, "Latin" as it was spoken outside of Rome fast became a cause of concern to language purists.[4] With the fall of the Roman Empire and the formation of regional feudal governments, widespread fragmentation of the already vague *romanice* manner took place. In its various forms, the adverb came to represent the individual Latin-derived speech of the areas of the Roman conquest. Still later, when regional literatures begin to emerge (roughly late twelfth and thirteenth centuries), *romance* (apocopation had dropped the unstressed penultimate *i*) is given a new meaning to distinguish those compositions in the vernacular that compete with literature, mostly by clerics and members of the clerical subculture, in Latin. The latter constitutes an unbroken tradition from the days of the Roman culture centered in Rome, while the new vernacular literatures, which will triumph in the fourteenth century with the beginning of the middle class, are a derivate tradition of basically Latin inspiration.[5] As we shall see below, in Spain the ballads are intimately linked to the epic and to the national chronicles, both of which are among the first extensive literary expression in the vernacular. Therefore, it is not surprising that during the period of ballad emergence (fourteenth and fifteenth centuries), this composition of almost exclusively non-Latinate derivation should come to be identified by the reflex of an adverb meaning in essence noncourtly and popular.

Nevertheless, despite the implication of the word *romance* and despite the long life which the ballad in Spain is to have as a form of popular, unrecorded culture, as Menéndez Pidal has stressed over and over again in his ground-breaking work on the subject, the Spanish *romance* is not in nature a popular work of literature.[6] While the meaning of "popular" that stresses "extensive and favorable reception" is appropriate to the Spanish ballad—uniquely so, as we have said, when one looks at the antiquarian nature of, say, the English or the Scottish ballad—"popular" in so far as it means "folk" or "anthropological as opposed to consciously aesthetic" is no longer an acceptable characterization of the *romance*. There is little doubt that the ballad in Spain, particularly when the compositions that we will be examining in this study were supplanted by the work of sophisticated court poets during the High Renaissance, entered the mainstream of folk literature in the Peninsula.[7] And there is also little doubt that folksingers that belonged to the lower classes mentioned by Santillana in his *Prologue* . . .[8] forgot, improvised, and generally modified the works that had become part of their popular tradition. The essentially inferior nature, from an artistic point of view and from the vantage point of the original compositions that have been preserved, of versions discovered from the last century on shows that the process of modification that has taken place during the last five hundred years has not been based on aesthetic criteria. Not that it should have been. The only point is that compositions, once part of the folk tradition, have undergone a treatment quite different from their handling during the period of formation by trained ballad minstrels.[9] As comments on reported versions have pointed out time and again, the folk tradition of the Spanish ballad, since it is dealing with an oral tradition and not a written and easily consulted one, has been subject to all of the garbling and changing for sociological and nonliterary reasons associated with any phenomenon of the nonliterate.

Thus the Spanish ballad is popular only in so far as it became one type of folkloristic song and only in so far as it was subjected to normal nonliterary modification by subsequent handling. At the same time, Menéndez Pidal and his followers have preferred to stress the word "traditional" rather than popular for defining the developmental growth and spread of the compositions that entered the mainstream of popular culture. By "traditionalism," ballad scholars have meant to give precise form to the concept of a composition or of a cycle of compositions related thematically that have not been preserved in any one original or primary form. Unlike the court poetry, which was written as a literary composition[10] and associated with an individual author, the *romance,* while it may have originated as a finished literary composition and of necessity must have been given shape at a particular moment by an individual literary consciousness, tended to be received and treated as an anonymous work open to all sorts of suggestions for improvement and change. Thus a minstrel might sing a new ballad, inspired by his knowledge of epic literature, of the chronicles, of legends. If the original singer did not himself modify his song in subsequent performances of it, anyone who heard it and—probably imperfectly—remembered it felt no qualms about making whatever changes and additions required to attract the applause of the audience. Thus, like common coin, the ballads, which to begin with did not have their origins in a courtly context conducive of individual authorial rights, passed from hand to hand, changing for the better or for the worse as they went. It is for this reason that the dominant critical position on the Spanish ballad deemphasizes individual poetic composition. Not because the ballad is popular in origin, but simply because any attempt to discover an "original" version, much less attribute it to an individual poet-minstrel, has proven to be quite simply an impossible undertaking. The scholar must content himself either with compositions preserved in literary documents and anthologies contemporary with the beginnings of the ballad tradition, or with songs remembered and recited to him by some obliging representative of the vanishing popular folklore.

Ballad scholarship has preoccupied itself with these two manifestations and has contributed an enormous amount of fascinating material for analysis. We now possess a healthy quantity of compositions preserved by written records of the fourteenth and fifteenth centuries. These compositions are called *romances viejos* (old ballads), in order to distinguish them from the *romances nuevos*/ *romances artísticos* (new or artistic ballads) which begin to be written by trained and known poets of the Renaissance. We also have, thanks to efforts in the field, abundant examples of the descendants of the *romances viejos* as they have been preserved—and modified in the traditional manner—by modern representatives of the lower classes of medieval and feudal Spain. This means works gathered, not only from the populace of Spain, but also from the Spanish-American countries (generally felt to be inferior, perhaps because of the destitute and exhausted spirit of much of those segments that formed the bulk of the colonial population),[11] as well as the remainders of the Sephardim, the Spanish Jews expelled in the late fifteenth century and who carried their distinguished traditions, one of which was a rich balladry, throughout the Western Hemisphere. Indeed, many of the important segments of the ballads are preserved today only in the Sephardic tradition, any contemporary written versions having been lost over the centuries.[12]

To summarize what we have been outlining so far, the Spanish ballads, which necessarily began with individual compositions, of which no discernible record remains or is likely to be discovered, were spread with immense modification during the fourteenth and fifteenth centuries by a trained and unquestionably artistically sensitive minstrelsy. They early entered the mainstream of contemporary folklore traditions and continued to diffuse and to undergo modification far beyond the time when they ceased to be of interest to the emerging Renaissance culture. Meanwhile, a new tradition of balladry, uniquely Spanish, sprang up during the flowering of sixteenth-century literary art, inspired by the original medieval ballads but committed to the aesthetic principles of the day. Given this new direction by the greatest period of Spanish poetry, the ballad as a literary form has to this day been a major manifestation of poetic art in Hispanic literature.[13] It is in these ways that we have said that the medieval ballad in Spain is intermediary. It cannot be called popular and folkloristic, nor can it be called "artistic" in the sense of the conscious poetry of the movements of courtly love and the fifteenth-century *Cancioneros* (anthologies of poems by major poets of the period).

The body of medieval Spanish ballads, called the *Romancero*

viejo, exhibits five basic types, the last one of which is distinctly
marginal and foreshadows the compositions of the Renaissance
(which is, therefore, called the *Romancero nuevo*). Historic ballads
(romances históricos), frontier ballads *(romances fronterizos)*, fictional or novelesque ballads *(romances novelescos)*, Carolingian
ballads *(romances carolingios)*, and minstrel ballads *(romances
juglarescos)* constitute the basic types of compositions found in
the Hispanic ballad tradition and in the collections which gathered
them together during the early decades of the Renaissance in Spain.
In the chapters that follow we shall have occasion to discuss each
type in considerable detail and to analyze in depth representative
selections of this enormously popular poetry. For the moment,
we need only consider the general characteristics of each type before
going on to consider their relationship to other literature of the
late medieval period.

The historic ballads are poetic reflexes of what have been established as the six major Spanish epic traditions. Since the latter have
been lost almost in their entirety, aside from any other value the
ballads on epic subjects may have, they do constitute one important
source of knowledge for the themes and the attitudes of the missing
works. It is with reference to these compositions that theories of
ballad origins have developed and major controversies been enter-
tained. Prevailing opinion today is that, when the epics left the
great halls of the feudal lords, whom they were composed to entertain and to animate in warlike courage, the most impressive and
dynamic segments of them gained favor with the populace in the
marketplace and fairground. Encouraged to repeat only those
portions important from the point of view of narrative action and
the popular values of the feudal society then dominant, the performers soon converted their repertoire of long epic compositions
(several thousand lines) into many short and pithy compositions
that were either one small part of a longer epic passage or an anthology of several parts, with one composition possibly running
together passages from widely separated segments of the epic
poem. These compositions are what we call the ballads, and their
reception and conservation by a nonaristocratic and nonartistic
populace and minstrelsy are what is meant by the term "traditional"
when it is applied to them.[14]

The most respectable theory that has emerged to account for
this proposed relationship is Menéndez Pidal's "fragmentation

theory" of traditional origins. What is meant is that, rather than preceding the epics and/or growing up alongside them as a separate tradition, the ballads—at least those which deal with historic themes —have their origin in the breakup of the epics, a breakup which is due either to a decline in their appeal to the original audience made up of the feudal aristocracy (is this why no texts remain?) or to the inappropriateness of the long epic compositions when taken out into the street and to the gathering place of the humble populace. The latter's lack of the relaxed *otium* required to hear a complicated epic in its entirety must obviously have played some role in the immense job of tailoring that the significant passages of the epic went through in their development from extensive songs intended for performance over a period of several days, to short songs that could be sung in a matter of minutes to an ebullient and distracted crowd.[15] Indeed, although an earlier position believed just the opposite, it is now an accepted principle that the shorter compositions bespeak the greatest amount of traditional evolution. Beginning as longish epic fragments, by a process of attrition and honing to meet the circumstances and the demands of the word, a ballad eventually acquired the succinctness and brevity characteristic of the remaining texts.[16] This general principle should not be taken to mean that all ballads were honed in this manner. Quite the contrary. Many, particularly those discovered during the last hundred years in the field, show that the dilution of a text by extraneous material also occurred, although one might reasonably argue that such inflation took place after the formative period of fragmentation. In addition, much corruption of thematic material took place, and several typical works reveal the contamination of one ballad by another, borrowing from more than one epic, and so on. That is to say, the historic ballads are not neat abstractions of the epic materials. Moreover, it is not to be assumed that the shorter the ballad, although it may be more "evolved" or "traditionally developed," the better its artistry. Although Spain's Gracián may have echoed a basic aesthetic premise when he said in the seventeenth century that "that which is good, if short, is twice as good" (*Lo bueno, si breve, dos veces bueno*), ballad compactness does not by definition lead to noteworthy poetry. It can also conceivably produce elliptic nonsense.

Despite the fact that the Spanish ballad is much touted for its expressive economy and for the frequent abruptness of its transitions and denouements (when the latter have been retained at all), one cannot naively take as an article of critical faith that these compositions are any better for the process of truncation. The process of compression may be a significant aspect of the ballads, but each composition must still be examined individually on the basis of its own intrinsic merits before the announcement that intense economy equals good art can be made. Needless to say, this intense expressive economy in the ballads was a factor in the interest devoted to them by the Spanish vanguardistic poets after the First World War. [17] In any case, whatever the artistic value to be assigned to these works, existing evidence is overwhelmingly in support of the interrelated theses of fragmentation and developmental condensation. [18] At the same time, the historic ballads, along with the Carolingian ballads, are the only parts of the *Romancero viejo* that clearly reveal an origin in early literary works.

If the historic ballads are later versions of established epics, themselves constituting "official" literary versions of national history, the frontier ballads are generally considered to be compositions contemporaneous with the events that they relate. Dealing with the general subject of the latter years of the Reconquest (completed in 1492), these compositions are similar to the historic ballads in their brevity and in their participation in the process of traditional preservation and transmission. [19] Not all critics, however, are comfortable with the prevailing belief that the frontier ballads are of roughly the same period as the historical ones and that the former are a manifestation of the worthiness of the tempestuous events of the last, decisive phase of the Christian campaign against the remaining Moorish society. [20] Indeed, the fact that within a century a modified version of the frontier ballad, the Moorish ballads *(romances moriscos),* is to gain favor as one type of Renaissance version—sentimentalized, stylized, and romanticized—of the struggle between the two civilizations of the Peninsula tends to argue for a more artistic origin for the frontier ballad than simply as one traditional manifestation of the *Romancero viejo.* [21]

Nevertheless, whatever the exact period of genesis, the compositions on events directly related to the Reconquest underwent the same process of traditionalization associated with the epic-related and fragmented historical ballads. As close examination of these works reveals, the frontier ballad is less securely tied to a controlling ethical and moral point of view, as are the feudal historical ballads.

Instead of being songs in praise of Christian virtues and the Christian campaign, the frontier ballads are often striking in their ability to capture a non-Christian point of view. One could argue from this circumstance that the frontier ballads reflect the very real context of the frontier: a not unusual cordial and respectful cohabitation of two cultures that had lived side by side for centuries.[22] Where the historical ballads are of interest for the acceptance and survival among the humble populace of works indicative of aristocratic feudal values, the frontier ballads in parts belie the antagonism that we would assume to have been a necessary and integral part of the Reconquest.

Another segment of the *Romancero viejo* which tends to support the fragmentation theory in its development from epic compositions is the one encompassing the Carolingian ballads. As the name would indicate, these works are in part reflexes of various versions of the French epics (the Matter of France) centering on the paradigmatic figure of Roland and his king, Charlemagne. The origins of the several important traditional items is not always clear. Many may have been imported from France as popular or semipopular songs that, in translation, gained an audience in the Peninsula. Also, there appears to have been a hearty reception in Spain given to the French epic, and enough evidence exists to assert that many were translated in whole or in part into Spanish. One must note, however, that any incursion into the Peninsula of the French epic must have been associated with groups other than those involved in the creation and performance of the Spanish epics. The latter, as we have pointed out, were a manifestation of local feudal society. The French epics—which we may assume were of the same origin in France, although this is by no means a settled question[23]—were likely to have been imported into Spain during the early thirteenth century when nascent Spanish literary culture was emerging in the monasteries.[24] The *mester de clerecía* (clerical minstrelsy),[25] as this early literary tradition is called, not only developed a religious literature influenced by Latin and French models, as well as local legends, but also shows an interest for more secular themes, as demonstrated by the anonymous *Libro de Apolonio (Book of Apolonius)* and *Libro de Alexandre (Book of Alexander)*. The fact that the *Chanson de Roland,* if not other epics, admits an anagogic religious interpretation that would be farfetched in the case of the Castilian Cid epic, may have also been a factor in the reception by

Spanish clerics of the Charlemagne stories.[26] Jules Horrent has studied this influence in detail[27] and Menéndez Pidal has analyzed one surviving fragment of a translation that likely served as the basis for some of the ballads.[28] Therefore, despite the foreign, exotic nature that the Charlemagne literature would have had in the Spain of the thirteenth century, there appears to be little question that a traditional ballad tradition developed based directly on Spanish translations and assorted reworkings of French epics.

In addition to those compositions representing fragments of longer versions of French epics, a number of the ballads that can be called Carolingian were composed as autonomous originals during the late fifteenth century when the older fragments first began to inspire a wave of independent creativity on the part of the popular minstrels. Nevertheless, as in the case of the historical ballads composed at this late date and the frontier ballads, of necessity composed later and as autonomous poems, the new Carolingian works entered the mainstream of the traditional process along with the older fragments to be discovered by field researchers during the last century. Perhaps it would be dangerous to generalize too much about the common nature of the Carolingian ballads. But it is true that their appeal does not reside in any reflection of Hispanic feudal values, and it is equally true that they derive from a literary tradition which, at least by the quantity and quality of remaining texts, did have an edge of sophisticated artistry over contemporary Hispanic poetry: no one doubts that the arts were given a greater impetus in France while Spain was still living from day to day with fratricidal feuds and the preoccupation of the Reconquest. Although it is possible to argue that any artistic artificiality of medieval French poetry is lost in the process of traditionalization, an issue open for discussion is whether or not the Carolingian ballads are important, rather than for national themes, for their quality as lyric poetry.

The fictional or novelesque ballads form a catchall category of generally exaggeratedly short compositions that easily rival any putative artistic excellence of the Carolingian works. Although some of them have been truncated to the point where one must appreciate frustrating ambiguity in order to assign them any value, many of them are among the most renowned and discussed examples of pre-Renaissance Spanish poetry. Their origins constitute an intriguing mystery. Some of them are about historical personages, suggesting some sort of relationship to historical, Carolingian, or frontier ballads. Others are characterized by a complete lack of reference to persons, places, or events that could serve as "fixes" for dating them or tracing their origins.

The last category of ballads is marginal to the *Romancero viejo* in that they are clearly the result of original composition rather than fragmentation from epics and similar longer works. We refer here to the minstrel ballads composed by the performers who took the epic fragments to the people. These performers in turn were probably filling a constant demand from their audience for more of the same, as well as satisfying an urge to turn their own skill in the revision of extant work to the creation of original texts. The origins of the minstrel ballads, then, must of necessity be miscellaneous. Some are inspired by the same epic fragments turned into historical and Carolingian ballads. Others are based on material from the emerging chronicle tradition, itself based in great part on the epic (indeed, some of our only evidence of the lost epics comes from the chronicles[29]). In the chapters that follow, we will not consider separately any of the minstrel ballads, but will consider them as one late manifestation of historical, frontier, Carolingian, or novelesque ballads.

Since these ballads were written as autonomous compositions ("written to form" is a common and descriptive phrase), they can be considered from one point of view as transitional phenomena, providing the link between the ballads which originated with the process of fragmentation and the acceptance in the late sixteenth and seventeenth centuries of the ballad as a distinct and valuable literary form deserving of the attention of cultivated poets. The quasi-sophisticated art of the *romances juglarescos,* while not prefiguring in any teleological sense the purposeful artistry of the *Romancero nuevo,* does bespeak a growing awareness of the appropriateness of the ballad form for original poetry.

Up to this point we have discussed the early Spanish ballads in terms of the thematic groupings that emerged during the medieval period of development. Let us consider briefly the common denominator of the Spanish ballad: its strikingly uniform pattern. Unlike the ballad traditions of other parts of Europe, and unlike the extant epic sources, the Spanish ballad early established a metrical format that continues to dominate even twentieth-century balladry. In the first place, the ballad is a musical composition, although our modern lack of training in medieval musicology and the loss of pertinent documents force us to consider the ballads almost exclusively in terms of nonmusical poetic compositions. In defense of this practice, one might add an often forgotten fact: much of the epic and lyric poetry composed prior to the decline of the Renaissance was intended to be accompanied by music. The relatively late practice of reading poetry to oneself in solitude— one result of the development of printing—effectively did away with the musical, and oral, performance of poetry. Nevertheless, these musical relationships are preserved in poetic terms such as *lyric, canción* and *cantiga* ("song"; both medieval forms), *sonnet* (literally, "little song"), and others.

Leaving aside the musical elements of the ballads constituting the *Romancero viejo*,[30] we find that the basic format is an indefinite number of sixteen-syllable verses, divided into hemistichs of eight syllables each; rhyming assonantally without strophic division.[31] (For analysis of what is meant by assonantal rhyme in Spanish, the reader is referred to the appendix at the end of this study.)There is no basic structural format for the development of a Spanish ballad, although we commonly find *ex abrupto* beginnings, excessively schematic or cursory presentations, and truncated or premature conclusions, with the narratively most important event suppressed and left to implication and our conjecture. We will have occasion to examine in detail these very generalized phenomena, in addition to characteristic rhetorical formulas, when we consider individual examples in the following chapters.

Although metrical variation often served in the epic to mark transition, the regularity of rhyme in the ballad obscures narrative shifts and dialogue changes; these difficulties are increased by the usual lack of punctuation—or its sketchiness—in premodern texts. While it is true that some of the most venerable examples of the *Romancero viejo* reveal more than one rhyme scheme, this is due more to the running together of selected fragments from parts of an epic with different rhyme schemes than to any attempt on the part of the several creators of a ballad to signal transitions.

What most identifies a Spanish ballad—its fundamental common denominator—is the narrative nature (shared, to be sure, with ballads in general), its relatively unique quasi-lyrical tone, the result of the intervention of some very talented performers and innovators, and the metrical composition on the basis of octosyllabic hemistichs and assonantal rhyme. In summarizing, then, the uniform metric characteristics, one cannot help but be impressed—if not puzzled—by the fact that an unvaryingly regular pattern emerged from sources that were not always poetry in the first place (chronicles, legends, etc.) and never metrically regular (the Hispanic epics, the

DEVELOPMENTAL REPRESENTATION OF THE SPANISH BALLADS

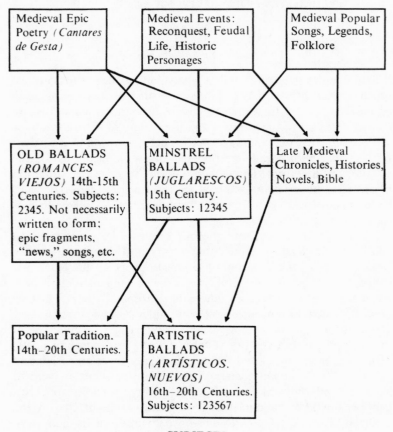

SUBJECTS:

1) Classics (The Roman Matter)
2) Historic (Peninsular)
3) Charlemagne and Carolingian history (The French Matter)
4) Frontier (The Reconquest)
5) Novelesque, Lyrical
6) Moorish (Post-Conquest Romanticization)
7) Religious

Spanish versions of Carolingian *gestes*). Although it may be true that the octosyllabic line is more "natural" for Spanish than others,[32] this hypothesis does not explain the other metrical regularities that are so outstanding in view of the irregularity of European non-Hispanic balladry.

As a synthesis of ballad forms in Spain, their chronological development and their relationship to their sources, the outline on p. 25 is provided.

II   *Theories of Ballad Origins*

Semipopular literature such as the ballad has been the center of much spirited debate between literary historians, anthropologists, and formal poets at least since the rise of Romanticism and folklore studies. Because of the richness and the variety of the tradition involved, the Hispanic ballad has occasioned discussion of a particularly intense nature and one that has major implications for the sociology of literature. Three main theories have vied for attention in the past; our brief analysis of them will bespeak the problems of ballad investigation as well as the formulation of an adequate concept of literary history.

Most popular during the nineteenth century—the period in which study of non-Western, noncontemporary and popular literature begins to attract the attention of serious thinkers—is the Romantic concept of the origins of literature in general, the ballad in particular. For the Romantics, an adequate concept of literary history would have to take into account the *folk* and *mythic* origins of poetry. Using the terms *Naturalpoesie* and *Volkspoesie,* theoreticians of the early nineteenth century sought to stress the source of poetic expression in the ritual and the occasional poetry of an earlier and more primitive human society. Their primitive societies were to be found only beyond Europe or in fossilized form in nonurban Europe, the latter having often been irremediably affected by the artificial "culture" of post-Renaissance civilization. In their view, not only did poetry have its beginnings in a context which was "primitive" (a word with little or no precise meaning, to be sure), but it was only among what was left of primitive society in the modern age that the philosopher or the poet could find evidence of both the true nature of poetic expression and what the poet should emulate in his attempt to "recover" the proper voice of literature. René

Wellek documents this strand of Romantic aesthetics,[33] and stresses the role of the Germans, particularly the Brothers Grimm, in formulating a concept of poetic origins that was to be used in discussing premodern forms of "popular" literature favored by many Romantics. In recovering the voice of folk poetry, the poet was to divest himself of the worn cloak of *Kunstpoesie,* art or "artificial" poetry, as the poetic expression of the trained, aesthetically oriented artisans of Antiquity and the Renaissance tradition came to be labeled. Although the modern poet could not hope to assume with success and honesty the role of the anonymous vatic poet of mythic folk ritual, he could nevertheless attempt to reflect with sincerity an interest in and an understanding of the "inner" voice of a people.

Not only, then, did the Romantic theories of "natural poetry" come to constitute a neofolk aesthetic; they came also to encompass a way of looking at the development of literature in human society and of approaching the earliest expressions of Western civilization. The two earliest expressions of Christian, post-Antiquity society were the epic and the popular song or ballad, and these works quickly attracted the attention of the Grimms and their colleagues. In contrast to modern theories concerning the development of epic literature, which stress the intimate relationship between Classical and at least the Romance vernacular literatures,[34] the Romantics saw the epic as a complete break with Classical tradition and the outpouring of local popular sentiment on the occasion of momentous events of local history. The epics were a vignette of folk expression. Put together with the edges smoothed over, the shorter compositions in time were transformed into the longer, more formal works that are the feudal epics.[35] In Spain, the discovery of the ballad tradition served to validate this thesis, and for many years the ballads were taken as the primitive, proto-epic fragments. Very early Ferdinand Joseph Wolf elaborated this concept of interrelationship between the surviving Spanish ballads and the missing, but known, Spanish epics.[36] Indeed, the very presence of an older body of ballads—the *Romancero viejo* gathered into partial and scattered collections in the sixteenth century—and a productive tradition of ballad imitations beginning with the Renaissance (the so-called *Romancero nuevo* or *artístico* from the sixteenth century to the present day), allowed Wolf to articulate with particular persuasiveness the Romantic position. This position made a clear and unreconcilable dichotomy between the "genuine" popular poems—the older ballads—and the artificial, inauthentic imitations of affected "art poetry" of the Renaissance and later.

The most immediate reaction to the dominance in the nineteenth century of Romantic theories concerning the origins of medieval poetry was the reemergence of an emphasis on individual rather than collective composition. In the France of the late nineteenth century, with positivism in full control of scholarship, there began an attempt to "correct" the Romantic notions about the nature of the French epic, and by extension, the Teutonic and Hispanic epic. Since France had no ballad tradition (a curious circumstance, analogous to the fact that Castile had no medieval lyric tradition of note), the sole emphasis of researchers was on the epic. Insisting, as the good positivists that they were, that the "scientific" study of literature could only concern itself with the "facts," the proponents of the individualist position dismissed the nebulous collective origins of vernacular literature and claimed that, no matter what previous, unrecoverable versions might have been, any given epic texts that the scholar might have at hand must of necessity have been the work of one or several individuals. Although they may have taken their material from unwritten, popular, or lost antecedents, whatever they did with it was a conscious, determined effort to construct a uniform work of art. Therefore, techniques used in the discussion of a signed poem by Ronsard, say, were just as applicable in the analysis of what is only unfortunately but insignificantly an unsigned epic.[37] Thus the epics were given no outstandingly different status as to origins and composition than any other work of literature in the construction of the positivistic histories of literature of the period. Although some recent research may threaten the hegemony of this empirical position,[38] it still remains the major theory of epic origins in France.

Taken together, the Romantic theory and the individualistic theory are basically complementary. Despite applications of the latter to the study of the Spanish epic, it was not conceived to deal with the fragmentary epics. Where the Romantic concept lacked the evidence that we now have that the epic preceded the ballads, the individualistic theory essentially skirts the issue of where exactly the anonymous ballads fit in and what their relationship is to the origins of the epic.[39]

The dominant theory among Hispanists is Menéndez Pidal's traditionalist or fragmentation theory which treats both epic and ballad development as a "traditional" process involving minstrel transmission and (re)elaboration. As we have indicated in discussing the historical ballads, all evidence, both empirical and stylistic, points to a breakup of the epics during the late Middle Ages and their survival in fragmentary pieces called *romances*.

Menéndez Pidal's theories—which are a careful and elaborate development of Milá's post-Romantic work[40]—are essentially historicist in the sense that they attempt to account for the development of literature in terms of the moment when specific developments take place. Put in terms of a pseudo-motto, literature must be examined in terms of the facts of its production—the period, the literary genre and tradition involved, attitudes toward literature, forms of transmission, and so on. Given the enormous amount of material to work with, not only in terms of the materials available from the late Middle Ages and the Renaissance, but on a chronological axis as well as with the volume of examples discovered in popular, rural, or semirural strata of society, Menéndez Pidal and his followers have been able to elaborate a series of conjectures, supported by the demonstrable interrelationships between traditional epic materials and traditional ballads, that have successfully resisted critical misgivings for seven decades.[41]

More recently, there has been a certain tendency, not to refute directly the thesis of collective transformation and transmission, but to bring to bear on the study of ballad origins modern, non-Romantic concepts of folkloristic expression. G. J. Geers[42] more than fifty years ago suggested the need to consider the implications of the emerging research on folk literature, pointing out that the novelesque ballads—the ones least valuable in support of the fragmentation theory—may be the oldest and the most popular. The great Romanist Leo Spitzer acknowledges this circumstance in his study of the "folkloristic prestage" of probably the most renowned example of this group.[43]

Of even greater importance is the work on the ballad by scholars with professional training in folk literature. Daniel Devoto's paper[44] is a closely reasoned and documented defense of the need to take folk literature into account and to acknowledge the no longer ignorable fact that there is an overt relationship between the motives of some of the ballads and the archetypal patterns described by Karl Jung *et al.* in their research on the collective unconscious of mankind. Particularly significant, within the framework of tradi-

tionalist theories, might be an explanation on the basis of the collective unconscious as to why certain ballads were unusually
attractive to the populace and as to what rationale might be given
for the particular changes brought about by the traditional process.[45]
While this work has not yet reached the point of returning full
circle to the Romantic theories, to reaffirm the collective, subconscious origins of literature, it does offer the study of ballad
criticism a wider scope than the historicist minutiae of traditionalist
research.

Menéndez Pidal's overwhelming body of research never revealed
any particular interest in the concerns of formal theories of literary
aesthetics as they began to emerge in this country and on the con-
tinent after the First World War. Thus it is in this area that the
critic is disappointed who believes that the academic study of literature must go beyond the issues of literary history, admittedly
sophisticated and complex in themselves. Although, unlike most
literary historians, who felt it was not their concern, Menéndez
Pidal brought to his work a true sensitivity for the human value
of literature and an awareness of the necessity to distinguish between good and bad poetry, the principal thrust of traditionalism
is the elucidation of problems that do not bear directly upon literature as a form of artistic expression. This is not meant as a complaint;
it is simply a characterization of the general tendencies of the studies
involved. In attempting to retrace the steps taken by a ballad or
a series of ballads as they passed through the process of traditionalization, research has had of necessity to deal with a great amount
of poetry that is far from excellent. To put it another way, the many
examples of truly superb poetry to be found in the *Romancero
viejo* are only a relatively small amount of the extant texts that
must be considered by anyone interested in reconstructing the
lines of development from epic to a ballad discovered, say, in
Asturias in the twentieth century.

To be sure, studies focusing on one ballad have tended to pick
ballads important for artistic as well as other reasons, and the
many anthologies that have emerged from ballad research under
the aegis of Menéndez Pidal reveal a secure ability to separate
good from bad poetry. Yet, the development of the theory down-
played the problems of artistic unity in order to highlight the complex problems of evolution. In considering the ballad as an artifact
that passed from hand to hand, traditionalism could not help but

stress the role of many miscellaneous poet-performers, rather than the autonomy that the several "finished" or "received" products might have as individual poems. Traditionalism does not deny the technical sophistication of the ballad; indeed, the role of well-trained minstrels during the early period of formation in the late Middle Ages is precisely the reason that the Spanish ballad is so far superior to ballads outside the Peninsula. But traditionalism does tend to gloss over the problems of conscious formal rhetoric that must have entered into the composition of the better pieces somewhere along the way. One need not imply that trained, court poets were involved. However, if one subscribes, as does this study, to the belief that good art is not by nature the result of accident (although some good art may be accidental), then poet-performers who did know what constituted excellent poetry were involved in the development of the best ballads. The critic, after he has understood the principles of Spanish ballad development, may want to approach a given body of texts from the point of view of what they are, after all, implicitly recognized to be: poetry. And good poetry, it seems inevitable to admit, is conducive to those analyses that will show how and why it is in fact good.

Basing ourselves without reservation on the traditionalist theories concerning the origins of Spanish ballads, theories which have been so minutely elaborated and validated by academic research, we will attempt in this study to approach the artistically most important texts to emerge from traditionalism. Although it will be imperative to characterize each text in terms of its relation to the totality of the *Romancero viejo,* we will underemphasize the issues of textual genesis taken up by studies cited in the Bibliography in order to place greatest emphasis on the artistry of the Spanish medieval ballads. In so doing, we will attempt to validate the frequently articulated intuition that these ballads represent some of the finest poetry of European literature.

III *Ballad Editions*

Before turning in the following chapter to a discussion of the principles of poetic theory that constitute the basis for our consideration of the individual ballads, an indication of the nature of the texts is necessary.

As we have stated, all evidence points to ballad emergence in

Spain in the fifteenth century, with some probable beginnings in the fourteenth. It has been noted that Santillana refers to *romances* in his famous *Prohemio* (1449), although it will likely remain impossible to determine if he is referring to the ballads or to other popular vernacular compositions, or to both (although the fact that Santillana himself was able to write only in the vernacular and not in Latin argues for a generic rather than a linguistic meaning for *romances*).

The first contemporary text of the *romances* dates from 1421, when a ballad text was copied by a Majorcan student in Italy into his notebook. Within fifty years, the ballads begin to enjoy a popularity among court poets and musicians, and many versions are reproduced in the fifteenth-century collections of their poetry, although, to be sure, often in "retouched" forms. This latter fact would indicate that, if the ballad was indeed reworked by the populace, it underwent no less tampering at the hands of nonpopular artists: indeed, here one finds the beginnings of the transition of the ballad from an anonymous semipopular form to the formal aesthetic composition of the Renaissance.

The first printed collection to contain only ballad texts is the so-called *Cancionero de romances,* or *Cancionero sin año* (literally, *Undated Songbook*), now known to have been edited by Martin Nucio in 1548 in Antwerp (which was then under Spanish domination). This collection is essentially a reprint of the *pliegos sueltos,* or loose-leaves, which was probably the most primitive form of distribution of printed ballad texts. Nucio's text went through several reprintings, with the addition of many new texts.

The middle years of the sixteenth century saw an interest in including the ballads in treatises on music, reminding us of this important aspect often overlooked by the literary scholar. It is during this period also that the publication of ballad collections attracts definitive interest (see the numerous listings in Simón Díaz, the first entry in our Bibliography). In addition, prose works such as Ginés Pérez de Hita's *Guerras civiles de Granada (The Granada Civil Wars),* published in 1595, and Cervantes' *Don Quixote* (1605 and 1615), use the ballads as basic narrative material and reproduce many contemporary texts. Finally, the beginnings of the *romance nuevo* among the Renaissance poets marks the final "civilized" acceptance of the importance and beauty of the ballad, culminating in 1600 with the publication of the *Romancero general* (1600–1605), which consists entirely of compositions by "professional" poets.

Despite the continued vitality of the ballad in the oral, popular tradition and its role as a major form of lyric and dramatic poetry, it is not until the research by the German Romantics in the mid-nineteenth century, described above, that we again find an interest in publishing collections of medieval texts. Durán's collections (1849–1851) and the Wolf-Hofmann anthology (1856) are the beginnings of modern interest in the *Romancero viejo*.

Unless otherwise indicated, all ballads studied will be quoted from Menéndez Pidal's anthology, *Flor nueva de romances viejos*.[46] Given the preference of researchers for other more scholarly editions (see listing in our Bibliography), some justification of this choice is necessary. Since we are not primarily concerned with the problem of textual variants and the evolution of several versions, it seemed best to make use of an anthology which is not only readily accessible to the Spanish reading public but one which is also known for the excellence and the diffusion of the variants chosen for inclusion. At the same time, the reader must be made aware of the fact that Menéndez Pidal has cast himself in his anthology in the role of a minstrel and some of his texts represent felicitous reworkings of several extant versions. Nevertheless, for the critic concerned with the relationship between thematic aspects and the form of their expression, Menéndez Pidal's procedure is potentially dangerous. Thus, in several cases—most notably all of the Carolingian ballads —we have felt it more advisable to quote "canonical" versions. Although we take up the matter in some detail in the following chapter, the reader should be advised that the selection of a ballad text for formal aesthetic analysis is fraught with potential embarrassment.

We provide for each text our own literal translation. One further note: it is to be assumed that all texts examined are from among those belonging to the period of ballad formation during the fourteenth and fifteenth centuries. We will indicate clearly whenever a ballad that might not belong strictly to the *Romancero viejo* is examined.

CHAPTER 2

The Ballads as Literature: Problems and Perspectives

IT should be clear from the presentation of hypotheses concerning ballad origins in the preceding chapter that any discussion of this body of poetry must take into account two separate but interrelated axes of controversy. Not only does ballad scholarship reflect the tension between an emphasis on individual composition at any one point in time versus collective transmission, resulting in innumerable variants, up to any one point in time (i.e., that of the medieval collections or of modern gatherings made by the folklorist). Also at issue is whether ballad poetry, even though we may accept its oral, anonymous, and "collective" nature, should be treated in its textual versions like any other poetry offered to the scholar for critical examination, or whether the recorded texts of oral-traditional poetry must be accorded a unique and distinctive critical status. Related issues are whether or not oral-traditional ballads can be called poetry at all in any aesthetic sense of the word, and what role the critic is to assign to the phenomenon known as "accidental (as opposed to consciously deliberate) art." This chapter will deal with these issues, some understanding of which and some critical position on which it is indispensible to possess before examining with significant perception the texts involved.

I Oral Versus Written Literature

Ballad scholarship outside of the Hispanic context is simplified somewhat by the virtual predominance of the oral over the written. Unlike the Spanish ballad, which possesses two textual traditions—one medieval and indicative of the formation of the genre, and one modern, indicative of Romantic and contemporary interest in folk literature—the English ballad, for example, is given written record only in modern collections.[1] Therefore, while the English or Slavic scholar may find some traces of formal literature in the oral ballad,

he generally is willing to concede that the ballad is an anthropological phenomenon and as such, by definition, lies outside the range
of interests of the literary scholar. Moreover, the latter, educated
to the analysis of poetry of aesthetic and generally aristocratic
pretensions, simply finds himself lacking the techniques and the
vocabulary appropriate to the discussion of folk literature.[2]

In Hispanic scholarship, then, we may say that the emphasis
on oral tradition as exemplified by the work of Menéndez Pidal
under the heading of "folkloric geography"[3] is two-fold in origin.
Not only does the ballad represent a literary manifestation that
is truly popular in the sense of the creative transmission of texts
from the Middle Ages to the present day, but the ballad as well
in its medieval origins was an oral, nonwritten phenomenon,
whether its audience was the feudal aristocracy or the curious masses.
The fact that in the Peninsula for one reason or another the ballad
was received with enough enthusiasm by a literate audience to
result in the practice of loose-leaf printing and the major collections
of the sixteenth century seems only to be felicitous happenstance.
While it may be legitimate to argue that such an enthusiasm was
born of the comparative excellence of the ballads in question, to
say that the Spanish temperament was more receptive to the ballad
may be more romantic speculation than valid sociological commentary.[4] Therefore, by virtue of the very nature of the ballad,
historicist criticism from the late nineteenth century on, concerned
as it is with the issues of "origin and development,"[5] has emphasized
as a matter of course the oral aspect of the ballad and the problems
attendant upon tracing the sources and the transmission of an oral
literature which at one point happily achieved written recognition.[6]
It is only to be expected, therefore, that the *romance,* even in the
case of written texts, because of its unique origins and unique
survival, should call for unique techniques of analysis. This position
implying that both oral and (medieval) printed ballads deserve a
special critical framework carries over to current anthropological
interest in the ballad.[7]

That the ballad may owe its enthusiastic reception by the people
to any suggestive embodiment of the collective unconscious—an
embodiment that would certainly be highlighted by the process of
traditionalization—is not all that significant. It is quite easy for
the folklorist to forget that the notions of collective unconscious
and mythic archetypes are all that much more valid for their ap-

plication to "conscious" as well as to folk art[8]—a concept that is disturbing to the literary critic who would have all art originating with the purely creative exercise of the intellect. If it is true that the ballad achieved popular recognition for its mythic potential, supposedly the same would be true of its impact among the non-lowly. Which is of course precisely what did happen and what did lead to the ballad anthologies by the literati, until the new aesthetic tendencies of Humanism and the Renaissance that were too com-pelling to be ignored shifted emphasis from the medieval originals to the equally excellent Renaissance creations. And the fact that the ballad, pseudo-popular as well as nascently manneristic, did consti-tute a major genre of the sixteenth and seventeenth centuries un-doubtedly must be of some fascination for the theoreticians of the collective unconscious.

A logical alternative view to the overwhelming emphasis on the ballad as popular and oral literature—a view totally unacceptable to canonical traditionalism to be sure—is that only individual, but unfortunately anonymous, poets of artistic maturity can possibly be responsible for the early ballads, at least those included in the sixteenth-century collections. A large number of these anonymous ballads unquestionably became part of the popular tradition and underwent transformation via oral transmission to become the often quite different versions still being recorded today on three continents. Meanwhile, the medieval ballad in its original form as found in the early-Renaissance texts "evolved" naturally into the ballad of the sixteenth-century *Romancero nuevo*. This observation is not intended as a rejection of the traditionalist view, a rejection which G. J. Geers[9] attempted unsuccessfully to stimulate earlier in this century. From our point of view today, eight decades of tradi-tionalist research, much of it highly sophisticated and unimpeach-able, cannot be argued away in one paragraph. What is intended, however, is, following Geers, to place a greater emphasis for treating at least the written texts of the *Romancero viejo* within the mainstream of nonfolkloric literature. It is one thing to observe that the oral ballad by definition cannot be subjected to formal literary analysis.[10] It is quite another to subject the textually pre-served medieval ballad to formal literary analysis and to succeed or fail in the undertaking to say something reasonably significant.

Another problem inherent in the conflict between the literary analysis of oral versus written literature is whether or not such a conflict does indeed exist. Is not the assumption that there must be an antagonism of major proportions between written and oral literature both a priori and prejudicial? Any belief that an expression must be written to qualify as literature, and that only that which is written can qualify for the label "good art," not only is a position without meaningful support but smacks as well of the genteel tastes in art of the late nineteenth-century bourgeois arbiters. Already in 1920, Geers could recall with disapproval the statement by Menéndez y Pelayo, that brilliant but stuffy originator of Spanish literary history, that "the songs of the people, if they are popular, are not good; and if they are good, they are not popular."[11] To believe that a text must have been consciously composed as "great literature" to be "literary" is a naive criterion for the modern sophisticated reader, schooled not only in the Great Books but also in primitive literature, folk music, and the contemporary committed writers who deny universal transcendency. Such a position emerged, one assumes, as a reaction to the Romantic ascendency of "natural" poetry over "art" poetry, and led to the unfortunate implication that only someone recognized by the "aesthetic establishment" is capable of art in any meaningful sense of the term. While there are many who would deny the aesthetic potential of folk or popular literature, the fact that many a modern reader might find the foregoing comments decidedly moot is in itself indicative of a shift in modern attitudes.

Of greater concern to the contemporary scholar in his assessment of any putative differences between oral and written literature, we suggest, are the concerns lumped together under the heading of "structure." In both anthropology (cf. the work on structuralism centering around the name of Claude Lévi-Strauss) and in literature (under the rubric of neo-Aristotelianism),[12] one finds concern for the way in which cultural manifestations organize themselves into *structures* of meaning and interrelationships. Although anthropology is preoccupied with the structure of a (primitive) society, folk literature as one cultural reflection of that society is also a proper concern.[13] Folk poetry—and the ballad where and if it is indeed a folk manifestation—is conceived of as possessing structural characteristics relevant to its intimate link with its social backgrounds. On the other hand, "formal" literature, literature written with aesthetic pretensions, also possesses a unique ordering of its content, an ordering indicative of whatever the goals of the artist may be as well as of the social backgrounds of the work itself.

We cannot pursue here whether literary structuralism is one manifestation of anthropological concerns[14] or whether their differing form—the totality of "primitive" culture vs. one artifact of "civilized" society—makes them essentially different undertakings. What we can do, however, is to ask if, on the basis of structuralism's preoccupation with the intrinsic form of a cultural manifestation, the ballad in general or the Spanish ballad in particular demonstrates structural concerns that set them off dramatically from those forms of literary expression acknowledged to be nonpopular and nonfolkloric. To put it another way, whatever the historical origins of the texts may be (i.e., the extrinsic factors), is there something intrinsic that enables us to separate oral from written literature and that furthers our critical goal of assigning each composition an artistic evaluation? The ways in which the Spanish ballad may or may not be structurally different, and the implications of those structural differences, constitutes one of the goals of this study. Not that this is an entirely original or contemporary line of inquiry. Parry and Lord's investigations during the early part of this century on formulistic diction in the oral poetry that survives among the south Slavic peoples was the attempt to isolate with statistical precision one phenomenon and to use it as a measuring stick in identifying and classifying popular poetry.[15] Their conclusions that formulistic diction was strictly an oral procedure of folk singers does give one type of stylistic validity to the dichotomy between oral and written literature. However, this one trait, no matter how ubiquitous it may be, does not answer the critic's question as to whether or not there are artistic reasons for treating oral and written literature as separate. In addition, there are the minor problems that we must deal with medieval oral texts given written form, rather than exclusively oral modern versions, and the fact that Parry and Lord's assertion that formulistic diction is exclusively popular is not conclusive.[16] To return to our original point of departure, the literary critic, aside from extrinsic considerations, lacks any intrinsic aesthetic evidence to support the claim that the artistically superior Spanish medieval ballad, admittedly involved in a proteic oral tradition, must be treated in its recorded textual versions any differently from any other form of important (medieval) poetry.[17]

II *Some Problems of Textual Instability and Accidental Art*

Elaborating on Ramón Menéndez Pidal's famous bywords, that the traditional ballads constitute a "poetry that exists through its variants," Ruth Weber notes in the conclusion to her study on formulistic diction[18] that "since ballads have been subject to constant modification by oral repetition, a given ballad can be said to have no [discernible] original text or any [one] final form. It has only versions and variants" (p. 248; additions given for clarity and emphasis).

Weber's comments touch here upon the one most single barrier to treating the written texts of the ballads as simply one unique manifestation of medieval poetry amenable to customary literary analysis. It is not so much the lack of any discernible original: literary criticism, if not literary history, can get along respectably without an *editio princeps*. Nor is it so much the fact that any written text, sixteenth or twentieth century, has captured only one form of a ballad that has many other versions and that will probably yield in the future several more. A working solution with regard to the latter difficulty is simply to assume for purposes of discussion that from the point of view of literary criticism some basis in the mind of the anthologizer must have existed for choosing that particular variant. It may have been the most popular, it may have been for him the most artistically appealing variant (but not necessarily the most popular), or it may have been that it was the only variant known to him. In the absence of any other medieval texts, the literary critic must willy-nilly make do with what he has at hand.

Rather, the principal difficulty presented by Menéndez Pidal's key phrase and Weber's comment in relation to it involves the danger of applying techniques of criticism that assume textual autonomy to a body of literature where all empirical evidence points to a gross textual instability. It would, of course, be objectionable simply to insist that the "alteration" of ballad texts through the process of traditionalization is analogous to the reworking by an individual poet of his work as part of the customary creative process of revision and preparation of definitive texts. The latter process clearly involves a sequence of versions that culminates in the one final text that the author wishes to have accepted as his contribution to literature. It is assumed that texts previous to the definitive version are working drafts, of interest only in demonstrating the development of the definitive text, but never to be given the status of the latter. Clearly, such a well-defined and biographically associated process is lacking in the development of the ballad. In the case of the medieval production which we are considering here, a process of modification spanning two hundred years is involved, as opposed to a far shorter period in the life of a poet. Moreover, were we to consider the development of a ballad text over the five-hundred-year-plus span of time from the period of ballad origins to the present day, the number of performer-poets and the potential diversity of variants involved suggest the absurdity of comparing the process of traditionalization with one poet's revision of one text.

Furthermore, as we have noted, the critic is bound to accept the final, that is, the definitive version of a known poet's text. It is a cardinal tenet of responsible academic criticism that we respect the integrity of the known author's text. This means not only *not* rewriting what the critic may feel to be a "weak" passage; it also means avoiding the discussion of what the author *might* have written, as well as acknowledging the primacy of the form in which the author left his work or presented it to the public. All of this in spite of what the critic in his learned omniscience may want to do to "better" the author's lamentable artistic failings. For better or for worse, the responsible critic must do his best to deal with what the *author* thinks to be the best form for his work.[19] Given the acknowledged circumstances of the texts captured in the *Romancero,* where we normally have no useful idea of primitive versions, of definitive texts, of the relationship between existing variants (although traditional methodology has established some workable principles here), it is easy to see that the accepted tenets of textual criticism are only remotely related to the problems of the ballads, written or oral. Where it is plausible for the Mark Twain critic to reconstruct the "ideal" text underlying the various versions of one work, such a procedure in the case of the geographically and temporally widely-scattered ballads is similar to the process of reconstruction in Proto-Indo-European: the reconstructed form is a phonologically impossible summary—really a symbol—of known descendant forms. No one takes this summary to be or to have ever been an actual form. In the case of the ballads, such a reconstructed text might be valuable as a summary of existing texts, but the reconstructed version would be worthless as a literary text in itself and impossible to discuss critically or analytically. Since the interest of the literary critic must be in texts about which he can say something interpretatively significant, clearly any attempt at the reconstruction of hypothetical ballad primitives will not serve his purposes.

The ballad critic's problem is doubly compounded. Not only are there an immense number of versions of any one "topic," but also any one text on a particular topic is but one of the variants to be discovered along two axes, one static and representing the variants existing at any one moment, and one dynamic and representing the potential variants produced by each previous variant over a period of time between, say, the period of ballad genesis and the sixteenth-century collections, or between the latter and the nineteenth- and twentieth-century gatherings. Given the issues presented by this chapter up to now, one may ask what option is open to the literary critic who would examine the medieval Spanish ballad in terms of its stature as poetic art? Once we have accepted the hypothesis that poetry of popular, nonaristocratic origins can qualify as art as much as can the well-developed courtly tradition of the fourteenth and fifteenth centuries, it is relatively easy to envision the discussion of the *Romancero viejo* as nothing more nor less than one manifestation of medieval poetry, despite the unique differences associated with any independent genre. One can legitimately proceed to focus attention on whatever texts have managed to survive from the medieval period.

While he must bear in mind that he is dealing with a small written segment of a far more immense oral tradition, the scholar cannot allow this comprehension to impede his critical activity. Little can be done to recover the unwritten texts of the *Romancero viejo,* and the latter's remnants among various surviving Hispanic oral traditions can only marginally compensate for the absence of a complete written record of the medieval corpus. Modification as a result of the process of traditional transmission has usually been far too extensive to enable us to speak of these remnants as medieval compositions; this situation has been well demonstrated by the research of traditionalist scholars. And in any case, our regrets concerning missing texts is mitigated by recalling that such is the circumstance in the case of all medieval literature: the medievalist must base his generalizations on what he knows to be only a very small part that has survived of the total production of the period. This is particularly true in Spain, where the richness of the surviving ballad tradition is offset by the loss of virtually the entire body of medieval drama, medieval Castilian lyric poetry, and all but a smattering of the epic.

Within this context it should then become easier for the critic to justify the concentration of his discussion on the ballads that were set down in the important sixteenth-century collections. He constantly reminds himself that what he is treating is considerably removed from the actual dynamic process of medieval Hispanic balladry, which grew up and developed with little concern for a written tradition. Nevertheless, he is able to justify his orientation on the simple fact that the *Romancero* collections are undoubtedly poetry of one sort or another, that much of it is good poetry, and— probably most important of all from the standpoint of literary history—that it is to a great degree this representation of the ballad which has had an impact upon the development of Spanish litera- ture and which has firmly established the Spanish ballad as a unique and significant segment of the European literary tradition.

III   *A Further Problem*

There is one other problem of concern to literary criticism that must be raised in connection with the Spanish ballad. The question of what role has been played in the development of the *Romancero viejo* by the phenomenon known as "accidental art"—the creation or occurrence by accident of something that is recognized after the fact as art. That this question is pertinent to our discussion here is revealed by the critical comments on the famous ballad of Count Arnaldos (see below, pp. 115 ff.), perhaps one of the most widely known of all Spanish medieval ballads. In the case of this ballad, the text preserved by the sixteenth-century anthologies and the text considered by literary histories is now known to be only a fragment of a much longer version. Reading the longer version not only destroys much of the charm of the truncated fragment; our inter- pretation of the work is drastically altered also. To what degree is truncation a circumstance of accidental art, and what is to be our critical attitude with regard to this famous text in one or the other or in both versions? Again, the casual reader may find the matter moot.

Nevertheless, a central issue of textual criticism has been the belief that acts of nature (the beauty of a sunset) and acts of chance (the beauty of an accidental splash of paint) are to be sharply distinguished from art which has been consciously created for aesthetic purposes. Aside from the practical fact that our tradition has given us methodologies and a vocabulary to deal only with the latter, confusing with conscious art the former two types of beauty would imply a denial of Western belief in art as the result of the aesthetic efforts of a disciplined sensitivity and intelligence. Such a denial might be salutary, particularly at a time when both philosophers and artists are dedicated to undermining some of the sacred tenets of Western thought. However, textual criticism is conservative—some would say reactionary—enough to continue to see a problem in the treatment of accidental art in the same way as conscious art is treated. James Thorpe has devoted a closely reasoned article to this problem, and his conclusions may not help us in the case of the Spanish ballad or other oral literature, but they are convincing.[20] Of course, if one assumes, as did the Romantics, that all art is the creation of some Divinity or Unknown Spiritual Force, with objects and anonymous individuals as only the means to an end, then the blurring of the lines between what happens by chance in art and what happens because of the artist's conscious creative choices makes some sort of sense. Most academic critics, however, would agree with Thorpe's basic position: "Since the work of art is an intended aesthetic object, the idea of either a random or a natural work of art is self-contradictory. Human intelligence was purposefully engaged in the creation of the work of art, but it may not have been successful; the term 'work of art' is thus descriptive rather than evaluative, and it includes failures as well as successes. The language of the literary work, whether judged a success or a failure, is a fulfillment of the author's intentions" (p. 466).

What, then, are the implications of these principles for the treatment of the medieval Spanish ballad? Traditionalism has provided one means of escaping the dangers of erecting a critical interpretation on what may be an accidental text. Menéndez Pidal early in his investigations proposed that we accept tacitly the idea that any modification in a ballad results from the conscious act of a performer-poet. While traditionalism is mostly interested in suppressing attention for the activities of the individual in creating and transmitting the *Romancero,* preferring to stress the anonymous and collective nature indicated by its special and temporal diffusion, the scholar cannot deliberately brush away the role that must have been played at each point by some individual involved in the process of modification. To be sure, many changes resulted from the failings of the poet-performer: weak memory, bad taste, impatience with overly long texts. All of these factors could lead potentially to major revisions in the form of the text. Indeed the latter—impatience with an overly long text—may have been involved with the truncation of the ballad of Count Arnaldos. The poet simply felt that the shorter segment constituted a good enough unit and perpetuated that abbreviation with remarkable success. It is idle speculation to attempt to guess whether the shorter form of the ballad came about because of the performer's failings or because he just preferred to shorten the text, or because he may have felt that concluding the work at a particular point improved the ballad and made it that much more pregnant with meaning. Any one or all of these factors could have entered in at the time of one performance or as the result of a series of several performances by a single minstrel or by several different minstrels. Thus, while we have no evidence to allow us to say that Text A became Text B through the deliberate changes by an individual poet, neither do we possess the evidence to say that Text B resulted accidentally from Text A. It is this conscious but anonymous role played by the performer-poet that is of such fascination to the traditionalist and that gives the Spanish ballad a position midway between more formal poetry and the "splash of paint."

Nevertheless, the accepted validity of Menéndez Pidal's hypothesis concerning the creative role at any one moment by the usually artistically sophisticated performer-poet enables us to assume for want of contradictory evidence that, despite the morass of versions and variants, each one is a conscious, creative manifestation of ballad art. We are therefore entitled to subscribe to Thorpe's observation elsewhere in his article concerning the problem of multiple definitive versions left by the known author: "The basic proposition which I submit about works created by authorial revision is that each version is, either potentially or actually, another work of art" (p. 477). Speaking later of the two published versions of Auden's "In Time of War," he summarizes: "From our review of what takes place in revision of private and public versions, I hope it is clear that the two versions of the Auden collection are equally 'real.' They stand, side by side, as two separate works, and each has every bit of the dignity and integrity with which an author can endow any work of art" (p. 480).

The ballad tradition which we are considering here is, of course, totally public in both its written and its oral form. Since no one author is involved in the *Romancero viejo* in originating, in revising, and in giving public form to a ballad, all of the versions and all of the variants can only logically be considered as unique and individual works of art. To the degree that we cannot divide the versions into primitive texts, transitional working texts, and definitive versions—as a textual critic does with the various notebooks, manuscripts, and editions of a known author's work—we have no choice but to adopt the position proposed by Thorpe. In the case, then, of the ballad of Count Arnaldos, there is no other viable option except to consider Text A (the longer version) and Text B (the famous truncated segment) as simply two separate poems that overlap verbally. The fact that students of both versions have been in agreement as to the different poetic moods created by the two separate versions, as well as the totally different meanings suggested by the two separate structures, leads us naturally to the conclusion that two separate works of literature are involved, the second one having occurred as the result of the normal "tamperings" occasioned by the process of traditional transmission. In our discussion of the medieval Spanish ballad, we will assume without further comment that the preceding discussion adequately validates the decision to treat each ballad version as a unique and autonomous poetic entity, whatever its extrinsic relation might be to other existing or supposed ballad texts.

IV *The Discussion of the Spanish Ballad as Good Poetry*

While the medieval ballad is usually included in an introductory course in Spanish literature, along with the unmistakably courtly poetry of the late fourteenth and fifteenth centuries, it is not at all clear from the vast body of research that scholarship is willing to accord the ballad "aesthetic stature" and to study it as a literary manifestation. Both the interest in the ballad vis-à-vis folklore and the oral and traditionalist concern with the popular preservation and transmission of the ballad—if not with one aspect of its composition—have combined to isolate the *romance* fairly effectively from the technical preoccupations of literary criticism. While these preoccupations have challenged the hegemony of nineteenth-century history in the academic study of literature during the last fifty years,[21] the Spanish ballad has remained firmly the province of investigations whose interest, although it may acknowledge the poetic brilliance of the ballad, is not essentially in the study of the *romance* as literary art.

The semifolkloristic nature of the ballad, as well as the critical problems associated with anonymous works, do little to explain this lack of aesthetic attention. The strength of Menéndez Pidal's voice in ballad investigations of course is implicated here. Nevertheless, from the point of view of contemporary literary criticism interested in the problems of good vs. bad poetry, the unique origins of the Spanish ballad are of only a secondary concern. As a matter of fact, it is this aesthetic interest that has been a leader in the controversy over recognizing the autonomous status of artistic excellence, regardless of the problems of genesis associated with a work of art. Whether a work be evaluated "anachronistically"—that is, without reference to the age and the socio-aesthetic standards involved—or whether the critic insists on taking the "literary backgrounds" into consideration in his evaluation, the result is a value judgment relatively unrelated to the central issues of literary history.

Within the latter context, we may posit as a working hypothesis the assumption that within a given literary tradition—late medieval culture in the case of the original Spanish ballads—literary and aesthetic bases are uniform, despite the unrelated origins of any given set of works. Thus, a sonnet and a ballad may have different sociological geneses: court vs. marketplace. As poetry, nevertheless, both are equally "literary" in value and subject to identical aesthetic evaluation. This would appear to be an obvious principle in view of the "democratic" tastes of the twentieth century: that which is good is good, not because of its origins, but because it satisfies our criteria of excellence, which are therefore oriented in terms of the audience (pragmatic) rather than the creator (subjective).[22] Although literary history is bound to record the origins and diffusion of literature, without prejudicial regard to its intrinsic quality, literary criticism is under no necessary obligation to recognize any type of literature as potentially inferior or superior because of its genealogy. In other words, neither the Romantic view that all popular poetry is by definition superior, nor Menéndez y Pelayo's statement quoted above implying that all popular poetry is by definition inferior strikes us today as particularly valid. The sophisticated student of literature, not to mention the educated and mature general reader, is by and large interested simply in literature which is artistically good and humanly valuable, no matter what the analysis to which it is subsequently subjected may be. The "objective" historian of literature—not that many scholars believe any more today in the possibility of a "science of literary scholarship"—may deplore this apparently Crocean relativism, but in greater or lesser manifestations of sophistication it has come to constitute the common denominator of literary studies in our age.

What the foregoing remarks concerning contending focuses for the academic study of literature mean for the ballad is that, once the meticulous cataloging of the traditionalist school has compiled a body of texts representative of the development of the ballad, it becomes the task of the literary critic to examine those texts in terms of what they represent as literature. Rejecting a priori assumptions as to whether they are good or bad by reason of their origin, the literary critic is interested foremost in examining each text in terms of itself, in terms of its literary backgrounds (if he believes this necessary, and the present writer so believes), and in terms of the criteria of artistic excellence applied to similar and contemporaneous poetry.

For the critic concerned with questions of literary aesthetics, the value of a ballad must go beyond merely the way in which it re-treats a given topic: the historical study of "re-treatment" implies an organic process that does not necessarily take into account the autonomous, intrinsic structure of a ballad text. One text possesses an autonomy regardless of its connections with an earlier version of its subject matter; the value and importance of any single ballad must be its totality, not just the curious ways in which it treats "with originality" its subject matter. This position concerning the importance of examining each ballad text "on its own" is far from novel; S. Griswold Morley tried without success more than fifty years ago to highlight the validity of giving a ballad greater stature than as simply one manifestation of an immense and proteic tradition.[23] As we have pointed out above, that Morley's position received less than its due has been the result of the dominant interests of prevailing ballad scholarship and the caveats which it has promoted on the dangers of according "oral and traditional" literature written status.[24] For, if there is any serious weakness in Spanish ballad scholarship from the point of view of the student of aesthetic and human values of poetry, it is the overwhelming emphasis placed on ways in which a ballad—or a variant/version as it might be more preferably called—comes to exist, rather than on what it may be from the beholder's point of view: a striking example of poetic art which the critic must elucidate and of which he must offer an appropriate literary appreciation. This latter position can be summarized with the phrase "artistic monuments," a phrase which reflects a more contemporary interest in the study of works which, although the critic may be bound to take into account all of the established issues of literary history in his discussion, are after all major examples of literary art and must be treated accordingly. While the literary critic finds that he cannot ignore the issues of literary history, it is nevertheless within the framework of the indisputable validity of the aesthetic structure of literature that we have approached the Spanish ballad precisely in order to provide critical substance to the claim that the *romances* are indeed poetry, and poetry of the highest order.

CHAPTER 3

The Historical Ballads

IT is appropriate that our actual examination of ballad texts begin with those based on historical or national themes. Not only is this the most extensive group of works; because of the immense number involved and the obvious relationship with other genres on "national" themes, such as the epic and the chronicle, the historical ballads have consistently been the point of departure for the elaboration and verification of hypotheses concerning ballad genesis and evolution. When one recalls that these ballads dealing with formative events of Spanish feudal society have also attracted the greatest attention of foreign translators and adapters and have had the greatest impact on subsequent Spanish literature, it is not difficult to understand their central importance in a comprehensive examination of the ballad.

Consideration of the historical ballad usually follows the chronological classification of the six known epic materials; King Rodrigo and the invasion of the Peninsula in 711 by the Moors; Bernardo del Carpio, a pseudo-historical figure created to counterbalance French treatment of Peninsular events (e.g., in the Roland materials) for his defense of Castile against Leon and Navarre; the Seven Infantes of Lara, whose story is revealing for the values of Spanish medieval feudal society; the Siege of Zamora, concerning the fratricidal upheavals of the mid-eleventh century; and the Cid, the most famous epic figure of Spanish literature for his embodiment of nonroyal feudal values and his work for the unity of the Peninsula. Due to the virtual loss of all epic materials, we have only a rather vague notion of the epic texts upon which the ballads of the historical cycles are putatively based.[1] Moreover, the foregoing list is chronological (covering the span 711–1090) in terms of the epic topics. It does not show the relative chronology of the ballad versions of those topics, nor does it indicate any accurate correlation between the treatment of a subject by the epic and its treatment in the ballads.[2] Indeed, the impossibility—if not the danger—of correlating the "world" of the epic with that of the ballad is shown

by the ironic fact that the Rodrigo cycle, although the oldest chrono-
logically, derives most likely, not from an early epic poem, but
from other traditional materials (legends, chronicles, etc.). In
addition, the ballads that we will examine appear to be some of
the latest of the traditional compositions on historical material.

The reader and the student of the historical ballads must therefore bear in mind the following caveat: although the traditional
ballads are understood to have derived from earlier epic material
—supposedly epic poems—either through fragmentation of texts
or reelaboration of prose accounts, there is a distinct difference in
approach between source and ballad. Not only are differences
resulting from understandable shifts in attitude from one period
to another involved. The very fact that a ballad text may be literally
torn from its larger epic context must make us realize that the
isolated fragment may have a different meaning on its own than
it had in conjunction with the forgotten (and often lost) context.
To be sure, the fact that one or more anonymous minstrels focused
on a selected fragment implies, it would seem, a desire to alter the
tone of the material by ignoring the larger and probably more
explanatory context. Another factor is also involved: where the
epic poem is a closed entity with an internal structure and meaning,
a ballad cycle, composed of several "miscellaneous" texts, may
derive from many text sources. The result may be a wide variety
of tones and points of view, some in direct conflict with the epic
poems with which they are paired. This is precisely the case with
many of the *romances* on the Cid: some are related directly to the
Poema de Mio Cid (mid-twelfth century) and reveal a sympathetic
attitude toward an exemplary individual. Some, by contrast, are
derived from later prose and rhymed chronicles and are by far less
sympathetic if not overtly hostile toward the Cid's forceful personality. Thus, while the scholar may recall the relationships between
epic and ballad for purposes of elucidating the development of the
latter, the reader is well advised to appreciate the ballads in terms
of their own particular "sense" of history and of the individuals
involved. Certainly, such an attitude will contribute toward accept-
ing the ballads as autonomous poetic compositions rather than as
simply abstracts of epic materials, no matter how closely they may
be historically related to the latter.

I *The Ballads on King Rodrigo*

It should be clear from what has been said above that the ballads surrounding the historical figure of King Rodrigo, the last of the Visigothic kings, enjoy a somewhat different position among the traditional medieval *romances* on national themes.[3] Not being based on an established epic poem contemporaneous with the events involved and therefore potentially "more accurate," but rather deriving from a well-developed and more free-wheeling version in the chronicles, the compositions that belong to the formative period of the *Romancero* are less epic fragments than they are autonomous fictional works. Indeed, it is not surprising to find Pedro del Corral's *Crónica Sarracina (Saracen Chronicle)*, ca 1430, adjudged to be the major source of the early ballads, characterized as a full-blown historical novel far-removed from what are assumed to have been the actual historical facts.[4] In addition, because of the momentous events described—nothing less than the destruction of a Christian empire by invading hordes of Islamic infidels—and the story of sin, guilt, and betrayal that legend came to attach to the principals involved, the relatively small body of original ballads (by comparison with the Cid) have had a great appeal to imaginative literature of later periods.

The essential texts with which we will be concerned derive from at least the late fifteenth century; being based on a narrative chronicle, they possess a greater unity from one composition to another than is usually found. Thus, while we can point to no poem giving the subject matter epic treatment (cf. however the late thirteenth-century French epic, *Anseï de Karthage,* based on early Rodrigo legend materials), the important medieval and traditional texts form a coherent cycle according the fall of the Visigoths an almost tragic dimension. As has been frequently observed, the lateness of the ballads and the restricted range of their sources have resulted in a clear-cut "novelistic" progression from one text to another. However, probably the most striking result of these characteristics is the nature of the modifications wrought by the ballad tradition upon the actual historical facts. While there is a certain background accuracy recalling the circumstances of betrayal and internal disorder leading to the spectacularly successful invasions beginning in 711, the Rodrigo ballads are of special interest for equating Christian defeat with the private immorality of the last of the Visi-

CARNEGIE LIBRARY
LIVINGSTONE COLLEG.
SALISBURY, N. C. 2814

gothic rulers. Rodrigo's sinful indiscretions are given in legend and in ballad as the immediate cause of the invasions, which are seen as the scourge of an angry Jehovah visited upon a ruler and his people in retribution for the former's moral guilt. We find, then, a dimension of Christian symbolism, borne out by the details and allusions of the texts involved, that is singular to the Rodrigo ballads, singular to the extent that religious issues are notably lacking in Hispanic epic material in general and in the medieval ballads in particular.[5] Perhaps it is dangerous to speculate too much concerning this shift of emphasis, but one cannot help but note that the focus of these ballads is Rodrigo's personal loss, in feudal rather than national terms, of Spain for his sinful transgressions. Thus, the ballads do not dwell on the fall of Spain to the Moors, but rather use the fall as the backdrop for the elaboration of one man's confrontation with the consequences of his own actions. Such a shift is indicative of a mythico-poetic desire to create texts of literary merit and broad human appeal, rather than simply to rhyme history.

Our first text concerns the encounter between Rodrigo and Cava, the woman who is to be the object of his immoral lust. Bespeaking what has come to be an almost universally described feature of the Spanish ballads, the following text is significant for its "open" conclusion and for what it leaves unsaid:

Amores trata Rodrigo,	(Rodrigo is talking of love,
descubierto ha su cuidado;	his intent has been revealed.
a la Cava se lo dice,	He tells Cava about it,
de quien anda enamorado.	with whom he is in love.
5 *Miraba su lindo cuerpo,*	He looked upon her lovely body,
mira su rostro alindado,	upon her embellished face;
sus lindas y blancas manos	her pretty white hands,
él se las está loando.	which he is praising.
—Sepas, mi querida Cava,	"Know, my beloved Cava,
10 *de ti estoy apasionado;*	that I am afire for you.
pido que me des remedio,	I demand you give me remedy;
yo estaría a tu mandado;	I will be at your command.
mira que lo que el rey pide	Consider that what the King requests
ha de ser por fuerza o grado.	must be his by force or willingly."
15 *La Cava, como discreta,*	Cava, as one who is discreet,
en risa lo había echado:	answers back laughingly:
—Pienso que burla tu alteza	"I think Your Highness is joking
o quiere probar el vado;	or he wants to test the water;

	no me lo mandéis, señor,	don't order me to do it, sire,
20	*que perderé gran ditado.*	for I have much to lose."
	El rey le hace juramento	The King swears to her
	que de veras se lo ha hablado;	that he has spoken with truth;
	ella aún lo disimula	she still dissembles
	y burlando se ha excusado.	and jokingly excuses herself.
25	*Fuése el rey dormir la siesta;*	The King went to sleep his nap;
	por la Cava ha enviado,	he has sent for Cava.
	la Cava muy descuidada	Cava carelessly
	fuése do el rey la ha llamado.	retires to where the King has summoned her).

(pp. 44–45)

Surviving in several versions, this is one of the most widely diffused ballads on the legend of Rodrigo and Cava. The text given above is not the earliest version; Menéndez Pidal gives it in his anthology because of its economy of expression—i.e., because it is indicative of a "well-traditionalized" composition. Several basic characteristics are demonstrated that we will recognize time and again in the pages that follow. In addition to the aposiopesis involved in suppressing the description of actual immorality between Rodrigo and Cava, we note the summariness of the three major movements of the ballad (physical description, dialogue, implied denouement), the extreme instability in verbal tense,[6] and the almost symbolic or metonymic fashion in which essential characteristics of personality or meaning are given. Consideration of these various features will facilitate this first orientation in the medieval Spanish ballad.

An initial approximation to this ballad must note the balanced tripartite division: eight verses of introduction, which stresses Rodrigo's reaction to Cava's beauty, twelve verses given over to an exchange between Rodrigo and the woman, and eight more verses that hint at the subsequent sexual relations between the two. Each part may be called "underdeveloped" to the extent that the audience must understand more through implication than direct statement. For example, in the first segment of the poem the *juglar* sets out to impress upon us Rodrigo's advances toward Cava and the high pitch his passion has reached due to the sensual beauty of the woman. When one compares this text with a sixteenth-century artistic ballad, "De una torre de palacio" ("From a palace tower"), which describes Rodrigo's furtive contemplation of Cava's luxurious bath—recalling Actaeon of Classical mythology—the enormous stylistic difference can be appreciated between the latter, Renaissance ballad which dwells on decorative detail and the elliptic, cursory treatment given by our medieval text. In eight lines, the ballad has barely space to refer to the meeting between the two, to refer to Rodrigo's aroused emotions, and to give no more than a suggestion of the woman's body. Absent are the extended formulaic descriptions of courtly love and the poetry of the fifteenth-century *Cancioneros (Songbooks)*. Only the slightest of references are needed to establish the poem's main point, Rodrigo's lustful involvement.

The second segment of the ballad is given over to the principals' own words. This is an important structural feature of this and other ballads. Having established a context of some major significance, the poem allows the heroes and the villains, so to speak, to reveal themselves with their own words. Soliloquies and dialogues do unquestionably lend dramatic intensity to oral or pseudo-oral literature, and the Spanish ballad is noted for placing the characters of these narrative works directly before the audience without the overtly intervening voice of the minstrel. More important, such dialogism promotes the "directness" in terms of action and human motivation associated with the *romances* that is in such sharp contrast to the nonnarrative and often tedious psychological introspection of contemporary fifteenth-century lyric poetry. Here, the few words uttered by each immediately serve to fix in the audience's mind their characters which are so pivotal in the elaboration in subsequent texts of the theme of sin and punishment.

The twelve verses are given in turn a balanced division into six for Rodrigo and six for Cava. Rodrigo's words are ambivalent, perhaps meant to be taken as indicative of his less-than-proper approach to the woman.[7] On the one hand he seems to hint at the formulas of courtly love when he begs a "remedy" (a frequent euphemism of courtly love; cf. its use in the *Celestina*) and when he promises to do her bidding, as, one assumes, a good liege lover (lines 9–12). On the other hand, Rodrigo makes it quite clear that he is ready to exercise his royal prerogatives (lines 13–14). Cava, in turn, is both discreet and worldly. We can safely guess that the ballad intends to portray her as willing and able to take advantage of her lord's passions. Her laughter and her clever words reveal, not the blushing timidity of the frightened maiden, but a skill at handling bold advances more suited to a courtesan. Although the actual physical encounter between the two is not detailed, the last line of the ballad, understood in terms of Cava's words, leaves little doubt as to her eventual compliance with Rodrigo's desires. Thus, the exchange between the two principals fulfills a double function in the economy of the poem: to present succinctly the pivotal character of each one and to provide the background necessary to grasp the implication of the elliptic conclusion. Key statements throughout the *romance*—the "metonymic fashion" referred to above—serve to avoid moral or epic discussion of the basic issues involved in order instead to focus simply on what the basic conflicts are and to imply their consequences.

What the consequences are to be of Rodrigo's advances toward Cava constitute the interest of subsequent ballads. The one transcribed below is another important medieval text and takes up the "story" with Cava's father learning of his daughter's dishonor. We might note that later ballads were composed to describe Cava's realization of her fall ("Bañando en sudor y llanto" ["Bathing in sweat and lament"]) and her decision to tell her father ("Cartas escribe la Cava" ["Cava writes a letter"]).

	En Ceupta está don Julián,	(Don Julián is in Ceuta,
	en Ceupta la bien nombrada:	Ceuta the well-named;
	para las partes de allende	to parts beyond
	quiere enviar su embajada;	he wishes to send his embassy;
5	*moro viejo la escrebía,*	an old Moor wrote it for him,
	y el conde se la notaba;	and the Count notarizes it;
	después que la hubo escrito	after he had written it
	al moro luego matara.	he then killed the Moor.
	Embajada es de dolor,	It is an embassy of grief,
10	*dolor para toda España.*	grief for all Spain.
	Las cartas van al rey moro,	The letters go to the Moorish king
	en las cuales le juraba	in which Julián swears to him
	que si de él recibe ayuda	that if he receives aid from him
	le dará por suya a España.	he will give him Spain as his.
15	*Madre España, ¡ay de ti!,*	Mother Spain, woe to you,
	en el mundo tan nombrada,	so well-named in the world,
	de las tierras la mejor,	the best of lands,
	la más apuesta y ufana,	the most gallant and proud,
	donde nace el fino oro,	where fine gold is born,
20	*donde hay veneros de plata,*	where there are silver lodes,
	abundosa de venados,	abundant in game,
	y de caballos lozana,	luxuriant in horses,

	briosa de lino y seda,	elegant in linen and silk,
	de óleo rico alumbrada,	enlightened in rich oil,
25	deleitosa de frutales,	delightful in fruit orchards,
	en azafrán alegrada,	gay in saffron,
	guarnecida de castillos,	adorned with castles,
	y en proezas extremada;	most towering in feats;
	por un perverso traidor	because of a traitor
30	toda serás abrasada.	you will be devastated.)

(pp. 47–48)

Menéndez Pidal's text here is shorter by half than other versions, which are characterized in the concluding segment by invectives against Julián for his traitorous decision to enlist Moorish support for his revenge and against Cava for having been the instrument of Rodrigo's transgressions. The latter point is significant for reinforcing the negative portrayal of Cava in the previous ballad and for implying that, as Adam lost Eden because of Eve, Rodrigo loses equally idyllic Spain (cf. lines 15–30). The thirty-verse version that we have given is neatly divided into two counterposed segments, one a description of Julián's decision and the other an encomium of Spain that recalls Isidore of Seville's *Laus Hispaniae,* all that more noteworthy for having been composed less than a century before the events described.

The first fourteen lines derive their poetic impact from the somber tone established by the anaphoric repetition in the first two verses. Between the first poem and this one, events have transpired that are to have momentous consequences, and this ballad must drive home the circumstances of treachery and revenge that will become the instruments for the divine punishment of Rodrigo's sin. In understanding the correlation made by the Rodrigo legend between the personal revenge of Julián and a divine punishment for Rodrigo, the reader must keep in mind he is considering literary examples of a cultural tradition that saw nothing ludicrous in assuming that the outcome of armed combat faithfully reflected God's judgment of the combatants and that God's will would unerringly manifest itself in trial by ordeal. In other words, when Rodrigo is to lose militarily in the face of the descending Moorish hordes, it is precisely because he no longer has the Lord on his side. (Indeed one insignificant text from the Rodrigo cycle deals with "combat justice." See "En la cibdad de Toledo" ["In the City of Toledo"].) It is against this background of a stern Germanic feudal code that we must appreciate the ballad's subtle interplay between divine castigation and personal vengeance. The effect of this first segment of the ballad derives, then, from the somberness accorded the details of Julián's preparation for treachery. We are shown the Count dictating his letter to the Moors, the letter which will offer them his assistance in the invasion of the Peninsula. A great amount of the effect of the scene relies on the sudden shift in line 8 from the circumstances of the letter to the killing of the old Moor who draws up the document. His execution in order to preserve secrecy is a typical metonymic procedure: the one suggestive action bespeaks all of the horror of the blood feud and high treason that constitute the backdrop of the ballad. The abrupt shift in tone and the symbolic value of the killing must have been most effective in sending a shiver of excitement through the minstrel's audience.

The remainder of the first fourteen verses are somewhat anticlimatic to the extent that they refer to the contents of the document sent by Julián to the Moors and serve to reinforce the audience's intuition as to its nefarious mission. Again the ballad makes use of repetition, this time the reiteration of *dolor* in lines 9 and 10. Perhaps the use of the word is meant to be double: in line 9, with reference to the document itself, we are reminded of the circumstances under which it is composed; in line 10, reference is made to the consequences which it is to have for all of Spain. Indeed, line 10 is introductory, and the verses that follow speak of the letter's destination and of its contents. With these references, the ballad shifts emphasis from the personal perspective of the dishonored father to the Spain that will suffer the scourge of his vengeance upon her leader. The last half of the poem is distinctly different in tone and function. It is, as we have observed, an encomium of Spain. Although at first we might think that two separate and unrelated poems have been run together here—a not uncommon circumstance in the early *Romancero*—several characteristics indicate that there is in fact a subtle relationship. We note that both parts have the same assonantal rhyme (*á-a;* see Appendix for a discussion of ballad metrics). Usually when disparate parts are run together, each retains its original rhyme.

Moreover, there is a certain importance to be attached to the use of the adjective *nombrada* in lines 2 and 16. In the first instance it is used to describe Ceupta (a Visigothic dependency on the Moroccan coast of which Julián was governor); later the adjective is used to

describe the Spain which is to be lost. That is to say, the adjective
serves to correlate not only two locales, one related to the source
of the invasion and the other the object of the invasion; it also
juxtaposes the personal and the national, a recurring feature of
the Rodrigo ballads. Thus, when the ballad shifts in the second part
from narrating Julián's steps to betray Spain to a stylized encomium
of the Peninsula, the anonymous minstrel is simply furthering the
relationship established by the source legends and chronicles between the invasion and a personal feud. In the last two lines of the
ballad, the encomium is explicitly related to Julián's treachery,
returning thus to the narrative point of departure and establishing
a convincing unity for the two segments.

We have given a rather detailed description of the particular
type of unity associated with these ballads in order at this early
stage in our discussion of the important medieval works to underline
what are common procedures. We are proceeding on the assumption
that the ballads reveal characteristically expressive patterns and
that those patterns deserve comprehension if we are to attribute
any artistic importance to the major ballad texts. Although the
critic may insist that the ballads are poetry deserving of close
structural analysis, he cannot escape the fact that circumstances
of composition and transmission have left their imprint. Elliptic
allusions, sudden shifts of narrative focus and tone, as well as the
imaginative correlation of historically unrelated events, often make
a ballad difficult to follow. At the same time, once we understand
the unity underlying any one ballad, we are in a better position to
appreciate the quality of the dramatic effects achieved by the skilled
minstrels.

Subsequent texts center on Rodrigo and his personal involvement
in the loss of Spain to the Moors. The impression, then, that one
receives from the interrelated ballads concerning Rodrigo and the
fall of Spain is that of a concerted effort on the part of legend and
ballad tradition to give some sort of personal dimension to the
Moorish conquest, to explain, as it were, in human terms what
must have been a disaster comprehensible at that time only as a
divine judgment. Hence the elaboration of a sequence of events
where one man's sinful lust serves as the mainspring for the castigation of an entire people. Although the major ballads show some
ambivalence toward the principals, now condemning Rodrigo,
now condemning Julián, now sympathizing with the king's loss,

there is no question that underlying unity rests ultimately upon a pseudo-epic vision of the fall of the mighty through their own sin, a vision which E. M. Wilson has accurately described as a recurring tragic dimension of the early Spanish ballads.[8]

II *The Infantes of Lara*

Rivaling the Rodrigo legend in dramatic intensity and narrative interest are the ballads dealing with the blood feud between the seven Infantes (Princes) of Lara (also called Salas) and their maternal uncle, who orders them killed out of spiteful vengeance. Set in Castile during the late tenth century, when Count Garci-Fernández, son of the legendary Fernán González, ruled, the story of the seven brothers attained epic stature in lost texts that have been roughly reconstructed on the basis of fourteenth- and fifteenth-century chronicles.[9] An unusually rich ballad tradition has derived from the lost epic texts, and the critic is confronted by an embarrassingly divergent selection of variants that complicate his presentation of the major examples of the sequence. In addition, some of the most important appear to derive from the blending together into one ballad of several scattered segments of the epic, with the result that key texts are far too long to quote in their entirety in a critical study.[10] The discussion which follows, therefore, can only pretend to give the outlines of the material and to indicate some of the salient poetic characteristics of the important ballad texts.

Menéndez Pidal prefaces his selection of texts in the anthology from which we are quoting with the following passage in imitation of the chronicles: "Of how [the seven Infantes of Lara] were betrayed and killed by their uncle Rodrigo Velázquez, during the times in which Count Garcí-Fernández saw Castile threatened by the conquering companies of the Moor Almanzor; and our story tells also how the death of the Infantes was later avenged by Mudarra González. It is a most piteous story of how a small insult grows into great discord, causes mortal enemies and a fearsome vengeance; the vengeance feeds long hatreds that wither the heart; the old hatreds engender new life, and the new generation is raised for hatred and for vengeance" (p. 101). Clearly, Menéndez Pidal's intent is to set a mood of Old Testament proportions, a mood in keeping with a blood feud involving the greatest of the realm and intercepting in its course the turbulent political events associated with the shifting instabilities of the post-Visigothic Christian kingdoms and their relationship with the firmly entrenched Moorish nation. It is a mood calculated to recall the harsh times of the tenth century when strange alliances and the complex interweaving of political, personal, religious, and economic relationships between Christians and Moors bespeak the coming-to-terms in the Peninsula between the fragmented Christians and the infidels, whose advanced culture and political organization was an ever-present and inescapable reality. It is important to note that, as in the case of the Rodrigo legend, the Infantes' murder is effected through the enlistment by their uncle of the help of Moorish troops. Moreover, and indicating the attempt of popular tradition to seek a counterbalancing force for the nefarious role of the Moorish troops, revenge for the dead brothers is sought successfully by Mudarra, the Infantes' half brother and the son of a Moorish maiden. Thus, the cycle achieves a synthesis between Christian and Moor—both are equally implicated in the treacherous circumstances where the clash between evil hatred and manly virtue transcends the limits of religious differences. But in another way, for popular tradition it would appear that an appropriate working out of feudal virtues was held in higher esteem than religious and political conflicts. And, indeed, historians and sociologists have frequently underlined this conclusion.

The first text that we will consider is both long and unstable in the number of versions and variants recorded. Approximately the first half is devoted to describing the convening of the marriage party of Rodrigo Velázquez, uncle of the seven Infantes. We are told of the preparations for the period of celebration, in particular the setting up of the *tablado,* a mock castle which contestants attempt to knock down with heavy darts. It is against this background of a feudal game, a game which, as in most societies, bespeaks the concerns and the values of the contestants, that the central action of the legend is presented:

En el arenal del río,	(On the river's strand,
esa linda doña Lambra,	pretty Doña Lambra
con muy grande fantasía,	with great artistry
altos tablados armara;	has set up a *tablado.*
75 tiran unos, tiran otros,	These ones throw, those ones throw,
ninguno bien bohordaba.	but none does well in knocking it over.
Allí salió un hijodalgo	There appeared an *hidalgo*

de Bureba la preciada;
caballero en un caballo
80 y en la su mano una vara,
arremete su caballo,
al tablado la tirara,
voceando: —¡Amad, señoras,
cada cual como es amada!,
85 que más vale un caballero
de Bureba la preciada,
que no siete ni setenta
de los de la flor de Lara.
    Doña Lambra que lo oyera,
90 en mucho se holgara:
¡Oh, maldita sea la dama
que su cuerpo te negara;
si yo casada no fuera,
el mío te lo entregaba!
95 Oídolo ha doña Sancha,
responde muy apenada:
—Calléis, Alambra, calléis,
no digáis tales palabras,
porque aun hoy os desposaron

100 con don Rodrigo de Lara.
—Mas calléis vos, doña Sancha,
que tenéis por qué callar,
que paristeis siete hijos
como puerca en cenagal.
105 Todo lo oye un caballero
que a los infantes criara;
llorando de los sus ojos,
con angustia y mortal rabia,
se fué para los palacios
110 do los infantes estaban;
unos juegan a los dados,
otros juegan a las tablas.
Aparte está Gonzalvico,
de pechos a una baranda:
115 —¿Cómo venís triste, ayo?
Decid, ¿quién os enojara?
Tanto le rogó Gonzalo,
que el ayo se lo contara.
—Mas mucho os ruego, mi hijo
120 que no salgáis a la plaza.

from Bureba the prized,
a knight on a horse
and a dart in his hand.
He spurs his horse
and throws at the *tablado*,
shouting: "Love, ladies,
each as she is loved,
for a knight
from Bureba the prized
is worth more than seven or seventy
of the flower of Lara."
    Doña Lambra who heard him
was quite pleased:
"Oh damned be the woman
who would deny you her body;
for if I were not married,
mine would be yours!"
    Doña Sancha heard this,
she replies with great pain:
"Quiet, Alambra, be quiet,
don't say such things,
for just today have you been married
to Don Rodrigo de Lara."
"Be quiet yourself, Doña Sancha,
for you've good reason to be quiet.
You gave birth to seven sons
like any quagmire pig."
    All this is heard by a knight
who had raised the Infantes.
Crying with great sobs,
in anguish and dire rage,
he went to the palace
where the Infantes were.
Some are playing dice,
others checkers.
Gonzalvico is to one side,
leaning over a railing.
"Why are you so sad, tutor?
Tell me, who made you angry?"
Gonzalo begged him so much
that the tutor told him.
"But I beg you, my son,
not to go to the square."

No lo quiso hacer Gonzalo,	Gonzalo did not want to heed him
mas su caballo demanda;	and demands his horse.
llega a la plaza al galope,	He comes to the square at a gallop,
pedido había una vara,	asks for a dart
125 *y vido estar el tablado*	and sees that no one
que nadie lo derribara;	had knocked down the *tablado.*
alzóse en las estriberas,	He rose up in his stirrups,
con él en el suelo daba.	and knocked it to the ground.
Desque lo hubo derribado,	After knocking it down,
130 *desta manera hablara:*	he spoke in this fashion:
—Amad, amad, damas ruines,	"Love, love, base women,
cada cual como es amada,	each as she is loved,
que más vale un caballero	for a knight
135 *de los de la flor de Lara,*	of the flower of Lara
que cuarenta ni cincuenta	is worth more than forty or fifty
de Bureba la preciada.	from Bureba the prized.")

(pp. 102–15)

What is most striking is the fact—made almost too obvious—
that the sequence of events is set in motion by an entirely gratuitous
insult made about her hosts by doña Lambra, the bride. That it
is made in terms of the game in progress and that it concerns the
skill of rival groups is significant. This detail not only plays on the
fragmentation and bitter rivalry between Christians; from the point
of view of the development of the ballad, having the insult that
will lead to murderous treachery made within the context of a game
of war justifies the initial segment of the ballad in which the game
is set up as part of the marriage festivities. In addition, the game
itself becomes a foreshadowing of events in which the hostilities
engendered by it will be transformed into the blood feud of treachery,
revenge, and vengeance. In the segment reproduced, the insults
involving rival groups convert the game in which a mock castle
must be knocked down into a symbolic exercise in hostile challenge.
Claiming Cordoban superiority over the Laras, doña Lambra is
to see the *tablado* easily demolished by the youngest of the brothers
in defiant proof of their superiority. In the concluding segment of
the ballad, which we do not include, the bride angrily demands
revenge from her husband, who is only too willing to accede.

From what we have said, it should be apparent that the ballad
is far from "facile" or "charmingly ingenuous," dubious value

judgments of a more Romantic orientation. Although there is, as in the majority of major examples, an unadorned directness resulting from traditional compression of source materials, we find nevertheless subtle organizational features. In the first place, the use of the inconsequential game to prefigure more somber events, events which are foreshadowed in the descriptive first half of the poem (cf. lines 31–32: "The marriage is now arranged,/oh Lord, at what an unlucky hour!"). The significant segment of the ballad is based on a correlation between the Cordoban who first tries his skill with moderate success (lines 80–83) and the youngest brother, whose success is more definitive (lines 124–29). Between the two attempts is the shift from game to earnest challenge. Parallel to this correlation is the formula repeated by both men (lines 83–88 and lines 131–37). It is the first occurrence of the formula, uttered by one of Lambra's compatriots, that occasions her insult to the Laras and in particular to doña Sancha, the Infantes' mother (lines 101–4). When Gonzalo utters the formula in his successful attempt at the *tablado,* it is clear that it is no longer to be understood as part of feudal competition, but as a serious challenge to his new aunt. The ballad immediately makes a transition to Lambra's demand to her husband Rodrigo, a transition indicating at once that the whole tone of the game has changed radically. Indeed, although Menéndez Pidal's text is more restrained in suggesting the nature of the shift in meaning of the formula of challenge by alternating "ladies" (line 83) with "base women," some texts are more explicit by having Gonzalo say "whores."[11] The latter reading is certainly more telling in indicating the deterioration of events.

Another characteristic of the ballad's narrative procedure is the absence of the Infantes when the insult takes place; they are represented, so to speak, by their tutor, from whom Gonzalo learns what happens. This absence heightens dramatic effect on the one hand by keeping the Infantes offstage until the climactic moment. It also allows for greater parallelism of structure: Gonzalo is able to ride up to defend his name and his family in the same fashion as the Cordoban has insulted them, thus providing greater rhetorical balance in the ballad.[12] Mention must also be made of the geographical carelessness of the ballad: Calatrava la Vieja and Córdoba were at the time outside Christian territory and therefore inappropriate locales for the wedding and Lambra's family. Such carelessness —found also in names and dates—is only a further indication of a well-recognized ballad trait: that the interest of the *romances* lies, not in repeating historical events as such, but in using those events for the beliefs, the traditions, and values which they symbolize.

Perhaps the most famous of all of the Lara ballads concerns the lament of the brothers' father. Prisoner of the Moor Almanzor in—ironically—Córdoba, Gonzalo Gustios is brought the heads of his murdered sons by Alicante, the Moor whose troops laid the trap for the Infantes. In one of the most moving passages of the *Romancero,* Gonzalo laments before his sympathetic Moorish captors the fate of his sons and their tutor (the reader becomes aware of the fruitless task of attempting to untangle the confusion of personal names used by the father):

	Así razona con ellas	(He speaks to them thus,
	como si vivos hablasen:	as though they were alive:
	—¡Sálveos Dios, Nuño Salido,	"God save you, Nuño Salido,
	el mi compadre leal!,	my loyal comrad!
35	*¿adónde son los mis hijos*	Where are my sons
	que yo os quise encomendar?	that I entrusted to you?
	Mas perdonadme, compadre,	But pardon me, comrade;
	no he por qué os demandar,	I must not press you so,
	muerto sois como buen ayo,	for you are dead like a good tutor,
40	*como hombre muy de fiar.* [. . .]	like a trustworthy man."
	Tomando la del menor	Taking the youngest's head,
	el dolor se le doblaba:	his grief doubled:
	—¡Hijo Gonzalo González,	"My son Gonzalo González,
100	*los ojos de doña Sancha!*	the apple of Doña Sancha's eyes!
	¡Qué nuevas irán a ella,	What news will go to her,
	que a vos más que a todos ama!	who loved you above all others!
	¡Tan apuesto de persona,	So fine in your person,
	decidor bueno entre damas,	articulate with the ladies,
105	*repartidor de su haber,*	generous with possessions,
	aventajado en la lanza!	excellent with the lance!
	¡Mejor fuera la mi muerte	Better were my death
	que ver tan triste jornada!	than to behold so sorrowful a day!"
	Al duelo que el viejo hace,	All Cordoba lamented
110	*toda Códoba lloraba.*	the old man's grief.
	El rey Almanzor, cuidoso,	King Almanzor, attentive,
	consigo se lo llevaba	took him along
	y mandaba a una morica	and sent a Moorish maiden
	lo sirviese muy de gana.	to serve him willingly.
115	*Ésta le torna en prisiones*	She returned him to his prison

y con amor le curaba;	and cured him with love.
hermana era del rey,	She was the King's sister,
doncella moza y lozana;	a young and elegant girl.
con ésta Gonzalo Gustios	With her Gonzalo Gustios
120 *vino a perder la su saña,*	came to lose his anger,
que de ella nació un hijo	for from her was born a son
que a los hermanos vengara.	who would avenge the brothers.)

(pp. 111–15)

This unusually long ballad is divided into three major movements (and derives directly from surviving epic fragments); we have repeated part of the second and all of the third. The first segment concerns the delivery of the severed heads of the seven brothers to the Moorish king Almanzor by Alicante. Being of Christians, the heads are put before Almanzor's captive, Gonzalo Gustios, who recognizes them as the tutor and his sons. This initial segment is not intended to characterize unfavorably the Moors involved. Rodrigo forces Alicante to cooperate with his scheme and it is he who arranges to have the heads delivered to where the father will see them; the latter's grief is part of his sadistic plan. Thus, the Moors are only unwitting instruments, and the ballad is careful to present them neutrally in this introduction; no suggestion is made that their presentation of the heads to Gonzalo is anything other than deference to the captive's possible interest in the death of "men of noble blood."

The central segment runs from lines 25 to 108 and is a series of eight encomia, as Gonzalo takes each head in turn and pronounces a eulogy of the dead man. In order to give some sort of rhetorical coherence to this portion of the ballad, the creative tradition has stressed for each man symbolic feudal virtues. Thus, the tutor and his seven charges are converted into exempla of manly traits held in esteem by the supposed audience. For example, the tutor is praised for his loyalty, a loyalty that led him innocently to the same fate as the Infantes. In lines 41ff. Gonzalo praises his seven sons. The first son is commended for his goodness, a virtue not merely indicative of a generous and pleasant disposition, but bespeaking the perfection of Christian grace. In terms of the dramatic effects manipulated by the ballad, lines 49–50 are important, not only for the pathetic scene of the father's tears cleansing the bloody head, but for giving added narrative function to the manner in which the father recognizes his sons. The action involved in taking up

each head in turn is made static briefly while mention is made of
a symbolic virtue, only to be brought out again by some sort of
transitional gesture as the father moves on to the next head. What
we have is a competent fusion of stylized eulogy and vivid narrative
action.[13] Of particular concern is the eulogy of Gonzalo, the youngest
of the sons and, as we have seen, the focal point of insult, challenge,
and revenge. As we will point out in the discussion of the last of
the Infantes ballads, Gonzalo's presence underlies the vengeance
of the brothers' murder. Gonzalo is praised first in terms of his
relationship with his mother (see comments on the conclusion of
the following ballad). Rather than illustrative of any one feudal
virtue, Gonzalo's personality is indicative more of a general nobility
of spirit and overall perfection of person, as his father refers to his
appearance, his courtesy, his generosity, his prowess. There is the
constant presence of the family unit at this point, and the father is
most concerned with the effect which Gonzalo's death will have
upon doña Sancha. Representative of all of the brothers together,
Gonzalo's death evokes from the father (after whom he is significantly named) the adynaton of lines 107–8 that synthesize the man's
unrelenting grief.

It would have been understandable for the ballad to terminate
with Gonzalo Gustios' final words; certainly their pathetic intensity
constitutes a superb climax. However, the poem does not conclude
at this point, and a third segment has been preserved from the source
material which lays the basis for the vengeance of the eight deaths.
Rather than shifting abruptly at this moment of transition in focus,
the ballad dwells on the pathos of Gustios' lament and describes
its effect on the Moorish audience. It is at this stage that we are
assured, so to speak, that the Moors are not conscious parties to
Rodrigo's perfidy. We have mentioned already the synthesis sought
by medieval tradition through the ballads of this sequence between
the Christians and the Moors, who are seen joined together by a
common sense of justice and decency even though they may be
separated by antagonistic religions. Thus, the ballad under consideration stresses the Moors' role in laying the basis for the
vengeance of the treachery of which they were an unwitting part.
Almanzor's solicitous behavior toward Gonzalo in sending his
sister to the captive is more than just generosity born of the
Christian's piteous lament. Seen in terms of the concluding verses,
as well as in terms of the next ballad, what Almanzor is basically

doing is providing Gonzalo with the opportunity to beget a son of mixed blood who will avenge not only the Christians but the Moors as well. Thus, the ballad implies very clearly a dominant concern, not with political and religious allegiances—probably of little importance and comprehension anyway to the more popular audience of the minstrels—but with issues of evil and justice. In a popular and traditional ballad, where social values are reduced to more clearly folkloric and mythic perspectives,[14] the need for primitive justice to triumph over the unacceptable evil represented by Rodrigo neutralizes any meaningful conflict between Christian and Moor. To repeat a cliché of ballad commentaries, conflict is here reduced to fundamental human values.

In contrast to the pathos of the preceding text, the last ballad—in terms of the "story" of the Infantes—returns to the somber and forbidding tone associated with the treachery of the brothers. Nonverisimilar in the complete isolation of the two men, the ballad is a masterpiece of economy for its omission of events leading up to the encounter of Rodrigo and Mudarra—the Moorish half brother who is destined to avenge the Infantes—and its exclusive concentration on the encounter itself and the realization of vengeance:

A caza va don Rodrigo,	(Don Rodrigo is out hunting,
ese que dicen de Lara;	he who is said to be from Lara.
perdido había el azor,	He lost his goshawk
no hallaba ninguna caza;	and found no game.
5 *con la gran siesta que hace*	On account of the great heat,
arrimado se ha a una haya,	he has rested against a beech,
maldiciendo a Mudarrillo,	cursing Mudarillo,
hijo de la renegada,	the son of the renegade.
que si a las manos hubiese	If he had him in his clutches,
10 *que le sacaría el alma.*	he would tear his heart out.
El señor estando en esto,	As the man was engaged in this,
Mudarrillo que asomaba:	Mudarillo came into view;
—Dios te salve, buen señor,	"God keep you, good sir,
debajo la verde haya.	beneath the green beech."
15 *—Así haga a ti, caballero;*	"The same to you, knight,
buena sea tu llegada.	be welcome."
—Dígasme, señor, tu nombre,	"Tell me, sir, your name,
decirte he yo la mi gracia.	and I will tell you mine."
—A mí me llaman don Rodrigo,	"They call me Don Rodrigo,
20 *y aun don Rodrigo de Lara,*	better, Don Rodrigo de Lara,

	cuñado de don Gonzalo,	brother-in-law of Don Gonzalo,
	hermano de doña Sancha;	brother of Doña Sancha.
	por sobrinos me los hube	My nephews were
	los siete infantes de Lara.	the seven Infantes of Lara.
25	*Maldigo aquí a Mudarrillo,*	I'm cursing Mudarillo,
	hijo de la renegada,	son of the renegade.
	si delante lo tuviese,	If I had him here before me,
	yo le sacaría el alma.	I would tear out his heart."
	—Si a ti dicen don Rodrigo,	"If they call you Don Rodrigo,
30	*y aun don Rodrigo de Lara,*	better, Don Rodrigo of Lara,
	a mí Mudarra González,	they call me Mudarra González,
	hijo de la renegada,	son of the renegade,
	de Gonzalo Gustios hijo	son of Gonzalo Gustios
	y alnado de doña Sancha;	and Doña Sancha's stepson.
35	*por hermanos me los hube*	My brothers were
	los siete infantes de Lara;	the seven Infantes de Lara;
	tú los vendiste, traidor,	you sold them out, traitor,
	en el val del Arabiana.	in the vale of Arabiana.
	Mas si Dios ahora me ayuda,	But if God will help me,
40	*aquí dejarás el alma.*	here you leave your soul."
	—Espéresme, don Mudarra,	"Wait for me, Don Mudarra,
	iré a tomar las mis armas.	and I will go for my weapons."
	—El espera que tú diste	"The wait you gave the
	a los infantes de Lara;	seven Infantes de Lara;
45	*aquí morirás, traidor,*	here you will die, traitor,
	enemigo de doña Sancha.	Doña Sancha's enemy.")

(pp. 116–17)

Bénichou is accurate in calling attention to what might be at
first glance the unusual circumstance that the focus of the ballad
is not the avenger Mudarra, but the traitorous Rodrigo.[15] Of basic
interest is the composition's balance of emphasis: both initial segment and first speech are accorded Rodrigo, while Mudarra is
allowed to speak only at the end when he identifies himself and
proceeds to execute Rodrigo. Traditionalists have been hard put
to explain both the source of the ballad and the shift in emphasis
to Rodrigo.[16] On the one hand, "A caza . . ." appears to be far
closer to "free" or "individual" composition than Menéndez
Pidal's investigations would tend to permit. There are lacking even
faint echoes of lines found in other ballads, of lines found in surviving epic material or prose versions. The best that can be done
is to appeal, as does Bénichou, to some vague notion of latent tradi-

tion: "In summary, there is between the ballad and previous tradition no textual coincidence that would oblige us to believe in any sort of affiliation. It appears that scattered memories have gotten organized into a poem with the help of formulas characteristic of traditional poetry, especially of the epic. . . . We can speak of the birth of the poem as a new initiative, as the work of poetic renovation on the basis of data, patterns, impressions that survived in the memory of their forgotten formal expression" (pp. 50–52). This is perilously close to admitting the presence of a unique poetic text, striking for its departure from existing chronicle material and its apparent *creative autonomy*. Although there is an understandable reluctance to venture such an affirmation in Bénichou's comments, his informative analysis of the ballad centers on the important uniqueness of the composition in suggesting a premonition and resignation to inevitable fate on Rodrigo's part (cf. p. 59), the exclusion of all but the two protagonists, and the execution of the traitor on the spot, in contrast to the protracted revenge described by the contemporary chronicles.

Turning more closely to the text itself, we have already noted the tripartite division into introduction, Rodrigo's speech, and Mudarra's speech. Of particular significance, especially in terms of the interrelationship of the texts on a particular subject so characteristic of the historical ballads, based as they are on a series of epic materials of some thematic unity, are the implied references to the omen preceding the Infantes' murder. Whereas in an earlier text, Rodrigo is represented in the omen by the sparrowhawk in full command of its strength, in the present text, the uncle's hunting azor—the goshawk—has gotten away from him and he is unarmed and defenseless. Strengthening the internal references between the two ballads, the omen takes place in a pine tree; here Rodrigo is resting against another tree, a beech tree that is to be the site, this time, of his own death. (Some texts are more specific than Menéndez Pidal's version quoted above and show Rodrigo impaled mortally against the beech by Mudarra's lance, distinctly recalling the death by laceration in the omen. [cf. Bénichou's text, p. 46, lines 26–28].) Finally, although Mudarra identifies himself by that name, Rodrigo addresses him in some texts as Gonzalo or Gonzalillo (the former name is used consistently in the prose version in the mid fourteenth-century *Arreglo toledano de la Segunda Crónica* [*Toledo Arrangement of the Second Chronicle*]). Indeed, our text (line 41) can probably be called an example of editorial hypercorrection not justified by known texts (cf. approximately line 23 in sixteen-syllable versions; line 40 in octosyllabic ones). The whole point, as one may have guessed, is the fact that the ballad involving the warning to the brothers focuses metonymically on Gonzalo in order to show the unwise refusal to appreciate the validity of the omen. Gonzalo is both the central figure in the ballad involving Lambra's insult, and his words in another text are the ironic prelude to the massacre. Thus it is only appropriate that the younger brother be recalled in the vengeance of the treachery. It is symbolic enough that Mudarra be a half brother and that he be half Christian and half Moor—vengeance is to come from within the family and by the hand of one who represents the two groups implicated in the assassination of the Infantes. It is only natural, then, that some texts should cast the avenging brother as a new Gonzalo, the synthesis and the quintessence of the martyred brothers' noble virtues.

All of this is, we suggest, the implied background to the encounter between Rodrigo and Mudarra. They are alone in this encounter, and their solitude heightens the decisive confrontation between the figure of Evil and the figure of Good. In the opening lines of the ballad, Rodrigo's solitude is underlined by his defenselessness, already cast in our analysis as of major consequence. Whether his inner thoughts and his almost expectant posture are indeed a premonition and a resignation to the necessary and ultimate triumph of virtue over evil, or whether the ballad simply uses these lines to establish context and principals, is a matter of speculation. Certainly, little doubt is left for the audience as to who is involved and—on the basis of lines 7–10—how Rodrigo is to strike the audience. His violent thoughts—possibly the consequence of another omen in reverse or the warning of a messenger—reinforce his characterization as a figure of fratricidal evil.

The basic feature of the verbal exchange between Rodrigo and Mudarra is the parallelism of their presentation to each other. Lines 19–28 and lines 29–40 constitute identical rhetorical units involving name, family, relationship to the seven Infantes, and threat to the opposing interlocutor. Stylized expression of this sort has many functions; perhaps the most frequent is to formalize the material and to lend it somberness and dignity of noncolloquial formulaic procedure. Moreover, in this ballad the parallelism in expression may be interpreted as a further attempt to make overt the antagonism and antithesis between the two men. It is significant to note that Mudarra's speech is two lines longer than Rodrigo's and that this slight variation in parallelism comes as a result of adding to the mention of the Infantes the crucial statement of denunciation contained in lines 37–38. Thus, the rigidity of stylized expression is disturbed only to intercalate Mudarra's accusation. Both the force of his words and the deviation from the parallelism serve to emphasize the point of departure for Mudarra's vengeance. The concluding lines of the poem move quickly to the denouement. Again, the actual climactic moment of Rodrigo's death is suppressed in some texts, as it is in ours, and the execution of justice is left implied. As has been pointed out, such suppression is frequent in the *Romancero*. Like good pornographic literature, the Spanish ballad exploits the greater vividness and lasting impact of that which is competently implied rather than merely described. Thus, we are told only the last exchange of the two, involving reference to Rodrigo's defenselessness and Mudarra's assertion that Rodrigo will die, like the Infantes, without being able to defend himself.

One last detail deserves comment. Why does Mudarra invoke Sancha (his father's legal wife and mother of the Infantes), rather than Gonzalo Gustios, the Infantes' father? Doña Sancha's reaction to her sons' death is absent at least from the major ballads, whereas the father's lament is the subject of one of the most famous texts. One explanation is that it is simply the remnant of doña Sancha's larger role in avenging her sons related in the prose chronicles. There she is cast in a most fearsome role. However, if it is true that "A caza . . ." contains no lines that are merely reflexes of source material (cf. Bénichou's comments discussed above), reference to doña Sancha here may fulfill another more intrinsic function. We suggest that reference to her here is meant to correlate with the role of her sister-in-law in instigating the murder of her sons. Whereas Rodrigo acts in the first instance because of his wife's demands for revenge against her new husband's family, the implication of our ballad is that Sancha is the motivating force behind Mudarra's vengeance. Thus, the two women, antagonists from the moment of the insult in the first ballad, are implicated in the final working out of the tragedy. Lambra is the source of the insult and the treachery, and Sancha is introduced at the last to imply her presence as the guiding force of the denouement. Between the two women stands Rodrigo, husband and brother and the dominant individual of this last ballad. Through him does the revenge occur and upon him do the final castigation of virtue and the reprobative judgment of tradition fall heavy.

The first two groups of historical ballads are thus seen to deal with events of a distinctly tragic dimension. Both are concerned with blood feuds and both articulate on an impressive scale values associated with medieval Spanish society, values related to fundamental religious and feudal concepts of guilt, retribution, and vengeance.

III *The Cid*

The most extensive and most outstanding historical segment of the *Romancero viejo* is made up of those ballads dealing with Rodrigo (or Ruy) Díaz de Vivar, el Cid. A historical figure (1043–1099), the Cid, who has come to be Spain's medieval national hero, is sharply differentiated from King Rodrigo and the Infantes in not being of royal or noble lineage, but rather a member of a warrior class that today we might call middle class. The ballads concerning this figure are divided into two quite different groups: those concerning his youth, in which he is presented as a rebellious and headstrong individual; and those concerning the exploits recounted in the *Poema de Mio Cid* (1140), Spain's only epic surviving virtually intact, in which the Cid is elevated to the stature of a symbol of emerging Peninsular unity and an embodiment that puts those of noble birth to shame of their own feudal values. The impressive popularity of the Cid as a national hero would appear to derive from this crucial blending of nonnoble birth with the highest sense of those virtues held to be most noble in a man. The trajectory of the Cid ballads—that is, the texts seen in terms of their chronological presentation of a maturing and aging warrior—dwell pointedly on this circumstance.

The first two ballads which we will consider belong to the *mocedades del Cid,* to the period of the Cid's youth, the most important event of which is his feud with the woman who is to later become his loving and faithful wife. These ballads, although they refer to a biographically earlier period, appear to derive from a source later than the twelfth-century *Poema de Mio Cid,* the *Mocedades de Rodrigo (Rodrigo's Youth),* composed during the fourteenth and fifteenth centuries. This body of narrative material, the source of the Spanish and French Renaissance dramas on the Cid (the *Poema* is "lost" between the late Middle Ages and the eighteenth century), portrays a more romanticized Rodrigo, a youth characterized by a temperament and a haughtiness out of keeping with the serene nobility that comes through in the earlier epic. The general gist of the first set of ballads concerns Rodrigo's conflict between his love for Ximena and his obligation to avenge her father's insult to his enfeebled father. Rodrigo accepts his manly duty, is successful, only to see Ximena demand (understandably) satisfaction from the king, her protector. Given this conflict and its resolution in the final marriage of the two, it is easy to see why this pseudo-courtly story—of as much tragic dimension as one will find at this period—enjoyed an immense popularity during subsequent centuries.[17] Our first text concerns the unfortunate test of filial duty with which the young warrior is confronted:

Pensativo estaba el Cid	(The Cid was pensive,
viéndose de pocos años	seeing how young he was
para vengar a su padre	for avenging his father
matando al conde Lozano;	by killing Count Lozano.
5 *miraba el bando temido*	He contemplated the fearful band
del poderoso contrario,	of the powerful opponent,
que tenía en las montañas	who had in the mountains
mil amigos asturianos;	a thousand Asturian friends.
miraba cómo en la corte	He saw how in the court
10 *de ese buen rey don Fernando*	of that good King Don Fernando
era su voto el primero	his voice was the first
y en guerra el mejor su brazo;	and his the greatest arm in battle.
todo le parece poco	All this seems to him trivial
para vengar este agravio,	in avenging this insult,
15 *el primero que se ha hecho*	the first ever to come
a la sangre de Laín Calvo;	to the blood of Laín Calvo.
no cura de su niñez,	He is not concerned about his youth,
que en el alma del hidalgo	for in the hidalgo's heart
el valor para crecer	courage to grow
20 *no tiene cuenta a los años.*	does not take account of years.
Descolgó una espada vieja	He took down an old sword,
de Mudarra el castellano,	the Spaniard Mudarra's,
que estaba toda mohosa,	that was all rusty
por la muerte de su amo.	due to its master's death.
25 *"Haz cuenta, valiente espada,*	"Take heed, valiant sword,
que es de Mudarra mi brazo	for my arm is Mudarra's

	y que con su brazo riñes	and with his arm you fight
	porque suyo es el agravio.	because the insult is his.
	Bien puede ser que te corras	Well it might be that you are vexed
30	*de verte así en la mi mano,*	seeing yourself thus in my hand.
	mas no te podrás correr	But you cannot be vexed
	de volver atrás un paso.	by taking a step backward.
	Tan fuerte como tu acero	As strong as your steel
	me verás en campo armado;	will you see me in the armed field;
35	*tan bueno como el primero,*	as good as the first one
	segundo dueño has cobrado;	you have found a second master.
	y cuando alguno te venza,	And if someone should overcome you,
	del torpe hecho enojado,	angered by the clumsy event,
	hasta la cruz en mi pecho	up to the hilt in my breast
40	*te esconderé muy airado.*	will I hide you in my fury.
	Vamos al campo, que es hora	Let us go to the field, for
	de dar al conde Lozano	it is time to give to Count Lozano
	el castigo que merece	the punishment deserved by
	tan infame lengua y mano."	so infamous a tongue and hand."
45	*Determinado va el Cid,*	The Cid departs with determination,
	y va tan determinado,	and he goes so determined
	que en espacio de una hora	that in an hour
	mató al conde y fué vengado.	he killed the Count and was avenged.)

(pp. 132–33)

As in the ballads in general, the effect of this text depends on and derives from the immediate establishment of fundamental narrative action. We are placed here before the Cid as he struggles with the problems presented by the need to avenge an insult to his father. The first half of the ballad (lines 1–20) are to be understood in terms of the initial characterization of the Cid's mood as "thoughtful." Thoughtful, the Cid considers the implications of what he is about to do because he must. It is fascinating to observe how the creative process—be it the work of one minstrel or of several—organizes these first verses in order to bring out the Cid's concern. On the one hand he must consider the strength of the enemy (*miraba* . . . [line 5]); on the other hand he must consider his reputation at court (*miraba* . . . [line 9]). Both constitute serious cause for reservations. The balanced anaphora of these lines suggests the weighty issues involved, weighty issues which are, however, brushed aside in lines 13–16, when consideration of the proportions of the offense dispel definitively any hesitation. The next four lines are, in fact, a justification of the Cid's decision and an attempt to have the audience understand the manliness involved in the youth's sure resolution. At this point, thoughtfulness, the opening note of the ballad, has given way to unwavering commitment. The buildup to this commitment is accomplished through the clever displacement of the tension suggested between the reasons given for the Cid's reservations and his unquestioning and ultimately triumphant sense of filial duty.

The second segment of the ballad is anticlimactic in structure. In the first place, it recounts the Cid's "psychological" preparations to do battle, preparations that follow naturally from the resolution arrived at in the preceding lines. This segment is also anticlimactic in the use of the adjective "determined" in lines 45 and 46 to characterize the Cid's mood during the moments before he leaves to do battle. The adjective provides a characterization which is by this point in the poem obvious. However, its use is appropriate in another sense, for it serves to correlate with the opening adjective of the first line. That is to say, the two juxtaposed segments are provided a focal qualifier that characterizes the significant mood of the warrior at two crucial moments.

The transition from "thoughtful" to "determined" is exactly representative of the trajectory of the Cid's behavior that the ballad sets out to describe. In this respect, it is worth noting that the ballad does *not* detail the joined combat between Rodrigo and Count Lozano—this is not the principal concern of the composition. Rather, its principal concern is the psychological process involved in the youth's arriving at the proper decision to accept his responsibility as a man. For this reason, the Cid's "conversation" with the sword of Mudarra—an interesting detail in that it shows how the ballad will make do with a limited stock of well-known facts and items valuable for their recognition potential and symbolism—is an important and necessary feature of the ballad in that it demonstrates the scope of his now unshakable resoluteness. The anthropomorphization of the sword elevates it to the level of a symbol of manly worth, and the Cid's promise to be deserving of its prowess or to die by it is a hyperbolic passage intended to glamorize as much as possible. The almost offhanded way in which the Cid's success in his encounter with Lozano is described serves only to further emphasize the ballad's overwhelming interest in motivation and personality. The Cid emerges from this well-executed ballad as a

striking and attractive figure, a figure calculated to appeal to a
feudal audience who will keep this "strength of character" in mind
when exposed to the furious attacks of Ximena in her grief for her
dead father.

The second ballad to be considered dealing with the youth of
the Cid recounts his visit to Fernando's court and portrays what
was considered to be the man's deplorable contempt for royalty.
The ballad, "Cabalga[ba] Diego Laínez" ("Diego Laínez rode"),
is too lengthy to quote in its entirety. However, the length is the
result of what must be considered the composition's most significant
device. The major issue is the Cid's aloofness from the other nobles
with whom he is traveling to Burgos to greet the king. It is an aloofness that derives in part from his fundamental sense of superiority,
but also in part from the nobles' discussion among themselves
of his successful encounter with Count Lozano. In Burgos, Rodrigo
further alienates the nobles by challenging anyone who regrets
the Count's death to step forward and defend his sentiment. Only
the careful persuasion of his father (Diego Laínez) can move Rodrigo
to properly greet his king, but Rodrigo cannot suppress the tempta-
tion to insult Fernando gratuitously by making it obvious that the
audience does the young man no great honor.

Throughout the ballad Rodrigo's aloofness is given characterization by contrasting him with the rest of the nobles and by giving
rhetorical form to this contrast through the use of anaphoric repetition. The first segment of the ballad, prior to arrival in Burgos,
characterizes the Cid, the "haughty Castilian," in the following
manner:

Cabalga Diego Laínez	(Diego Laínez was riding
al buen rey besar la mano,	to kiss the King's hand;
consigo se los llevaba	with him he was bringing
los trescientos hijosdalgo;	three hundred hidalgos,
5 *entre ellos iba Rodrigo,*	among which rode Rodrigo,
el soberbio castellano.	the haughty Castilian.
Todos cabalgan a mula,	All rode on mules;
sólo Rodrigo a caballo;	only Rodrigo on a horse.
todos visten oro y seda,	All were dressed in gold and silk;
10 *Rodrigo va bien armado;*	Rodrigo is well armed.
todos guantes olorosos,	All with scented gloves;
Rodrigo guante mallado;	Rodrigo with a mailed glove.
todos con sendas varicas,	All with their own javelins;

	Rodrigo estoque dorado;	Rodrigo with a golden rapier.
15	*todos sombreros muy ricos,*	All with rich hats,
	Rodrigo casco afinado,	Rodrigo with a polished helmet,
	y encima del casco lleva	and on top of the helmet
	un bonete colorado.	a red hat.)

(p. 137)

The procedure is to alternate references to everyone—"the others"—with references to Rodrigo. Such a formulaic device both serves to set the man off from the others and to underline the contrast between Rodrigo's more warlike dress and the rich raiment of the other horsemen. In addition, the device stylizes the presentation of Rodrigo: the repetition of the contrast is an appeal to the audience to appreciate the extent of the man's exaggerated aloofness. It is significant to note that the first pairing off of Rodrigo and the others (line 8) prefaces his name with the adverb "only," an adverb that is the axis of the subsequent contrast. When Rodrigo challenges Fernando's entourage in Burgos, the audience is prepared to comprehend the seriousness of his words: it is obvious that he is all too ready to make trouble at the first opportunity. Repeating the word "everyone," of paramount importance as a result of the contrast between the Cid and everyone else posited by the introductory verses of the ballad, the poem shows vividly Rodrigo's powers of intimidation but at the same time the extent of the ill will that he has engendered:

	—Si hay alguno entre vosotros,	("If there is anyone among you,
	su pariente o adeudado,	relative or retainer,
	que le pese de su muerte,	who regrets his death,
	salga luego a demandallo;	let him come forward to make his suit.
	yo se lo defenderé,	I will prevent it
35	*quiera a pie, quiera a caballo.*	either on foot or on horseback."
	Todos dicen para sí:	Each says to himself:
	"Que te lo demande el diablo."	"Let the devil make the suit.")

(p. 138)

When everyone else moves forward to kiss the king's hand, *only* Rodrigo remains behind (lines 39–42), until persuaded by his father to comply with the demands of courtesy. It would appear best to see the ballad in terms of a juxtaposition between an initial segment, in which the Cid's aloofness and the antagonism of the nobles are skillfully introduced (lines 1–38), and the remaining half of the composition in which the Cid's initial refusal to kiss

Fernando's hand and his childish remarks when he does are presented
via direct dialogue. Juxtaposition, as a contrast resulting from
a shift in technique or tone, derives from the change in mode of
presentation between the two parts as well as the manner in which
the Cid's person comes off. There is a juxtaposition of the stylized
characterization with the more or less unmannered directness
achieved in the second part by the use of dialogue, and there is
a juxtaposition with respect to the haughty self-isolation on the
one hand and the immaturity of behavior on the other. The overall
effect of this ballad is a rather severe portrait of one who is to become a national hero. Typical of the unflattering materials from
which it is derived, this composition is singularly successful in
representing an attitude and a comportment on the Cid's part
that are calculated to inspire negative reaction from the audience.
In turn, the negative reaction which the Cid inspires in the nobles
with whom he comes in contact might be understood as a basis
for his persecution in later years. Although subsequent ballads
treat this persecution of Rodrigo by the nobles, their source in the
laudatory *Poema* results not only in a more decidedly sympathetic
portrait of the man, but the absence of any real explanation as to
reasons for the grudge borne him by the nobles. The later epic
materials, the inspiration of the ballads that we have just examined,
suggest to be sure some rather compelling reasons.

The next text to be considered belongs to the ballads dealing with
the siege of Zamora which space will not permit us to examine in
detail. However, the one text is significant for the light which it
throws on the royal and noble disfavor incurred by Rodrigo,
a disfavor that is the backdrop to the *Poema* and the Cid's struggle
to regain his king's respect and recognition. The ballad refers
to events that are the aftermath of the siege of Zamora. The story
is complicated, but the major events concern the Cid's suspicion
that King Alfonso, in order to extend his power, was an instigator
in the murder of his brother Sancho during the siege. The Cid,
as the vassal of Sancho, has the right to demand that Alfonso
swear his innocence. It is this demand that becomes the central
conflict in the ballad. A historical fiction, the episode of the oath
became a part of the Zamoran epic and ballad materials and served
to link these with the *Poema de Mio Cid,* providing an additional
explanation for Alfonso's stubborn hostility to an otherwise faithful
and obedient Rodrigo.

The ballad is as follows:

En Santa Gadea de Burgos	(In Santa Gadea de Burgos,
do juran los hijosdalgo,	where hidalgos swear their word,
allí toma juramento	there the Cid takes the oath
el Cid al rey castellano,	of the Castilian King
5 *sobre un cerrojo de hierro*	on an iron bolt
y una ballesta de palo.	and a wooden crossbow.
Las juras eran tan recias	The oaths are so strong
que al buen rey ponen espanto.	that they frighten the good King.
—Villanos te maten, rey,	"May peasants kill you, King,
10 *villanos, que no hidalgos;*	peasants, not hidalgos;
abarcas traigan calzadas,	may they wear sandals,
que no zapatos con lazo;	not shoes with laces;
traigan capas aguaderas,	may they wear waterproof cloaks,
no capuces ni tabardos;	not hoods or tabards,
15 *con camisones de estopa,*	with long shirts of burlap,
no de holanda ni labrados;	not of cambric or embroidered;
cabalguen en sendas burras,	may they ride each his own mule,
que no en mulas ni en caballos	mules not horses;
las riendas traigan de cuerda,	may the reins be of string,
20 *no de cueros fogueados;*	not of cured leather;
mátente por las aradas,	may they kill you in the fields,
no en camino ni en poblado;	not on the highway nor in a town;
con cuchillos cachicuernos,	with horn-handled knives,
no con puñales dorados;	not golden daggers;
25 *sáquente el corazón vivo,*	may they rip your heart out alive
por el derecho costado,	on the right side,
si no dices la verdad	if yo do not answer truthfully
de lo que te es preguntado:	the question put to you:
si tú fuiste o consentiste	whether you were in or consented to
30 *en la muerte de tu hermano.*	the death of your brother."
Las juras eran tan fuertes	The oaths were so strong
que el rey no las ha otorgado.	that the King has not agreed to them.
Allí habló un caballero	There a knight spoke up,
de los suyos más privado:	one of his closest:
35 *—Haced la jura, buen rey,*	"Give the oath, good King;
no tengáis de eso cuidado,	don't worry about this,
que nunca fué rey traidor,	for a King was never a traitor,
ni Papa descomulgado.	nor a Pope excommunicated."
Jura entonces el buen rey,	The good King then swears
40 *que en tal nunca se ha hallado.*	that he was never in on that.
Después habla contra el Cid	Then he speaks out against the Cid
malamente y enojado:	extremely angered:
—Mucho me aprietas, Rodrigo,	"You press me hard, Rodrigo;
Cid, muy mal me has conjurado,	Cid, very wrongly have you urged me.
45 *mas si hoy me tomas la jura,*	But if today you take my oath,

	después besarás mi mano.	later you will kiss my hand."
	—Aqueso será, buen rey,	"That may be so, good King,
	como fuer galardonado,	as if it were a reward,
	porque allá en cualquier tierra	because in any land
50	*dan sueldo a los hijosdalgo.*	they give knights a stipend."
	—¡Vete de mis tierras, Cid,	"Be gone from my lands, Cid,
	mal caballero probado,	now proved a bad knight,
	y no me entres más en ellas	and do not return
	desde este día en un año!	until a year from today!"
55	*—Que me place—dijo el Cid—*	"That suits me fine," said the Cid,
	que me place de buen grado,	"just fine,
	por ser la primera cosa	for it's the first decree
	que mandas en tu reinado.	of your reign.
	Tú me destierras por uno,	You exile me for one,
60	*yo me destierro por cuatro.*	I exile myself for four.")

(pp. 167–69)

The concluding twenty-two lines of the ballad describe the departure of the Cid and his men from Burgos: "The Cid now departed/
without kissing the king's hand." Aside from the function of these
verses, in according to the figure of Rodrigo and his men a stately
dignity in sharp contrast to the venial rage of Alfonso, they show
a remarkable similarity to the opening lines of "Cabalgaba Diego
Laínez." Although the stylized repetition is absent, the references
to the men (there are again three hundred in the band) and their
appearance show a probable textual interrelationship.[18] More
significant than the accuracy of reference is that in the context of
the Santa Gadea text the material is used to magnify the Cid's
character, whereas in the previous ballad it is used to underscore
his unacceptably conceited sense of superiority. Such a circumstance bespeaks the way in which the *Romancero* tradition will
transfer lines and whole segments freely—almost indiscriminately—
from one ballad to another. Although such textual interrelationships are of importance in establishing lines of development within
the tradition, from the point of view of understanding any one ballad
text it is of far greater importance to consider the way in which the
borrowed material is utilized within the context of the ballad in
question. The result of such a consideration is a comprehension
of how related materials may be used for totally different purposes
depending upon the overall perspective, organization, and poetic
rhetoric of the composition.

To return to the quoted portion of Santa Gadea, leaving aside the eight-line introduction, we find that the ballad exploits an important antithesis between Rodrigo and Alfonso. After impressing upon us the awesomeness of Rodrigo's demand that Alfonso swear his innocence (lines 7–8), the poem confronts the Cid's demand with Alfonso's enraged response. It should be evident from our foregoing discussion that such a procedure involving juxtaposition, antithesis, contrast, and so on, is of particular value to at least the historical ballads. Speculation as to why this is so might emphasize the frequently found observation that the ballads differ from their longer source materials in their attention to a single event or circumstance of overwhelming significance in terms of the feudal and Christian values of the people concerned: characters, minstrels, audience. The most common type of event of such dominant importance would logically be a conflict of values, particularly a situation in which an unquestioned value is seen placed in jeopardy by antagonistic forces. Another event of similarly high tension involves the clash between principles, or representatives of principles, which are equally transcendent but which have suddenly come into opposition with each other. Thus, the recurring juxtapositional structure of the historical ballads seems to be the reasonable result of not only the epic and heroic subject matter, but also the clear preference for seeing issues in terms of dramatic conflict.

It is the latter type of conflict of principles that we find in Santa Gadea. On the one hand, the Cid is completely within his rights to demand an oath of innocence from the new king. On the other, the king is also justified in his displeasure with the intensity of his new vassal's words and with Rodrigo's refusal to humble himself before Alfonso. The banishment of the Cid, whose haughtiness again comes through at this moment, is the direct result of his refusal to kiss the hand of the king, who has satisfactorily sworn his innocence. What is most impressive about the ballad is the manner in which the Cid's demand is presented. In a long diatribe, Rodrigo warns Alfonso in no uncertain but nevertheless impressively untactful terms what may be the consequences of the monarch's presumed guilt. Manifesting a carefully selected rhetorical procedure, the ballad has Rodrigo frame his demand in the form of a long series of indirect commands that are to apply *if* Alfonso is guilty. The *if* segment of Rodrigo's statement is contained in five brief verses (lines 27–30), while the series of threatening subjunctives takes up eighteen lines, a disproportionate distribution that makes it obvious that the Cid is not prepared to accept Alfonso's innocence.

Reinforcing the organization of the vassal's challenge is the balanced arrangement of the subjunctive statements. The composition makes use of the "A, not B" formula familiar to rhetoricians who would contrast prejudicially two contending possibilities. In this instance, what Rodrigo is contrasting is the ignoble fate which will befall Alfonso (the "A" possibilities, of which there are nine), as opposed to a fate a little more befitting royalty (the rejected "B" possibilities, of which there are also nine), *if* he is guilty of complicity in his brother's death. Thus, for example, in the first pair (lines 9–10), Rodrigo cries for Alfonso to be killed by peasants ("A"), *not* by noblemen ("not B") if he is guilty. Or later (lines 21–22), if Alfonso is guilty, may he be killed ignobly in the fields ("A"), *not,* as more befitting a royal execution, on the highroad or in town ("not B"). Through a series of nine pairs of this sort Rodrigo lashes out against the frightened king before concluding the far briefer "if" segment of his terrible challenge. All in all, a quite impressive buildup to Alfonso's actual oath.

When the ballad finally turns its attention to Alfonso, the effect of Rodrigo's words is reinforced by the hesitation of the monarch, who proceeds to swear his innocence only after an astute counselor reminds him cynically that kings are never found to be traitors just as Popes are never excommunicated. Alfonso's hesitation, rather than designed to reveal any guilt on his part—the Cid and legend had already firmly established his complicity in the murder —is more important as a further way of giving emphasis to the awesomeness of Rodrigo's threat to set in motion the vengeance of Sancho's death through royal treachery.

Nevertheless, once the Cid has exhausted his rage, once he has been successful in humiliating Alfonso by his challenge, the vassal once again is thrust back into his socially inferior position. The fact is brought out vividly by the shift in roles of power that occurs in line 41ff. Having complied with Rodrigo's demand that he swear his innocence, the king is now able to reassert his authority over the rebellious warrior. This he does by reminding the Cid that: "If [since] you have made me swear/you shall later kiss my hand" (lines 45–46). The importance of this assertion is not only a demonstration of Alfonso's understandable fury with what the vassal has done, nor is it just a casual return to the proper roles of lord and vassal. Alfonso's statement is a very obvious correlation with the Cid's long diatribe based on the same type of conditional sentence. That is to say, the ballad underscores the fact that, once having been forced to accede to Rodrigo's tactless demand, based on the conditional threat "if that, then this," Alfonso reasserts his dominance by presenting his new vassal with the same sort of condition. Although far less significant, both from the point of view of ideological importance and dramatic effect, the monarch's condition is nevertheless calculated to impress Rodrigo with his proper role vis-à-vis his lord.

Rodrigo's reply is not entirely unexpected; it certainly recalls the unfavorable portrait of the *Mocedades* material. The words "good king" demonstate unmistakably a continued mistrust of Alfonso. It is a mistrust understandable to an audience familiar with the ballads that precede this one in the narrative of the siege of Zamora. The effect, then, is to diminish Alfonso's futile attempt to reassert his authority more than it is to point to the Cid's disrespect for royalty. This basic perspective on the clash between the two men is reinforced when Alfonso attempts to impose exile on Rodrigo. In the place of the monarch's year of exile, the Cid will impose upon himself four. It is a move on his part that serves, from the point of view of the ballad's development, to reinforce hyperbolically the inverted dominance of vassal over lord portrayed from the very outset of the poem. Said differently, Rodrigo's self-imposed exile only serves to further embarrass an already humiliated and enraged Alfonso. In this context, the use of "the good Cid" in line 61 is not only meant to be taken literally; it is meant to parallel the Cid's own sarcastic use of this epithet when he addresses Alfonso in line 47. A compositional detail easily lost in such a long and dramatic ballad, this parallelism is nevertheless a touchstone for appreciating the fundamental relationship between the two men. It is a detail that speaks favorably of the ability of the anonymous minstrel/poets to structure their material so as to make overwhelmingly clear the exact way in which the audience was to understand the importance and the resolution of the conflict portrayed.

From the point of view of subsequent events concerning the Cid narrated by the traditional historical ballads, the strong assertion in this text of the dominance of the Cid is of no mean significance. One of the major points made by the epic poem and preserved in the ballads is that, despite the greater feudal authority of Alfonso and the great nobles, the strength and the extent of the Cid's challenge to this authority rests on the very simple circumstance that he is morally superior.[19] In addition, the epic and other ballads are careful to show the Cid submitting to the feudal authority of Alfonso, while growing in moral stature as the result of the petty persecution of the nobles. It is this aspect of the hero which we wish to emphasize in our consideration of further examples from the vast number of ballads on the Cid.

Although there are any number of important ballads dealing with the Cid's military exploits against both Christians and Moors during the years of various exiles and successful campaigns (it will be recalled that he gets the name Cid from a title of respect, meaning "lord," accorded him by the Moors), limitations of space make it more advisable to restrict our range of interest to those ballads dealing with Rodrigo's final "feudal rehabilitation." One reason for this is that the traditional process has resulted in particularly excellent texts for the episode concerning the injurious treatment of the Cid's daughters at the hands of the arrogant but spineless Counts of Carrión and Alfonso's swift response to the father's demands for justice. It is our opinion that the two texts discussed below are superb examples of ballad artistry, probably better in their successful focusing on a crucial conflict in the Cid material than the ballads of military exploits, which tend to be somewhat less intense in organization and perspective. One reason for this circumstance is, of course, the fact that actual military scenes in the epic *Poema de Mio Cid* are few in comparison and importance to those scenes that portray the nuances and the complex development of the Cid's relations with Alfonso.

Our first text concerns the insult to the Cid implicit in the mistreatment of his daughters by the Counts, their husbands. Although the Cid has been generous to the Counts, he has not been able to hide his lack of respect for their courage, which is blatantly deficient, and they in turn have given ample indication of their sense of social superiority. As we have pointed out elsewhere in independent research on the *Poema*,[20] the insult to the Cid through his daughters, an episode which occurs near the end of the epic and which culminates in his final and definitive "rehabilitation" in Alfonso's eyes, is basically a cameo of the underlying conflict of the poem. In miniature, the epic puts before us the innate nobility of the Cid challenged unwisely for one last time by detestable men who are his social superiors, but who, in their dastardliness, reveal once and for all their own moral inferiority and the indomitable nobility of the once "haughty Castilian." Here is the first ballad based on this circumstance:

De concierto están los condes	(The Counts are conspiring,
hermanos Diego y Fernando;	the brothers Diego and Fernando.
afrentar quieren al Cid,	They wish to insult the Cid,
muy gran traición han armado,	and they have planned a serious treachery.
5 *quieren volverse a sus tierras,*	They want to return to their lands,
sus mujeres demandando;	claiming their wives.
y luego les dice el Cid,	The Cid then says to them
cuando se las ha entregado:	when he has yielded up the latter:
—Mirad, yernos, que tratedes	"Look, my sons-in-law, treat
10 *como a dueñas hijasdalgo*	my daughters as proper ladies,
mis hijas, pues que a vosotros	for I have given them to you
por mujeres las he dado. [. . .]	as your wives." [. . .]
45 *Apéanlas de las mulas;*	They get them down from their mules,
ambas las han desnudado;	and strip off their clothing.
cada uno azota la suya,	Each beats his own wife
con riendas de su caballo;	with his horse's reins.
danles muchas espoladas,	They wound them with their spurs,
50 *en sangre las han bañado;*	and leave them bathed in blood.
con palabras injuriosas,	With injurious words
mucho las han denostado.	they have terribly insulted them.
Los cobardes caballeros	The cowardly knights
allí se las han dejado.	have left them there.
55 *—De vueso padre, señoras,*	"Of your father, ladies,
en vos ya somos vengados;	we are now avenged through you,
que vosotras no sois tales	for you are not such
para connusco casaros.	as to be married to us.
Ahora pagáis las deshonras	Now you pay for the dishonor
60 *que el Cid a nós hubo dado*	that the Cid did us
cuando soltara el león	when he loosed the lion
y procurara matarnos.	and tried to kill us.")

(pp. 185–86)

The reference in the final lines is to the famous episode in both the epic and the ballad (cf. "Acabado de yantar" ["Having eaten"]) in which the brothers' lack of courage is brought out in their womanish fright over an uncaged lion, which is easily tamed by the manly Cid. It is an event skillfully deployed both to bring out comically the Counts' cowardliness as well as to provide an event humiliating enough for them to justify in some way their revenge in the Corpes forest. Again we find that the poem is bipartite. The first segment relates the departure of the newlyweds; the second half describes the assault on the daughters. Of course, the assault itself is an even more damning revelation of the two men than the lion episode. They are unable to confront Rodrigo directly to avenge the presumed insult. It is only by attacking pusillanimously the defenseless daughters that they can be "brave" enough to get back at the Cid. There is little question that the events chosen and the form which they are given are meant to be a powerful indictment of the Carrión brothers and the nobility which they feel themselves to represent.

The ballad achieves its dramatic effect by counterposing elements of the two segments. For example, after making it quite plain that the brothers are planning to avenge their humiliation, we are quoted the Cid's amiable words of farewell (lines 9–14). These words are clearly ironic in function, as the audience is well aware that the Counts have already prepared to ignore them. When the actual mistreatment of the daughters takes place (lines 45–54), one cannot help but recall their father's earlier recommendation. It should be noted how the ballad is so straightforward in characterizing the principals, and the oxymoronic phrase "cowardly gentlemen" in line 53 is really unnecessary in terms of the overall tone of the work. At the same time, the ballad accords a greater sense of premonition to Rodrigo than does the epic. In the latter, we are not told of his sense of foreboding, and Ordoño is simply sent as a retainer. The ballad, on the other hand, makes a point of contrasting the Cid's happy rejoicing in line 20 and his tearful farewell—a forshadowing of his later tears of anger and distress— in line 24. At the same time, the ballad retains the one dominant note of foreshadowing to be found in the epic: the use of the stylized setting whose forbidding shadows prelude the dark deed.[21] This latter feature is one of the most obvious literary devices of the epic, and tradition has done well to retain it. However, the inclusion of references to Rodrigo's actual premonition of treachery, while reinforcing the rhetoric against the Counts, serves in the ballad only to dispel the tension created between the father's early words and the detailed description of the actual assault.

Another example of correlation between the two segments concerns part of the Cid's speech and Diego's and Fernando's comment to his daughters after having beaten them. In lines 10–11, the Cid makes reference to the stature which his daughters have in his eyes: they are ladies of the minor nobility who deserve respect. Later, the brothers are to throw this opinion in their face when they tell the women that they are not worthy to be married to men of such high rank (lines 57–58). If the Cid's recommendation is ironic in terms of the brothers' treatment of their wives, the brothers' assertion is ironic in terms of the Cid's description of his daughters. The ballad is designed to make it obvious that, rank by birth aside, the Cid and his daughters are much more worthy than the perfidious "noble" duo, probably the most infamous villains of medieval Spanish literature. It is easy to see how the conflict exploited by this ballad has been used to place in definitive perspective the moral superiority of Rodrigo in his struggle against the pettiness of his social betters.

The last historical ballad to be presented is one of the most memorable, based as it is on the Cid's successful suit against the Counts of Carrión before the assembled nobles, which is recounted in the closing segments of the surviving twelfth-century epic. Although brief in comparison to other texts on the Cid material, the following ballad is particularly indicative of procedures that can be termed truly literary:

Tres cortes armara el rey,	(The King has called three courts,
todas tres a una sazón;	all three at the same time:
las unas armara en Burgos,	he has called courts in Burgos,
las otras armó en León,	others he called in León
5 *las otras armó en Toledo,*	and also courts in Toledo,
donde los hidalgos son,	where the hidalgos are,
para cumplir de justicia	in order to accord to the lesser
al chico con el mayor.	the justice of the great.
Treinta días da de plazo,	Thirty days he has given,
10 *treinta días, que más no,*	thirty days and no more,
y el que a ellos no viniese	and he who does not come by then
que lo diesen por traidor.	will be considered a traitor.
A los viente y nueve días	On the twenty-ninth day
los condes venidos son;	the Counts arrive.
15 *treinta días son llegados*	Thirty days have gone by
y el buen Cid no viene, non.	and the good Cid does not come.
Allí hablaran los condes:	Then the Counts spoke up:

	—Señor, dadlo por traidor.	"Sire, consider him a traitor."
	Respondiérales el rey:	The King answered back:
20	—Eso non faría, non,	"That I would not do,
	que el buen Cid es caballero	for the good Cid is a knight,
	de batallas vencedor,	a winner of battles,
	pues que en todas las mis cortes	and in all my courts
	no lo había otro mejor.	there is none better."
25	Ellos en aquesto estando,	While they were engaged in this,
	el buen Cid allí asomó.	the good Cid appeared.)

(pp. 189–90)

William Rose mentions this ballad in his comments on numero-
logical symbolism in the *Romancero*.[22] Although Rose does not
attempt to attach any symbolic meaning to the occurrence of three
(and its multiple thirty), he does point out the organizational
value of any numerical reference that is given some sort of internal
development. Here, the introductory verses of the ballad are colored
by the formality and the implied importance of there being *three*
courts convened in different parts of the realm and the fact that
each is mentioned in turn in phrases that are syntactically parallel.
While the three may have no particular importance and while the
locales may be more incidental than significant (actually the three
cities are important feudal capitals), the rhetoric of the first seven
lines is calculated to impress.

It is possible, on the other hand, to attribute some sort of internal
importance to the period of thirty days. A natural division of time
—i.e., the average length of a month—the thirty days are meant
to evoke a sense of mounting tension as day after day Alfonso and
his court await in vain the arrival of the Counts and of the Cid.
It is not until the twenty-ninth day that the Counts arrive; Rodrigo
arrives after them at the last possible moment when all have written
him off as a traitor. The Cid's last-minute arrival is not only a high-
point of tension; arriving after the Counts, the defendants, is the
judicious move of the confident claimant. Reference, then, to the
longer period of time and to the consequences which are to result
from not complying with the stipulated period, is a further indication
of literary skill on the part of some minstrel, who, in freely modify-
ing in these ways the epic source material, evinces a conscious
interest in structural procedures associated with competent literary
composition. The effect is to reduce the presentation of the setting
for the Cid's suit against the Counts to a set of concise circumstances

which, in their implied importance, symbolize the magnitude of the principals involved and of the conflict between them.

In this respect it is interesting to note how the nobles are all too ready to dismiss the Cid as a traitor when it appears that he will fail to arrive on time. Their words in lines 17–18, after Rodrigo is referred to by the narrative voice as "the good Cid" in line 16, serve to remind the audience of the very unwarranted antagonism that underlies the whole series of ballads dealing with the adulthood of the hero. In contrast, however, to previous ballads, Alfonso shows himself willing to be charitable toward the Cid before his less sympathetic nobles. This is probably due to a change in attitude inherited from the epic poem. The Cid, despite his exile and harsh treatment at the hands of the nobles, has remained a faithful and useful vassal and has slowly but surely won the respect of a monarch who is his moral inferior. It is a change in attitude, as we have mentioned, of no little complexity from the narrative and structural point of view of the extended epic, and we cannot recount all of the details here. Suffice it to say that, as this ballad demonstrates, Alfonso is now a supporter of Rodrigo, a fact which is attested not only by his cooperation in calling the courts (which the Cid has demanded rightfully under feudal practice), but as well by his warm words of praise. Moreover, these words are significant both for the change in attitude which they bespeak and for the fact that they are directed against statements made by the jealous nobles with whom Alfonso showed himself earlier more than willing to side. (One will recall that Alfonso swears only after having accepted the advice of a nobleman who is clearly unsympathetic toward the young Rodrigo.) It would seem not inappropriate to compare the two demands registered by the Cid under feudal law: his challenge to Alfonso in Santa Gadea, and his claim against the Counts of Carrión. The shift in Alfonso's attitude toward Rodrigo between the first and the second demands is not just due to the fact that the monarch's honor is supposedly not implicated in the second challenge. As a matter of fact it is: legend has it that Alfonso proposes the disastrous marriage between the Carrións and the daughters.[23]

More at issue is the "rehabilitation" of the Cid that has taken place over the years between the two narrative moments represented by the two ballads. Rodrigo has shown himself to be a gentleman of the highest feudal order, magnificent in stature and integrity, but useful as well to the weaker Alfonso. Thus, Alfonso's words possess in their brevity an enormous value within the context of the ballad and within the still larger context of the legend of the Cid perpetuated and popularized by the ballad cycle. They can only be understood as signifying that Alfonso is prepared to defend against his own nobles the superiority of the Cid. This he does, as subsequent ballads show him favoring Rodrigo's case, a case which must nevertheless be resolved in decisive combat. However, the triumph of the Cid's representatives in combat against the Counts of Carrión is essentially anticlimactic. Alfonso's words are enough to prefigure the inevitable outcome.

If this middle segment of the ballad is of paramount importance in revealing the final and complete acceptance of Rodrigo Díaz de Vivar by his lord and king, it is certainly well organized. Throughout the entire ballad, the Cid is held offstage; we have no diluting of tension here, as was the case with the preceding text. Although not present physically, there is no question as to who constitutes the center of attention. The Cid and his suit against the highborn counts is shown to be uppermost in every mind. It is only when this psychological milieu has been firmly established, only when the ballad has made it abundantly clear how Alfonso's attitude has shifted, only when we have assessed the alignment of support, that the Cid is allowed to appear. His appearance is all of a sudden. Interrupting as it does the conversation between Alfonso and his nobles, it is an appearance of impressively dramatic dimensions. Skillfully, the Cid is not allowed to speak: there is little that he can or need say this moment. It is simply but appropriately the appearance of a man of epic stature. The conflict between Rodrigo and his monarch apparently having been resolved, the moral superiority of the man having been securely demonstrated, the Cid's silent appearance at the last moment to prosecute his complaint against the two brothers who are the epitome of an untrustworthy nobility, is the stroke of unquestionable poetic genius.

IV   *Summing Up*

One conclusion would appear fairly evident from the historical ballads that we have discussed in this chapter: that the overwhelming majority of the important texts which must be discussed in a general survey of this sort do not lend themselves to an exclusively autonomous critical treatment. That is to say, despite the proposal in our introductory chapters to attempt in so far as possible to examine the medieval Spanish ballad as above all a poetic manifestation, it is nevertheless impossible on many occasions not to have recourse to historical fact or to references to other ballad texts. Although many critics would insist that the decision to treat a composition as primarily a work of literature implies the willingness to limit oneself to dealing only with the text at hand, the very obvious interrelationships and circumstances of origin and transmission make it often more appropriate to treat the historical ballads, at least, as a cycle of closely-knit compositions rather than as isolated poems on the same subject. While there are several major ballads that can be satisfactorily dealt with from a more or less unified autonomous point of view (the ballad on Mudarra's vengeance might be one; the oath of Santa Gadea another), it is more likely that the analytic critic will be attracted by examples of mature artistic virtuosity embedded in ballads which otherwise possess less than ideal coherence.

As a result of the foregoing observation, it is easy to see how the historical ballads provide internal validation for the traditionalist's theory. Not only is there the external evidence relating ballad to epic poem and prose chronicle; in addition, we find textual characteristics associated with the independent texts that argue for their consideration within the larger framework of literary history. At the same time, however, our remarks have tried to illustrate, along with their characterization of the importance of the principal *romances históricos,* the ways in which interpretive and analytical considerations may be also brought to bear upon the ballad compositions in the attempt to justify their significance from the point of view of literary issues of a more purely structural and aesthetic nature.

CHAPTER 4

The Frontier Ballads

THE traditional ballads called *fronterizos* have rightly been acclaimed throughout the centuries as one of the most intriguing segments of the *Romancero viejo*. Such an interest and popularity is due not only to their intimate relationship with the closing decades of the protracted conflict between Christians and Moors—indeed, their name derives from events which occurred along the spiritual as well as geographical frontier between the antagonists in the fifteenth century. Their importance stems equally from the proficient and mature minstrel art which they evince, an art which is far more individual than "cumulative," as is the case with early historical ballads that are considered to have taken form far more gradually. All *juglarescos*—that is, written to form as finished ballad texts by nevertheless anonymous balladeers—the most important examples demonstrate a poetry of unusual brilliance.

Gerald Brenan, in his popularized but nevertheless informative history of Spanish literature,[1] contrasts the historical and the frontier ballads in the following manner in order to highlight the attraction of the latter:

> The historical and frontier ballads contain some of the grandest poetry in Spanish literature. [. . .] The frontier ballads, on the other hand, are more subdued: they deal with war, not vengeance [as do a great share of the historical ballads]: their tone is realistic and the sense of tragedy inseparable from ballad themes is given by taking one to the Moorish camp and associating one sympathetically with their losses. [. . . The] Spanish *romances* do not jeer at the enemy, as the Hebrew and early Arab ballads do, but with an impartiality that is not far removed from sympathy allow us to see how bitter is the taste of defeat. The generosity of mind of the Castilian *caballero* and the secret feeling that binds him to his traditional enemy are well shown in these ballads [. . .]. (pp. 127–28)

The sympathy which Brenan describes for the enemy is, to be sure, the sympathy of the generous conqueror, and not a "traitorous" if timely sympathy for the weakening enemy. At the same time, a sense of unity between Christian and Moor[2]—despite the last final antagonism of the struggles recounted in the *romances fronterizos*—perpetuates the trait of the earlier historical ballads whereby the contest between Good and Evil, in which both Christians and Moors are participants, transcends the more humdrum conflicts of religion and politics.

One of the major issues of the literary history surrounding the frontier ballads, an issue intimately linked with this sympathetic attitude toward Moorish defeat, concerns the probable period of composition. Referring to events of the fourteenth and fifteenth centuries—the time during which, as we have noted, the medieval Spanish ballads begin to appear—it is not altogether clear that this group of ballads was actually composed before the sixteenth century. Most scholarship has, however, accepted Menéndez Pidal's opinion that, despite having been composed by very professional minstrels, they were the result of an interest in and a demand for "news" of the frontier events of that tumultuous period.[3] On the other hand, the literary sophistication associated with the best of these ballads, the much-touted sympathy for the enemy, and the intense romanticization of Moorish culture which is to occur in the literature of the sixteenth century, have led to a body of dissenting opinion.[4] Rather than the result of a sort of eyewitness contact with events, the frontier ballads would have been created out of chronicles and other source materials. There is little doubt that the traditional frontier ballads are associated with sixteenth-century literature, as in the case of the texts gathered in Ginés Pérez de Hita's *Guerras civiles de Granada (Civil Wars of Granada)*, 1595, although this does not in itself prove late composition.[5]

Whatever the exact circumstances of creation, one thing is sure: the frontier ballads differ from the historical ballads in one important feature. Whereas the latter exemplify the process of fragmentation, the *romances fronterizos* bear no link whatsoever with longer source material. That is to say, it is generally acknowledged that a majority, if not all (and some critics would be willing to say all) historical ballads, are based on longer source materials; the ballads derive from them via a process of fragmentation, synthesis, condensation. Thus, it is usually said that the historical ballads were not written to form; i.e., were not written as closed or finished compositions, but rather assumed any sense of unity and completeness through the action of the traditionalizing process. Indeed, as we have pointed out, many examples are characterized by the absence of a sense of closed form associated with compositions by a single hand.

In contrast, and although a single hand may not have been present in their formation, the frontier ballads are generally believed to result from the events themselves rather than from the reworking of previous textual sources. To the extent that this is true, the individual compositions may be considered to have been written to form: they are compositions that are complete and autonomous for having been composed from scratch as a unified vision of the subject and for having little significant relationship with earlier nonballad treatments or with other contemporary ballads on the same subject. It will be recalled that one of the problems in treating the historical ballads was the interrelated, cyclical nature of whole groups of ballads on the same theme; this problem is absent in the case of the frontier ballads. In one sense, it is a feature more conducive to the examination of the texts as isolated literary documents. In another sense, from the critic's point of view, it is much more difficult to link the various ballads together in one analytical discussion. It will be necessary, therefore, simply to discuss a series of compositions that are famous for the theme which they treat and important for the artistic success of their composition.

I *"Abenámar"*

It is no exaggeration to label "Abenámar" as one of the most renowned Spanish ballads of all time. A great part of the attraction of the composition results from the sophisticated ironic interplay between the militarily triumphant Christian element on the one hand and the culturally superior Moorish element on the other. It is an interplay which, far more than recalling political and religious strife of seven centuries, speaks more directly and most emphatically for the Christian respect toward Moorish culture and the sentimentality generated by its passing in the Peninsula with the final ascendency of Christian unity:[6]

'¡Abenámar, Abenámar,
moro de la morería,
el día que tú naciste
grandes señales había!

("Abenámar, Abenámar,
Moor of Moorish lands,
the day you were born,
there were great signs!

5	Estaba la mar en calma,	The sea was becalmed,
	la luna estaba crecida;	the moon waxed large.
	moro que en tal signo nace	A Moor born with such signs
	no debe decir mentira.'	ought not lie."
	Allí respondiera el moro	Then the Moor replied,
10	bien oiréis lo que decía:	you will hear what he said:
	'Yo te la diré, señor,	"I will tell you, sire,
	aunque me cueste la vida,	although it cost my life,
	porque soy hijo de un moro	because I am the son of a Moor
	y una cristiana cautiva;	and of a captured Christian woman.
15	siendo yo niño y muchacho	When I was a child and a lad
	mi madre me lo decía,	my mother did tell me,
	que mentira no dijese,	that I must not lie
	que era grande villanía:	for it is evil.
	por tanto pregunta, rey,	Therefore ask, King,
20	que la verdad te diría.'	and I would tell you the truth."
	'Yo te agradezco, Abenámar,	"I appreciate, Abenámar,
	aquesa tu cortesía.	your courtesy.
	¿Qué castillos son aquéllos?	What castles are those?
	¡Altos son y relucían!'	How tall and shiny they are!"
25	'El Alhambra era, señor,	"That would be the Alhambra, sire,
	y la otra la mezquita;	and the other the mosque.
	los otros los Alixares	The others, the Alixares,
	labrados a maravilla;	whose workmanship is a marvel.
	el moro que los labraba	The Moor that did it
30	cien doblas ganaba al día,	earned 100 *doblas* a day,
	y el día que no los labra	and any day he did not work
	otras tantas se perdía.	he lost the same amount.
	El otro el Generalife,	The other is the Generalife,
	huerta que par no tenía;	whose garden is without equal.
35	el otro Torres Bermejas,	The other, Torres Bermejas,
	castillo de gran valía.'	a castle of greatest value."
	Allí habló el rey don Juan,	Then King John spoke,
	bien oiréis lo que decía:	you will hear what he said:
	'Si tú quisieses, Granada,	"If you would, Granada,
40	contigo me casaría:	I would marry you:
	daréte en arras y dote	I will give you in property and dowry
	a Córdoba y a Sevilla.'	Cordova and Seville."
	'Casada soy, rey don Juan,	"I am married, King John,
	casada soy, que no viuda;	married and not a widow.
45	el moro que a mí me tiene	The Moor who has me
	muy grande bien me quería.'	loves me exceedingly well.")

The unusualness of the encounter between Moor and Christian in this text has stimulated debate as to the historical accuracy and/or veracity of the incident.[7] While there is some scant evidence to the effect that the anecdote finds corroboration in several fifteenth-century events, an attempt to make the ballad into a quasi-historical document has remained inconclusive. The literary critic would be wise to heed Bénichou's conclusion,[8] arrived at after considering the historical arguments:

Each will select the historical hypothesis most appealing to him; as far as I can see none can be rejected on the basis of decisive arguments. The name Abenámar alone, with the historical reality of the person so uncertain, and an incident as vague as the conversation of don Juan and a Moor overlooking Granada, are not sufficient to make us read the ballad as a recollection or remembrance of an actual episode of Spanish history. The King Juan who discovers and covets Granada, if one wishes to fix his historical identity, can only be Juan II during his 1431 campaign. But, aside from the name, the ballad could refer equally to Enrique IV or to Fernando el Católico. And the Moor with whom the king speaks is even less individualized. We do not know who he is and we don't want to know; he is not even introduced as a prince or knight of Granada. Abenámar is not, in any sense of the word, a historical personage. His only function in the poem is to reveal, as a Moor, the unequalled excellence of the city and to increase the desire of the king. The ballad, then, only deals with a general situation, that of the Castilian kings in their relationships with Moorish Granada. (pp. 67–68)

Unlike the historical ballads, intimately related as they are to more particularized events, the later frontier ballads are more advanced artistically and are as a consequence capable of greater poetic license. In this composition, license is obvious in a number of details: the fiction of the encounter between Moor and Christian, the intensity of the latter's attraction to the city and his willingness to give up two major Christian cities in exchange for the one brilliant Moorish Granada, the anthropomorphization of Granada so that the city may engage in dialogue with don Juan, and the general tone of wide-eyed awe with which the obviously provincial Christian greets the splendor of Moorish civilization. All of these details cannot in any sense of the word be taken as indicative of a ballad intended to capture the spirit of the Christian Reconquest. It is, as Bénichou so aptly observes, a highly artistic piece of poetry in which the whole nature of the relationship between two antagonistic cultures in contact is synthesized with irony. As we shall attempt to point out, the irony central to the conflict of the encounter between Granada and don Juan is expressed in terms of an unmistakable Moorish superiority.

The initial segment of the ballad, lines 1–20, has attracted a great deal of puzzled attention, primarily for the emphasis on Juan's suspicion that Abenámar will lie to him. Since what is at issue from lines 21 on is only the identification of the city, it is difficult to justify Juan's caution, which is more suitable to the exchange of state secrets. Nevertheless, to the extent that the critic must assume that the organization of a literary text is intentional—the result of an attempt at artistic unity—the most judicious approach is to seek an affiliation between superficially disparate parts. It will be noted that these first twenty lines are bipartite and involve an exchange of some grandiloquence between Christian and Moor. The former speaks first, and his words are from the outset nonconversational. That is to say, the ballad is not recording a casual dialogue, but is capturing an expression of intense emotional involvement on don Juan's part; if necessary one can assume that the unconsequential formalities of greeting between the two men are understood to have taken place before the ballad opens. Juan's repeated exclamatory vocative to Abenámar is in itself an indication that his feelings are high-pitched. What follows—and the *adnominatio* of line 2 involving the root of *Moor* is a stylized rhetorical device for emphasis—is an extravagant compliment to Abenámar for the impressive circumstances of his birth. While it would be possible to recall the function served in medieval poetry by the commonplaces of the signs mentioned,[9] their symbolic detail is less important in the long run than the cumulative impact of their use. They lead up to Juan's explicit confidence that, as a result, Abenámar will tell him the truth. From one point of view, Juan is playing on Abenámar's horoscope to insure truthfulness. From another point of view, the suggestive importance of the signs themselves reinforce any attempt by the ballad to portray Juan's excitement.

Abenámar's response is equally hyperbolic, particularly in the implied importance of his mixed blood. Supposedly, it is the lesson of his *Christian* mother that will insure his honesty.[10] This is a rather gratuitous slur on the honesty of the Moors, and indeed some ver-

sions have line 13 as part of don Juan's speech, in which Abenámar
is called "son of a Moorish dog." Although early ballad criticism
was inclined to believe that this ballad originated in a Moorish
poem translated into Spanish, the presence of line 14 in the vast
majority of versions would seem to indicate the primacy of a Christian
point of view. In any case, what we are able to say about Abenámar's
speech as a whole is that it is far more urbane, despite the extent
to which he goes to "prove" his honesty. Again, there are several
possible interpretations of the function of the Moor's words. On
the one hand, they are simply the rhetorical counterpart of Juan's
impassioned speech. Their urbanity and general lack of emotion
contribute to underlining Juan's intense feeling upon discovering
the splendor that is Granada. From another point of view, both
the urbanity of the Moor's disavowal of any inclination to lie and
his indication of why he can only tell the truth may constitute a
subtle, if not sarcastic, irony. Abenámar would have sensed the
awe of Juan and measured the passion of his words, and, amused
by Juan's exaggerated demand for an honest answer, replies in
a manner calculated to impress the Christian at the same time that
it shows up his provincialism. Juan, of course, misses this and
thanks Abenámar for his courtesy in lines 21–22; realization of the
irony of the Moor's response rests with the audience and their
sensitivity to the contrast between the tone and content of the
two speeches.

That an analysis of the function of the opening segment as an
ironic context deriving from Moorish superiority is accurate is
borne out by the closing segment of the composition, to which we
will turn in a moment. What is important at this point is that we
stress an interpretation of these first twenty lines that justifies their
presence. It would seem difficult to justify Juan's demand for
honesty if we take into consideration only the content of his subsequent questioning. We are a little better off if we assess his initial
words as a device for revealing the intensity of his awestruck
reaction to the contemplation of the magnificent city. Nevertheless,
given the eventual direction which the ballad takes in its denouement, we propose that the first segment be understood not only
as an indication of Juan's surprise, but also as a foreshadowing of
the vision of Christian and Moorish relations with which the composition leaves us. The intense irony of the last eight lines, in which
the superiority of Moorish culture is unquestionable, is prefigured

by the urbane irony of Abenámar's overly diffident reply to Juan's boorish attempt to extract an assurance of honesty. It is only in this way that we are able to accord a segment that takes up just under half of the total lines an integral and significant role in the overall structure of the ballad.

The central portion of the text is best described as "descriptive/lyrical." Juan's (overly?) serious remark in lines 21–22 preludes his wonder-filled question and exclamation of lines 23–24. The foregoing lines have built up to this moment, and the full weight of the king's awe is gauged by the initial exchange with Abenámar. Again, we suggest that the ballad's main objective is to imply a fundamental provincialism on the part of Juan, and the candor of his overwhelmed senses in the presence of the architectural sophistication of Granada is meant to represent a telling revelation of this provincialism. Abenámar's reply shows once again the Moor's condescending urbanity, as he identifies the landmarks and repeats the circumstances surrounding their construction. The detail in lines 29–32 concerning the architect is worthy of a tour guide who carefully selects a "human-interest" anecdote that will impress an undiscriminating audience. (In other versions Abenámar goes on to relate how the architect was executed upon the completion of his commission so that his talent would not be used to rival Alixares.) While there is no doubt that one function of these words is to highlight the care taken to make Granada the most glorious of Moorish cities, it is not difficult to see them as also intended to play as unsubtly as possible on Juan's wonderment. Abenámar's brief catalogue of Granada's splendors both appeals to the audience's recognition of the importance of Granada as a symbol of Moorish culture—this is an aesthetic gesture of the poem—as well as it exploits Juan's predisposition to be impressed by what he is shown, the latter reinforcing the ironic tone of Abenámar's attitude toward Juan.

What we are essentially saying is that lines 23–36 are integrally linked to the first segment of the ballad. Having demonstrated the nature of the relationship between Juan and Abenámar through the establishment of an ironic context, the anonymous poet proceeds to lay the groundwork for the climactic moment of the ballad's juxtaposition of the superiority of Moorish culture and the frustrated covetousness of the Christian for what cannot be his—at least what cannot be his until the final triumph of the Reconquest in

1492, sixty-one years after the putative time of the encounter
between Juan and Abenámar. The groundwork which is laid is
fundamentally ironic also in tone. In this instance it is an irony
arising from Juan's gaping attention to the Moor's guidebook
identification of the splendors spread out before him.

The final lines of the ballad, 37–46, represent a brusque transition from Abenámar's display of Granada's beauty to the impetuous-
ness of the Castilian monarch's offer made on the basis of what
little he has seen. In terms of the poem's rhetorical techniques, it
is necessary to note how two lines are given over to introducing
Juan's words. This formula, used extensively in earlier epic material
and in the ballads, serves to call special attention to what is to
follow. What is hereby introduced is expected to be a statement
of unmistakable significance: a denunciation, a threat, a challenge,
a declaration of war, and so on. In the context of this ballad, however, the most transcendency that can be assigned Juan's subsequent
declaration is that it is significant for its indication of his awe, an
awe which has been clearly presented as an index of his lack of
cultural sophistication. Far from being simply another example
of the deployment of a hackneyed transitional formula, the words
to the audience in lines 37–38 are more valuable in preparing us
for the third and final irony of the ballad which is to follow. This
climactic irony is, of course, Juan's "proposal of marriage" to
Granada. It is a proposal noteworthy, not so much for its being
directed at a lovely city, but rather for Juan's extravagant offer of
a dowry settlement, which includes two Christian cities for the one
Moorish Granada.

Several interpretations are suggested here. First of all, Juan's
declaration to the city may be taken as nothing more than the
logical result of his display of awe up to this point. It is a hyperbolic
reaction which, in its candor and extravagance, is perfectly chosen
by the minstrel to bring home the effect that Granada has had upon
the Christian monarch. Indeed, the juxtaposition of this reaction
with what can be assumed to be the wealth and cultural resources
at hand in the Castilian court (which is reaching its first bloom of
sophistication under Juan's patronage) is a favorable comment
on the fabled magnificence of the Moorish court. At the same time
it is not difficult to see Juan's words as an affirmation that Granada
must be his, no matter what the sacrifice. Bénichou's analysis of
this ballad stresses the note of frustration in Juan's words. Granada

cannot be his, despite his own personal military prowess. Nevertheless the composition and the popularity of the composition come at a time when Granada has in fact become a jewel in the Castilian crown (having fallen in 1492, the date given as the successful completion of the Reconquest). However, to see Juan's words as themselves an ironic and veiled threat to Granada, a threat given realization in 1492 when she does indeed become a "widow," would be to miss the emphasis given throughout the previous portions of the text to the monarch's simple nature and his entertaining awe. That is to say, it would be a clumsy shift in tone were the ballad to suddenly transfer ironic focus from Juan's cultural inferiority in order to allow him in turn to prefigure ironically Granada's eventual fall to the Christians. The lack of any reference in the text to Juan's presence as an indication of a military expedition against Granada reinforces the foregoing conclusion. Juan's words, then, can only be seen as a procedure adopted for the final display of the man's wonderment.

In this regard, one might well ask why the ballad has Granada herself answer Juan rather than Abenámar, whose urbanity has on two previous occasions served as a revealing counterpoint to Juan's remarks. The most likely reason is that Abenámar can only speak for his own cultural superiority; however, he has no personal relationship with Granada, and therefore cannot answer for her when confronted with Juan's proposal and/or implied military threat.[11] Being neither ruler nor "guardian" of Granada's beauty, Abenámar is excluded from Juan's direct address to the city. Thus, it is more appropriate that Granada herself answer the Christian's words, and her blunt reminder to the monarch that she is already "wed," and "wed" to one who will know how to hold her becomes simply the final indication of the relationship between Juan and the Moorish reality with which he has so strikingly come in contact. Granada's reply is, in short, that of an indignant woman who is all too capable of putting a man who would make rash advances in his place. As far as the audience (and the now silent Abenámar) is concerned, Juan's humiliation is complete. We have seen him presented first as a somewhat rude and boorish man who unreasonably demands a trivial pledge of honesty from Abenámar; we have seen him in his delightful awe at the splendors of Granada; and, finally, we have seen his own sense of superiority and importance, which comes through in his inflated proposal to the city,

definitively crushed by the aristocratic and haughty reply of the
city herself. Juan has no choice, we are led to assume, but to retreat
in humiliated embarrassment.[12]

A résumé of the structure of the ballad "Abenámar," then,
would necessarily dwell on its organization in terms of three revealing ironic circumstances: Juan's demand, his question, and his
"marriage proposal." These three ironic contexts not only represent
a buildup to the monarch's humiliation by the haughty Granada.
They fuse to form a unified expression of the relationship between
Christian and Moorish life. Moreover, the trajectory of narrative
development emphasizes unmistakably the contrast between the
Christian's self-confidence at the outset and his subsequent re-
sounding rebuff by the Moorish city. There is little doubt that the
ballad is an intense and highly convincing "argument" to the effect
that not only did the Moors rightfully consider themselves culturally more advanced than the Christians, but that the latter were
only too willing to concur in this opinion and to humiliate themselves in their frustrated covetousness of a civilization that could
not be theirs to possess. This may be somewhat of an exaggeration
of the actual sociological facts of early fifteenth-century Spain,
on the eve of its grim destruction of the remnants of Jewish and
Moorish culture in the Peninsula. No matter; what is of far greater
significance than actual facts is the attitude, regardless of how it
is idealized, embodied by the composition. Literature is neither
historical nor sociological fact; it is the vision of a reality perceived
or imagined by the artist and as such must be accepted in terms of
its "inner coherency" rather than any correspondence with documentary evidence. As to the accuracy of its vision, the popularity
and the diffusion of "Abenámar" speak for themselves.

II   "¡Ay de mi Alhama!"

Not all ballads are emotional encomia of a sentimentalized
Moorish tradition. The popularity and brilliance of "Abenámar"
are rivaled by the following composition, of unusual interest both
for its total exclusion of the Christian presence and for the unique
use of epiphonema, which is excluded from the even-line assonance:

Paseábase el rey moro	(The Moorish king was riding
por la ciudad de Granada,	through the city of Granada,

desde la puerta de Elvira
hasta la de Vivarrambla.
5 Cartas le fueron venidas
cómo Alhama era ganada.
   ¡Ay de mi Alhama!
Las cartas echó en el fuego,
y al mensajero matara;
10 echó mano a sus cabellos
y las sus barbas mesaba.
Apeóse de la mula
y en un caballo cabalga;
por el Zacatín arriba
15 subido había a la Alhambra;
mandó tocar sus trompetas,
sus añafiles de plata,
porque lo oyesen los moros
que andaban por el arada.
20 ¡Ay de mi Alhama!
Cuatro a cuatro, cinco a cinco,
juntado se ha gran compaña.
Allí habló un viejo alfaquí,
la barba bellida y cana:
25 —¿Para qué nos llamas, rey,
a qué fué nuestra llamada?
—Para que sepáis, amigos,
la gran pérdida de Alhama.
   ¡Ay de mi Alhama!
30 —Bien se te emplea, buen rey,

buen rey, bien se te empleara;
mataste los bencerraes,
que eran la flor de Grana[da];
cogiste los tornadizos
35 de Córdoba la nombrada.
Por eso mereces, rey,
una pena muy doblada,
que te pierdas tú y el reino
y que se acabe Granada.
40 ¡Ay de mi Alhama!

from the gate of Elvira
to the gate of Vivarrambla.
Letters reached him
that Alhama was captured.
   Woe is my Alhama!
The letters he threw in the fire
and the messenger he killed.
He grabbed his hair
and pulled out his beard.
He dismounted from the mule
and rode out on a horse.
Up through the Zacatín he comes
to the Alhambra;
he ordered the trumpets played,
his Moorish pipes of silver,
so that the Moors would hear
that were out tilling.
   Woe is my Alhama!
Four by four, five by five,
a great gathering has assembled.
There an old sage spoke up,
his beard fine and gray:
"Why do you call us, King,
why our call?"
"So that you may know, friends,
of the great loss of Alhama.
   Woe is my Alhama!
"You have been dealt with well,
                        good King,
well are you dealt with;
you killed the Abencerrajes,
the flower of Granada;
you caught the renegades
of Cordoba, the famed.
For this, King, you deserve
a double grief:
may you and your realm be lost
and Granada finished."
   Woe is my Alhama!)

(pp. 226–27)

The loss of the city of Alhama in 1482 to the Christians serves
as the historical backdrop for this immensely popular ballad, which

survives not only in Spanish versions, but in Portuguese ones as well. It is apparent that the composition of the poem resulted from the attempt of the anonymous minstrels to express their concern for the increasing losses of the Moors to the Christians in terms of some sort of internal fault or guilt of their own people. This is, of course, a widely documented type of "justification": the enemy succeeds, not because of his overwhelming strength, but because of the immorality of the conquered which is divinely punished by defeat. We have seen that this formula is basic to the antihistorical ballads dealing with King Rodrigo's loss of Visigothic Spain, and to a certain extent, the present text is the Moorish counterpart to the earlier Rodrigo compositions. Where the Christian realm of the latter falls before the descending Moorish hordes as the result of his personal indiscretions, it is now the Moorish ruler who sees what remains of his territory lost to the advancing Christian armies in grim retribution for personal immorality.

The general organization of the ballad contrasts the ruler's private grief over news of the loss of Alhama with a public rebuke before his people by the sage, who lays before him the awesome interpretation of events. Intensity is lent the opening segment of the ballad by the initial delay in indicating the subject of the poem and in showing the unexplained consternation of the Moorish king, before we are told in lines 5–6 that Alhama has been lost. Following the epiphonema, which is a cry of grief over the loss (it is not clear whether this cry comes from the king or from the narrative voice—probably the latter, as the king otherwise speaks only in lines 27–28), the violence of his behavior serves to symbolize the immensity of the tragic announcement. For any audience not familiar with the actual historical events involved, the mention of the execution of the messenger is itself enough of a "narrative cue" to make obvious the importance to be attached to what has been related.

Such narrative cues are indicative of the so-called economy of the early Spanish ballads. While many of them may be superfluous for the scholar familiar with the historical or social circumstances surrounding the composition and spread of a ballad, for the popular audience that accounted in large part for the *raison d'être* of the traditional poems—not to mention the modern reader—narrative cues of this sort may function to intensify the mood of the passage as well as simply to suggest the significance of what is being recounted. In this sense, it is not even necessary that a reader realize what Alhama is and what it represented for Moors and Christians of the fifteenth century. It is sufficient that the internal development of the ballad is skillful enough to provide an unmistakable indication of its significance. We may not be able to identify Alhama geographically or historically; nevertheless, the epiphonema and the agitation of the Moorish king, in particular his violence toward the messenger, assure us that we are witnessing through the words of the balladeer a happening of terrible proportions.

At the same time it must be understood that the use of narrative cues such as the ones we have pointed out may not necessarily be meant to recall the importance of the event described. The cues may simply function to attribute more importance to what is being detailed than it, in fact, possessed. In this sense, the ballad is unquestionably a literary invention that may or may not faithfully reflect the true facts. As we have seen in the case of "Abenámar," it is not surprising, and is indeed natural, to find that a ballad will fabricate a moving vision of an event or a circumstance that is completely fictional. The narrative cues that call our attention to the meaning of what is being presented may be highlighting something of verifiable importance, or they may be pointing up the fiction created by the ballad. In the last analysis, it really matters little. We have insisted that literature reflects the true values of a period and/or a people, but few would join Plato anymore in damning literature because it lies in either fact or emphasis or both. Said differently, whatever the military and diplomatic implications were of Alhama's loss, the ballad sets out to create the illusion that it was of momentous consequence. Perhaps what we can say with assurance is only that the emphasis of the ballad captures the feeling that, if nothing else, the loss of Alhama to the Christians was or should have been a tragic blow to Moorish morale.

Thus, as the ballad continues, once we have been made aware of the value to be assigned what has happened, the king is seen to climb to the Alhambra—the eternal symbol of Moorish culture in the Peninsula—to share his grief with his subjects. At this point, the tone of the ballad shifts noticeably from the highly concise representation of the ruler's private grief to the direct discourse of his announcement to the people and the prophetic exegesis of the grim sage. This transition in tone is marked by the repetition of the epiphonema in line 20 (the structural midpoint of the poem).

In reality, from this point on the narrative is dominated, not by the king, but by the *alfaquí* who speaks first after the brief attempt at a formalized description in lines 21–22 of the gathering of the people. The sage speaks throughout the balance of the composition, with the exception of the king's reply to his query in lines 27–28 and the two final repetitions of the epiphonema in lines 29 and 40. Although not noting that it is limited to the words of the sage, González de Escandón has pointed out the stylized effect of repetition at this point in the ballad, stressing its presence in order to give a certain insistent sombreness to the content.[13] In reality, the "repetitions" in lines 25–26 *(llamas/llamada),* in lines 30–31 *(emplea/empleara)*[14] and, in some texts, in lines 39–40 *(pierda/ pierde* [in place of *acabe*]) are examples of adnominatio—the successive use of one base form with the addition of different affixes. In this case, the effect of reusing the same verb with a different syntactic value is an affectation intended to emphasize the gravity of the sage's speech, as opposed to the grief and agitation of his king's behavior. The shift in tone is due in part to this stylistic attempt to suggest the weightiness of the former's pronouncement, in sharp contrast to the emotional turmoil of the monarch.

That the sage has usurped the center of attention is made clear by the brevity of reply given by the king to the former's question and the extent of his fearsome tirade in response. In ten lines, the *alfaquí* changes the focus of the loss of Alhama entirely. When at first we are presented with the fact and with the king's understandable discomposure, the poet is careful to suppress any mention of a relationship between the event and the person of the ruler. The only admissible response is sympathy with his reaction to news of the tragedy. If we can accept the affirmation that the ballad is meant to implicate the emotions of the audience in the context that it establishes, implication is at the outset a clever deceit. For the prophecy of the sage not only warns the king of the impending doomsday for his treacherous perfidy; it also reveals to the audience the error of their emotional identification with the king. Since the ballad concludes with an unmistakable denunciation of the king and an attribution to his personal will of the disastrous event, one might well ask what purpose is served by allowing the audience to lament the loss of Alhama in terms of the king's own grief—i.e., by permitting an identification with his personal feelings. The best interpretation would be that the ballad sets out to damn the king and to damn him in the harshest terms possible. In part damnation is accomplished through the words of the sage, words whose import is well understood by the assembled public and by the audience of the ballad. However, the emotions of the latter are clearly meant to be involved in the circumstances presented, and the function of the epiphonema that is probably best attributed to the narrator himself is to awaken in the listeners the same intense sentiment that it expresses. The discovery that sympathy for the king has been misplaced can only in turn deepen our sense of his despicableness and the justice, at least, of his only too well deserved personal misfortune.

In truth, our appreciation of the justice of his fall must be somewhat ambiguous. For in his fall he is, according to the prophecy of the sage, to bring down all of Granada with him. It is the prophesied tragedy of the eventual fall of Granada which most damns the Moorish ruler. It is only fitting that he suffer personally for his mistakes. But that the whole realm must suffer innocently on his account raises damnation of his perfidy to inexpressible heights of sorrow. The last cry of the epiphonema is more piteous than grievous. When it is first uttered it seems appropriate enough to characterize the sorrow awakened by the fall of Alhama. But when we hear it for the final time, it is wholly inadequate to express the sense of doom that must attend the realization of the accuracy of the *alfaqui*'s prophecy. Or, from another point of view, we might say that the epiphonema, verbally identical in each of its four occurrences in the version quoted, acquires each time a deeper and deeper connotation of tragedy, until in its final enunciation it is best described as a piteous understatement of all of the impending disaster symbolized by the fall of the one city of Alhama. Superficial analysis might easily attribute to the repeated refrain a function such as "punctuation of the narrative" or "a sort of death knell of Moorish civilization." These descriptions would possess a basic ingredient of accuracy; the epiphonema does heighten in these ways the affective tone of the ballad. However, it is not difficult to overlook the way that a phrase that is repeated in a poem is colored by the successive contexts in which it occurs.[15] Iteration of the formula takes on a deeper meaning for the advantage of coming farther along in the lyrical development of the composition. In the case of this ballad, "Woe is my Alhama" is not just a repeated phrase, but rather a cry that shares at each utterance the increased intensity of feeling generated by the minstrel's depiction of the circumstances at issue. The trajectory of intensity attributable to the epiphonema reflects with artistic precision the carefully plotted development of the damnation of the Moorish ruler for his treachery and for the consequences of that treachery for all of Granada.

III *Summing Up*

A long study of the frontier ballads in comparison with the older historical ballads would be necessary before one could affirm with any respectable accuracy that the former represent a development in artistic maturity. We have seen that both groups, despite their claim on popular attention, do indeed represent, as Menéndez Pidal has repeatedly and convincingly claimed, poetry of the highest order. To be sure, critical analysis of the frontier ballads, although they too present the difficulty of multiple traditional versions, is facilitated by the relatively closed nature of composition: each ballad is more of a thematic entity than the historical texts, which tend to group themselves in cycles reflective of their origins. In the case of both groups, however, we have attempted, by examining in detail organizational structure, to underline the various ways in which these brief compositions seek—and, we are confident, achieve—a unity of expression and meaning. Such an examination and its corresponding conclusions can pretend no more than merely to give analytic substance to the esteem in which these ballads have come to be held.

CHAPTER 5

The Novelesque Ballads

THE novelesque ballads enjoy the unique status of representing perhaps the oldest segment of the *Romancero viejo*,[1] of being compositions on the one hand closest to what can be called folkloric and mythic reflections of society, and on the other hand of demonstrating some of the least narrative and most lyrical elements to be found in the ballads. While research has shown convincingly that the diffusion and the development of the novelesque ballads from the late Middle Ages on parallel the compositions of a dramatic and narrative nature considered in the previous two chapters, one must nevertheless admit that any consideration of their origins lies quite outside the theories focusing on epic fragmentation and reworking. While some of the poems—and there are numerous ones of a strikingly impressive artistic merit—bear clear resemblance to nonballad literature, others are either thematically *ex nihilo* or part of general European traditions equally vague in their sources. As indicated in the introductory comments on ballad classification, one cannot easily escape the impression that literary history has set these ballads aside as a pseudo-autonomous group for their lack of correspondence with the ballads developed out of Castilian or Carolingian epic material and frontier compositions. At the same time, the necessity to examine the major texts in strict terms of their intrinsic meaning and structure, rather than in relationship to putative sources and cycles, argues for a more convincing rapprochement with the nontraditional, "professional" court poetry of the late fourteenth and fifteenth centuries. Although the problem of anonymous traditional development and multiple versions still remains to plague the critic anxious to achieve such a rapprochement, the fact that these compositions have attracted the interests of folklore and nontraditionalist researchers and given rise to a greater range of anthropological, allegorical, and psychological interpretations speaks well for a general sense among critics of their greater independence from the questions surrounding the development of the other three major groups.

Our examination, as in the case of previous ballad categories, will involve the selection of a number of widely acclaimed texts, and their subjection to an analysis that will hopefully highlight their artistic unity and rhetorical organization. The texts selected fall into two broad groups: quasi-lyrical and fantastic, and amorous. The only purpose of this grouping is to provide some coherence of discussion for a selection of otherwise basically unrelated poems.

I *Quasi-Lyrical and Fantastic Novelesque Ballads*

"The Ballad of the Prisoner" is one of the best of the first group, not only for its remarkably appropriate brevity but also for its subject: evocation of sympathy for the imprisoned is always assured of popular appeal in Western society. Of fundamental importance in this composition is the sudden shift in tone and the use of the prisoner's own voice in order to engage audience sentiment:

	Que por mayo era, por mayo,	(In May it was, in May,
	cuando hace la calor,	when it is hot,
	cuando los trigos encañan	when the wheat is coming up
	y están los campos en flor,	and the fields are in bloom,
5	*cuando canta la calandria*	when the skylark sings
	y responde el ruiseñor,	and the nightingale answers back,
	cuando los enamorados	when lovers
	van a servir al amor;	go to do service to love.
	sino yo, triste, cuitado,	Except for me, sad, afflicted,
10	*que vivo en esta prisión;*	living in this prison,
	que ni sé cuándo es de día	not knowing when it's day
	ni cuándo las noches son,	nor when it's night,
	sino por una avecilla	but for a little bird
	que me cantaba al albor.	who sang to me at dawn.
15	*Matómela un ballestero;*	A crossbowman killed it
	déle Dios mal galardón.	—may God give him a bad reward.)

(pp. 213–14)

At first appearance, this ballad is deceptively simple; initial and casual comment might underline appropriately the presence of an "empirical-I" that indicates more than anything else the lyrical rather than epico-narrative nature of the composition. However, close analysis reveals several significant structural characteristics. It is not quite as possible as it was with the longer and more narrative ballads to speak of "movements" or divisions of the poem. We have rather somewhat of an overlapping of what could be considered the major points developed in the sixteen lines: the season of the year, the miserable incarceration of the prisoner, the role of the little bird, and the killing of the latter by the crossbowman. The fundamental question to be asked is how does the poem in so few lines engage our sympathy for the prisoner and make us sense the desperate emptiness brought by the bird's death.

The first half of the ballad is taken up by the indication of season. That it is the month of May is of immediate evocatory powers. May is the awakening of nature after her Winter slumber and the awakening of the senses of man to the primitive rites of Spring. Throughout Western tradition, May has come to symbolize the exaltation of man's sensitivity to and identification with Nature in the most mythical and spiritual meaning of that abstraction. It is not surprising to find that Christianity accommodated the traditions relating to Mother Earth to the Virgin Mary, and in a less secular context reference to May would evoke Marian rather than fertility festivities.[2] As it is, the ballad, reminding us of a dominant trait of the *Romancero viejo,* is decidedly nonreligious in outlook, and the initial lines of the composition are given over to a traditional evocation of that lusty month. Reading these eight lines, it would be difficult to dismiss as incorrect the research which has wanted to relate at least some groupings of the novelesque ballads to either folkloristic popular origins or to the primitive lyric poetry of the earliest Romance literature in the Peninsula. Certainly, the feeling of May as a stimulant for one's sluggish senses—and sensitivities— can arguably be traced to the mythical May festivities of remote popular origin. We will leave this nonliterary issue to folklorists. What we can say from a critical point of view, however, is just that the success of the appeal to our acquaintance with the primitive meaning of May is a highly successful literary device undoubtedly chosen calculatedly in order to exploit audience identification with the festivities of May, festivities in which the prisoner, of course, cannot participate. In other words, the meaning of May may recall vague prehistorical fertility rites; to any audience aware of popular European culture, a poet's general evocation of those rites through the mention of May is a first step in engaging their identification with his narrative.

In terms of an earlier poetic tradition, "The Ballad of the Prisoner" unquestionably recalls the parellelistic poetry of medieval Portuguese.[3] Without entering into the hoary academic debate of the influences on the *Romancero* of formal, courtly poetry,[4] we can nevertheless point to the unity of the first half of this ballad through the use of identical formal diction.[5] Parallelistic poetry is distinguished for its use of lines of identical or functionally similar syntax. Four anaphoras using *cuando* ("when"), followed by six present-tense verbs and their subject constitute the parallelism of these opening verses. Their function is to depict through the reference to easily identifiable circumstances of the month of May all of the glory of that awakening of man and nature. From a more precise stylistic point of view, the first five verbs are intransitives with their respective subjects. The three inanimate and two animate references are symbolic of the season. The last verb involves a reference to man and woman and their love, awakened and stimulated by the awakening of nature around them. It is interesting to note how the relationship between man and nature is established. In lines 5–6 a female bird attracts the attention of a male; in lines 7–8 we are presented with the suggestion of a similar attraction between lovers, whose "service to love" is, of course, a stylized game that brings out in intense detail the sexual attraction between men and women. Whatever the affiliation of the ballad to the formal love poetry of Portuguese literature[6]—an affiliation unproblematical in itself due to the inappropriateness of making any sharp distinction between medieval poetry written in the various Romance dialects of the Peninsula—there is little doubt that this composition exploits effectively the parallelistic structure in order to highlight the synecdochical elements that symbolize the "merry month of May."

When the ballad turns in line 9 to focus attention on the "I" of the speaker, an immediate conflict is established. The function of the first half of the poem has been to present a context which *does not* apply to the speaker. The pleasure taken by one in recalling with the poet's words the glories of the season is meant to be soured by the direct and harsh characterization by the prisoner of his situation. The juxtaposition that occurs exploits the rhetorical formula "A, but not B," a formula related to the one used to present the Cid in the ballad discussed in Chapter 3 (cf. p. 82). Here, the prisoner contrasts himself with the rest of mankind. He alone is unable to participate in the full awakening represented by May. The reference in lines 11–12 to being unable to distinguish night

from day is a synecdoche for the unbearable isolation of his imprisonment and the sense of frustration at being so cut off from the
mainstream of life. The poet effectively evokes here the unnatural
cruelty of physical and spiritual confinement that is the basis of
our pity for the imprisoned individual. Of course, this pity is not
diluted by reference to the reason for incarceration, and it is easy
enough to recall frequent injustices and miscarriages of justice to
make untroubled our identification with the spiritual agony of
the prisoner.

With all of the pity aroused by the first two-thirds of the ballad,
the main impact comes in the rapid conclusion of the last four lines.
We are told of the little bird whose singing alleviated the burden
of imprisonment by announcing the dawn. The obvious importance
of the bird to the man and the references to the birds who participate
in the awakening of nature in lines 5–6 serve to suggest a role for
the creature disconsonant with the brevity of allusion to it. Not
only is the bird a consolation to the prisoner for singing the arrival
of dawn—that is, for assuaging the synecdochical suffering of the
man by helping him distinguish night from day. The bird is clearly
meant also to serve as a link between the misery of his imprisonment
and the full glories of physical existence symbolized by the month
of May that are denied to him in his dark dungeon. Hearing the
bird's song, the prisoner is able to reconstruct in his tortured soul
the exalted meaning of Spring awakening. While the ballad does
not make explicit reference to this function of the bird, confining
itself rather to her song at dawn and its importance, it would be
difficult to comprehend the relationship between the first and second
halves of the poem if a more integral meaning were not intended.

The *avecilla,* then, brings to the prisoner the coming of dawn
just as she symbolizes in her literally lyrical integration with nature
the broadest sense of living denied the prisoner in his confinement.
The main impact of all this comes in the statement, little more than
a note after the parallelistic buildup and the "A, but not B" juxtaposition, that the bird has been killed by a Spring sportsman.
The intensity of the prisoner's curse is startling, coming as it does
upon the heels of the pathos and sympathy generated by his earlier
words, and therefore it is all that much more effective in strengthening audience appreciation of the man's unbearable suffering.
Reference to the bird and suggestion of what she symbolized in
bringing some scant mitigation of anguish to the prisoner calls

forth our relief that at least he has her song to look forward to in the tedium of his night. But the abrupt mention of the bird's death can only be meant to reinforce a sense of despair, destroying, as the crossbowman destroyed the bird, any glimmer of hope and alleviation of suffering.

From a rather innocuous beginning, pleasant for the references to May festivities, the ballad has been skillfully developed to engage our own forgotten despair as human beings for the suffering that can afflict man. Here that suffering is symbolized not only by the physical fact of imprisonment, but by a circumstance in which something that could have been construed as a soothing balm to that suffering has been destroyed, and destroyed with the irretrievable finality of death. The curse uttered against the crossbowman (representative in his unthinking sport of the injustice of the forces that imprisoned the man?) is both an expression of one man's hopelessness and helplessness as well as the chord of fury latent in every man's soul toward the destruction of his faint rays of hope. It is on the basis of this correlation that the ballad seeks our personal understanding of the plight of the prisoner, to evoke in us, carelessly enjoying the promise of May, the emphemeral fragility of that hope.

It is not difficult to see why this ballad has long been a favorite for the modern reader since the time of the Romantics. Not only is it striking for the use of a personal "I" rather than the third-person narrative characteristic of the ballad; it is a procedure attractive, to be sure, for the subjective orientation of much of modern poetry. But the bleakness of vision underlying the ballad, a bleakness not found in the ballads as a whole but certainly there in the literary tradition of the fourteenth and fifteenth centuries,[7] constitutes an appeal to all of those emotions in the individual that today are vaguely gathered under the umbrella of "Existentialism." Although it would be absurd to speak of this ballad as indicative of a medieval pre-Romanticism or pre-Existentialism, it cannot be denied that the bleakness of vision is there, supported with impressive mastery by the structure of the poem, and that that bleakness has been a major factor in identification between the poet and the audience of its composition and the modern reader who can scarcely imagine an anthology of the Spanish ballad without it.

II *"El conde Arnaldos"*

Rivaling in popularity and emotional content "The Ballad of the Prisoner" is the ballad of Count Arnaldos, or, as some texts identify him, Infante Arnaldos. Although for some the impact of this composition might be diluted by familiarity with surviving longer versions, in which the mystery of its conclusion is disappointingly dissipated,[8] if we consider the more popular shorter version and the longer surviving texts, in effect different poems, we will be better prepared to appreciate the surprising effect that it has upon the reader and to understand the problems of interpretation that it presents:

¡Quién hubiera tal ventura	(Would that I had such adventure
sobre las aguas del mar	by the waters of the sea
como hubo el infante Arnaldos	as the Infante Arnaldos
la mañana de San Juan!	the morning of St. John's Day!
5 *Andando a buscar la caza*	Looking for game
para su falcón cebar,	to feed his falcon
vió venir una galera	he saw a galley
que a tierra quiere llegar;	approaching to land.
las velas trae de sedas,	Its sails are of silk,
10 *la jarcia de oro torzal,*	the rigging of plaited gold,
áncoras tiene de plata,	anchors of silver,
tablas de fino coral.	planks of fine coral.
Marinero que la guía,	The seaman that steered it
diciendo viene un cantar,	was singing a song
15 *que la mar ponía en calma,*	that becalmed the sea
los vientos hace amainar;	and tamed the winds.
los peces que andan al hondo,	The fish in the deep
arriba los hace andar;	are brought by it to the surface;
las aves que van volando,	the birds that fly
20 *al mástil vienen posar.*	come to light on the mast.
Allí habló el infante Arnaldos	There spoke the Infante Arnaldos,
bien oiréis lo que dirá:	you will hear well what he says:
—Por tu vida, el marinero,	"Upon your life, seaman,
dígasme ora ese cantar.	tell me that song."
25 *Respondióle el marinero,*	The seaman answered,
tal respuesta le fué a dar:	this reply did he give:
—Yo no digo mi canción	"This song I tell to no one
sino a quien conmigo va.	except that he come with me.")

(pp. 203–4)

In reality, the figure of Arnaldos is insignificant as presented in the ballad. Although he speaks once (lines 23–24), he is but a named entity through whose eyes we experience the wondrous event that is the central and dominant concern of the poem. While the longer version of the ballad may give some further specific meaning to the person of Arnaldos in terms of his story of captivity and freedom, in the truncated text, the one most known to Hispanic tradition, he is really little more than a point upon which the happening turns. The assertion that Arnaldos may be considered only a presence is supported by the fact that the ballad gives initial, and therefore emphatic, weight to the voice of the narrator. The first lines, "Would that I had had such luck," focuses our interest first on the anonymous singer of the ballad. When in lines 3–4 he is to refer to the Infante, it is only to express whose luck it is that he would have shared. Thus, it is clear from the outset that Arnaldos' adventure with the sea is to be related to us, not in the vague terms of someone else's experience, but in terms of an experience of immediate appeal and attraction to the narrative voice. This is a circumstance which, in terms of the exclamatory opening adynaton, serves to engage the curiosity of the audience.

The first four lines of the composition are thus given over to the establishment of this "I/he" relationship between the minstrel and the Infante. Their function is both to facilitate a sense of immediacy through the creation of an identification with the latter's experience closer to the audience, as well as to create a tone of wonderment and suspense as to what that luck was that will color our subsequent contact with the narrator's tale. Although introductions of the ballad have spoken in one voice about the skill with which suspense and a sense of mystery and wonder are created by this brief composition, few have attempted to deal with how this is so. An obvious question that analyses might ask, which at first appears more facetious than critical, is why does the minstrel wish to have partaken of Arnaldos' adventure. It is the force of this adynaton, we suggest, that strikes the tone maintained throughout the development of the ballad.

The next four lines turn to an introduction of the Infante himself and the context in which the event occurred. Although the second line of the ballad implies that Arnaldos' luck comes on (sobre) the waters of the sea, these lines make it clear that he witnesses the arrival of the galley from the beach, and later verses neither state nor imply a shift in position. Of course, the longer version of the poem, as we have hinted, relates events aboard the vessel, which is implicated both in his kidnapping as well as in his rescue. Within the context of the shorter text, there are three possible interpretations: 1) the second line may be taken as meaning *on* literally and as foreshadowing the Infante's decision to accompany the seaman (cf. our comments below on Hart's decision to accept this reading); 2) the second line may be taken as a typical example of imprecise linguistic usage in the ballad—the locative preposition is only meant to be a vague indication of relative position; 3) *sobre* may be taken to mean "near" or "alongside of," a usage of wide attestation.[9] It may seem unnecessary to dwell on this point, but most commentaries and translations of the poem place emphasis upon the adventure having taken place *on* the sea. In a text which presents so many possibilities for conflicting interpretations, it is not amiss to accord a far closer attention to prepositions than one might wish to in examining other ballads. The second segment, therefore, barring liberal interpretations, fixes the meaning of the second line with great precision and depicts the Infante as engaged in the normal pursuits of a young nobleman when he sees the approaching galley.

The context given for this event is of considerable importance in estimating the relationship between Arnaldos and what he sees and hears. There is little doubt that the charm of the ballad derives in greatest measure from the unexplained and therefore mysterious nature of the galley, its helmsman, and the magical powers of the latter. All of these are put in extended juxtaposition to the humdrum activities of the Infante, who is out hunting with his falcon. That is to say, one is not stretching a point to suggest that the presentation of Arnaldos is based on his appearance in a role both indicative of and quite common for a man of his nobility. It is, in short, an expected and normal, if not daily, role. In order that we understand the impression of unusual wonderment which the galley is to make upon the Infante, it is necessary that we see him first in an activity that can possess no wonderment and nothing unusual.

What follows in the remaining portions of the ballad are the description of the galley and the dialogue between Arnaldos and the seaman which serves to indicate the reaction of the former to what he has seen. Fully twelve lines are taken up with the unusual apparition (lines 9–20), almost half of the total composition. Much could be said about the galley and the strange influences exercised by its helmsman. It must first be noted that the ballad makes it quite clear that it is the morning of St. John's Day—Midsummer—and a day, as the reader of medieval poetry in general well knows, supposedly filled with portent and strange happenings.[10] The mention of the day in line 4, then, is to be construed as a foreshadowing of what is to come, an indication that the day will not be lived in vain. What can one say about the details of lines 9–20? Aside from justifying them on the basis of the day on which the galley and its master appear, we might refer to the legend of the Flying Dutchman and numerous other legends and fairy tales concerning wondrous—as well as horrible—apparitions associated with the sea. Anyone familiar with schoolbook accounts of pre-modern superstitions surrounding the unknown expanses of the sea is able to appreciate the emotions awakened in Arnaldos as well as in the poet's audience by the strangeness of the vessel and its mysterious occupant.[11]

It would also be possible to pursue the generalized Western symbolism attached to the specifics used. While such a procedure might help in explaining a more intellectual effect for the apparition, it would not stress well how the latter is presented in the straightforward terms of a fantastic marvel. Our overall impression from what we are told is like that of Cinderella when her fairy godmother gets to work. For the audience at large, there is no particular symbolism in glass slippers and mice-drawn pumpkins, but rather just the awe-inspiring unusualness of it all. Fantasy is a chamber of the human mind that receives only infrequent visitation, lying vacant until some happening or event or circumstance permits us to escape daily tedium into an unknown which is universally characterized by its beauty, its perfection, and its spectacle. This is, of course, the attraction of fairy tales from the dark recesses of time unknown down to the Tolkiens of modern literature.[12] While the tale of fantasy may be only one narrative mode for commenting on the human condition, its superficial attraction alone is usually great enough to entertain our interest.

The principal effect, therefore, of the apparition of St. John's Day is the marvel that it awakens in a man who has just been described as engaged in a routine activity of no particular moment. Perhaps the principal reason that Arnaldos is presented in such passive and insignificant terms is precisely to highlight the dramatic nature of the galley's arrival and the man's subsequent enthusiasm. At this point in the ballad, the juxtaposition is between ordinary Arnaldos and the extraordinary sight which he descries on the sea. We suggest that the ballad's intent is to exploit this juxtaposition toward creating a sense of disruption by the unknown and the fantastic on St. John's Day of what is really quite a quotidian and normal reality for the Infante. To say that Arnaldos is seeking relief from the quotidian would be to generate more meaning than the text indicates. What we can, however, say with some basis on content is that the action of Midsummer day is to elevate the emotions of Arnaldos from passive involvement with a routine activity to a confrontation with a vision that cannot help but awaken in him the freeplay of his sense of the unknown, the fantastic, and the marvelous.

There is a pivotal contrast between the passivity of Arnaldos as he is first presented, a passivity seen against the excitement of the narrative voice, and the awakened excitement of his sense of the mysterious evinced by his plea that the helmsman share with him the words of his song. The adnominatio of the introduction to the latter's reply creates a brief moment of suspense reminiscent of the suspense created by the eight opening lines that preface so excitingly the description of the galley. The reply, of course, can only be as equally mysterious as the apparition itself. Anything else would have diluted and dissipated irremediably the sense of wondrous mystery evoked by the entire composition up to this point. It is quite unnecessary to ask why the seaman cannot share his song with Arnaldos unless accompanied by him. An answer to this based on an intellectual analysis of the symbolic meaning of galley and master would likewise dispel the charm occasioned by its unknown nature. Rather, we should first accept the response that closes the poem as a preservation of the autonomy of the fantasy, a fantasy that we cannot be allowed to penetrate to the extent that any knowledge of it would overwhelm and destroy its effect upon us.

On another level, the implied meaning to Arnaldos of the response must be an invitation to him to flee his earthbound reality and to escape into whatever mystery is given temporal and spatial form by that vessel on that significant day of the year. At the same time that we cannot know the meaning of the fantasy and continue to be touched by it in the same way, we likewise cannot know what the Infante's decision will be. The abrupt ending, truncating a longer poem that does indeed explain and therefore dispel our sense of wonder, can only have been chosen to maximize an overall inexplicitness as to meaning from an intellectual point of view. To be sure, if we interpret line 2 to mean "on" in the sense of "out upon" the waters of the sea, then the decision of Arnaldos to accompany the magician-seaman is made clear. By the same token, if we appreciate the meaning of Midsummer's day, appreciate its ephemeralness and the return to daily reality that follows the escapist festivities and happenings of that feast, then we ought to incline toward believing that Arnaldos, despite his awakened sensitivities to the unknown, must accept in the end his inseverable attachment to the normal routine of existence that characterizes man's life. Although we incline toward the latter interpretation (little in impact would have been lost by stating Arnaldos' acceptance to flee with the mysterious stranger) we need only appreciate the context which is established explicitly, a context which is sufficient in itself to justify the word *ventura,* "good fortune," used in the opening verse of the ballad. On that day of the year when the unexpected and the impossible become brief reality, Infante Arnaldos is presented with a vision that accomplishes one very important function of Midsummer festivities: to awaken in man his sensitivity to the fantastic and the marvellous which is submerged in his routine contact with the grayness of reality.

It is, of course, just for this reason that the fantasy is always a brilliant and splendorous "supra-reality." The popularity enjoyed by this ballad and the impact which it has had upon sensibilities that are in any way romantic clearly make it a unique masterpiece of Spanish literature. Not only is it unusual for the general absence of the fantastic in the Spanish ballad; aside from some medieval legends inspired by Arabic and general Oriental sources (cf. the influential *Libro de Calila y Dimna* [*Book of Calila and Dimna*], translated into Spanish in 1251 from the Arabic), there is a general lack of fantastic literature in Spanish when compared to Celtic and Germanic traditions.[13] Of course, it is not altogether accurate to describe the ballad of the Infante Arnaldos as fantastic. It deals less with a fantastic experience of Arnaldos than with the effect of such an apparition upon him. That is to say, the ballad itself is not a fairy tale; it is too much dominated by the narrative voice and the meaningful juxtaposition between the mystery of the sea and the earthbound reality, brought together momentarily but movingly on St. John's Day. Modern literature might impress upon us how man's fantasies are the intrusion of the subconscious on the conscious. But modern man preserves just enough of the primitive, prepsychological belief that the mysterious unknown is a force which disrupts his tranquility—and his boredom—from without to sustain the dramatic effect of this ballad upon our imaginations.

We should not close our discussion of this important text from the *Romancero viejo* without acknowledging T. R. Hart's sacramental interpretation.[14] After advancing the widely-held thesis that most, if not all, medieval literature should be read from the point of view of medieval scriptural tradition, a tradition that impregnated the literature of the period with allusions to the promise of Scripture and of the New Law of Christianity, Hart proceeds to analyze our ballad as a religious statement on the promise of salvation offered by the Church to man:

> Allegorically, then, our text says simply that a man has responded to Christ's appeal [the ship is the Church; its helmsman, Christ], he has become a member of the Church (in the sense, of course, of the whole body of those who believe in Christ), and by doing so has been saved. It may be objected that we are not told that Arnaldos accepted the boatman's veiled invitation to accompany him on his journey. But we know from the very first line that anyone would be glad to share Arnaldos' adventure, and this implies that Arnaldos does not refuse the boatman's invitation.   (pp. 283–84)

Hart's reading of the symbolism of the ballad is accurate in terms of scriptural tradition, and the details of his argument may be consulted by the reader not familiar with what are trite and overused allusions in medieval literature. Any hesitation to accept Hart's interpretation, then, cannot come from his understanding of the allegorical meaning of references, but from an error in critical judgment with regard to the unified tone of the work itself. Said differently, one must first accept Hart's premise that the ballad need of necessity be understood in terms of the symbology of the Christian promise. If one does not agree that all of medieval literature is elaborated around scriptural tradition, then he must consequently be willing to agree however that his ballad does pretend to advance a sacramental meaning for Arnaldos' adventure. We have argued elsewhere against the panallegorical interpretation of medieval literature because it imposes an extrinsic and rigid attitude toward literature that is unacceptable from the point of view of a creative principle that insists on critical discovery of meaning within the text rather than as an external *sine qua non*.[15] In terms of the possibility of the ballad's making it intrinsically obvious that a scriptural meaning is intended, the reader must be left to his own judgment and critical sensitivities. Our own analysis has made it plain that we do not accept Hart's interpretation, principally because it must be taken on faith. The text itself provides not one indisputable basis for supposing a scriptural meaning, unless one subscribes to the highly debatable assumption that the allusions can only have been used in terms of their Christian symbolism. We have no good cause to reject Hart's reading—it has the advantage of satisfying intellectually the mysterious unknown quantities introduced by the poem—but by the same token we are left with no good reason to accept it.

As a footnote to this discussion, we might add that perhaps the ballad is an implied criticism of the ecclesiastical meaning of St. John's Day, that is, as the feast of St. John the Baptist, who is the last of the great prefigurements of the Coming of Christ. As we know, the Church chose to repress the pagan Midsummer festivities by giving the day a religious significance, a procedure behind the dating of the majority of the important Church feasts. Such an accommodation in the case of Midsummer robs it of all of its ties with the fantastic and the unknown (of course, there is supposed to be nothing more "known" than the prophecy of the Coming of Christ). The ballad is significant for taking a reference to the Church feast and using it as a point of departure for evoking all of the wonderful fantasies which are shown vividly in Arnaldos' experience to continue to obtain. Needless to say, this footnote, rather than being an interpretation of the ballad as a criticism of the Church calendar, might only be an aspect which enriches our appreciation of Arnaldos' welcome of the marvelous apparition.

III *"Fontefrida"*

Fontefrida, Fontefrida,	(Fontefrida, Fontefrida,
Fontefrida y con amor,	Fontefrida and with love,
do todas las avecicas	where all the little birds
van tomar consolación,	go to find consolation,

5 *si no es la Tortolica,*	all except the Turtledove,
que está viuda y con dolor.	who is widowed and bereaved.
Por allí fuera a pasar	There came to pass by
el traidor de Ruiseñor;	the traitorous Nightingale;
las palabras que le dice	his words to her
10 *llenas son de traición:*	are full of treachery:
—Si tú quisieses, señora,	"If you like, madam,
yo sería tu servidor.	I would be your servant."
—Vete de ahí, enemigo,	"Be off, enemy,
malo, falso, engañador,	evil, false, deceiver,
15 *que ni poso en ramo verde*	for I do not light on any green branch
ni en prado que tenga flor;	nor in any field in bloom,
que si el agua hallo clara,	and if I find the water clear,
turbia la bebía yo;	I would drink it muddied.
que no quiero haber marido	For I want no husband,
20 *porque hijos no haya, no;*	nor any children as well;
no quiero placer con ellos,	I want no pleasure with them
ni menos consolación.	and less consolation.
¡Déjame, triste enemigo,	Leave me, sad enemy,
malo, falso, ruin, traidor,	evil, false, debauchèd, traitorous,
25 *que no quiero ser tu amiga*	for I will not be your friend
ni casar contigo, no!	nor will I marry you either!")

(p. 65)

Several features of this ballad make it somewhat strikingly unusual in a ballad tradition that deals almost exclusively with
historical and quasi-historical events and persons. Obviously influenced by the extensively developed medieval tradition (inherited
to be sure from Classical Antiquity) of the Bestiary and related
narrative fables, the almost exclusively lyrical ballad of the turtledove is quite an isolated case in the *Romancero viejo*. The ballad
is, basically, a fable itself, since a first approximation would indicate
how the encounter between the two birds and what they represent
constitutes a stylized artifice for the expression of certain ethical
or moral values. The Bestiaries were encyclopedic works dealing
with real and imaginary beasts that were discussed and analyzed
in terms of legendary qualities, the majority of which were related
directly to personal and institutional values of human society.[16]
The Bestiaries in turn influenced the development of the fable, a
fictional narrative in which stories dealing with conflicts and situ-
ations readily identifiable by a human audience were presented in

terms of animals, most of whom had become archetypes of specific vices and virtues. Scholarship has traced the development of the twin themes of the turtledove (feminine) and the nightingale (masculine) with special reference to their appearance in the Spanish ballad.[17] Thus there can be little doubt that at least this one composition demonstrates an enormous influence of the clerical (or scholarly) and nonpopular literature of the Middle Ages, an influence whose essential details can be traced back to Antiquity and forward in time in their frequent use by the sophisticated poets of the Renaissance and Baroque.

Asensio, however, is quick to point out in his comments the extent to which we may speak of the popular folkloristic elements in the ballad that derive from the semipagan rites of May which we have already discussed with reference to "The Ballad of the Prisoner." The fundamental issue here would seem to be the *fontefrida,* the cold fountain, associated in those rites with fertility and sensuality and in whose proximity the exchange between the two birds takes place. At the same time, as we shall point out, there are unmistakable references to the unique medieval traditions of courtly love and its literary formulas. It would appear, then, from the outset that, despite its superficial "delightful" simplicity of expression and popular appeal, we are dealing with a work of no mean literary antecedents.

We mentioned briefly in our preceding pages that one of the problems presented by one type of novelesque ballad was that of whether or not they should all be dealt with as ballads in the same context in which one examines the historical ballad. In other words, from what critical point of view is it justifiable to discuss "Frontefrida" and, say, one of the ballads of King Rodrigo as examples of the same literary tradition? The strongest arguments, usually more implicit than defended in the literary histories, is simply that both make use of the same poetic format, the ballad metre, and both have participated in the same process of traditionalization, having been accepted by popular tradition and subjected to the reworking and modification responsible for the absence of a fixed text and the presence of innumerable versions. These arguments are, of course, basically extrinsic, and their virtue in bringing together works that typify a unique aspect of Spanish poetry also has the vice of overlooking the very real differences of theme and technique. Although developing toward the close of the Middle Ages, and indeed not really having been recognized in print until the early Renaissance, the ballads have been more easily maintained as an autonomous genre due, we suggest, to the very real loss of whatever tradition of lyric poetry in Castile there might have been during early centuries.

Although we have ample evidence of the development of lyric poetry in Catalan and in Galician-Portuguese, only traces exist in Castilian to indicate that there might have been such a genre in Central Spain.[18] Spanish literary history, lacking until the fifteenth century a body of nondidactic poetry, has found it far easier to lump those relatively few ballads of a lyrical and nonepic nature together with the more properly-speaking historical texts. The result is the lack of an appropriate critical attention to the ways in which many of the novelesque ballads, "Fontefrida" in particular, bespeak traditions of poetry which in reality had very little to do with the emergence of epic literature and, later, the ballads derived from it. The overemphasis on popular acceptance and diffusion, with all of the problems attendant upon this process, does not deal satisfactorily enough with the value of the poem in terms of its unique status as a ballad and as a work of art. The recent philological criticism to which we have referred is important to the extent that it moves in the direction of considering the ballad, not within the context of the *Romancero,* but as a singular poetic text of affiliations with a quite different type of literature. Nevertheless, the dominance which traditionalist theories have exercised over these ballads of a nonepic nature is demonstrated rather amusingly by the preamble to Asensio's study, which is a tribute to Menéndez Pidal's *Romancero hispánico* and is quite unrelated to the arguments which follow in Asensio's paper.

Turning now to the text itself, our attention is first drawn to the context established by the ballad. The first four lines, opened with a repetition that suggests a song, present the cold fountain that serves as an erotic symbol of femininity, a meaning which is apparent both in popular tradition and in more formal poetry (one manifestation of which, one assumes, is the recurring image of the nude woman/nymph bathing in the stream). Our ballad, however, presents the fountain (or spring in the sense of a natural fountain) in terms of the female birds (*avecicas*) who seek consolation in its waters. (Since the subsequent encounter is to counterpose female and male bird, we assume that the *avecicas,* while semantically referring to all birds of either biological gender, is meant to refer in the poem only to female birds by virtue of the diminutive and by the popular association of the cold fountain with women. That the female turtledove rests near the fountain can be taken as a further indication of it as a feminine domain.) The purpose of this introduction of the fountain is to present the widowed turtledove in line 5 in terms of the formula "A, but not B." All of the other birds, but *not* the bereaved turtledove find consolation there. As we have pointed out in previous discussions of this formula, its function is to give a negative emphasis to an isolated circumstance that does not participate in the general circumstance.

The opposition between the turtledove and the nightingale loses subtlety in English. Since the names of these birds in Spanish (and in other Romance languages) are of opposite grammatical genders (feminine and masculine, respectively), they can be used to contrast biological or natural gender. This is a frequent type of relationship in languages where nouns are so marked: the grammatical gender of the Romance words for Earth and Death have resulted in the former being portrayed as Mother Earth and the latter as a woman (cf. the tradition of the Dances of Death). English shows some traces of this "sexual personification" by virtue of nouns taken into English from languages where the marked gender has already resulted in a traditional image. Most abstract nouns, for example, in the Romance languages are feminine, with the result in English, which borrowed many principally from French, of female personifications: Justice, Nature, Dame Philology, and so on. Since English early lost gender classification for nouns—which Anglo Saxon nevertheless had—the type of anthropomorphization reflected in our ballad does not have quite the same impact when translated into English, where either one must attach the clumsy adjectives of sex or suppress the distinction altogether.

The birds themselves present no particular problems of meaning or symbology. Even without Asensio's comments concerning the sources for their depiction in the ballad, internal evidence points clearly to the sad turtledove as representing virtue and fidelity—let us say simply Christian femininity—and to the traitorous nightingale as representing deceitful and sinful masculine aggressiveness. These roles the text makes plain; what we do gain by understanding that they are traditional representations in literature and other forms of art is an appreciation of how the ballad is probably designed to call, as did the fable, on the comprehension by the audience of a basic conflict of human virtue. This is, naturally enough, the usual motive for the use of clichés: they are readily identifiable and usually represent a whole panorama of meaning which therefore need not be made explicit. In this case, the main point of the ballad is the virtuous fidelity of the turtledove to her deceased mate, a fidelity difficult for the modern reader to appreciate but easily understandable in terms of the Church's early efforts to maintain the indissolubility of the marital union even in death.[19] The deceit of the nightingale is basically a challenge to the fidelity which the turtledove attempts to maintain and which should be obvious to the male bird because of the widow's separation from the other birds, who are free to indulge in the sexuality symbolized by the fountain. On the most immediate level of a fable, therefore, the ballad addresses itself to the virtuous continence that the widowed turtledove would observe in the presence of the sexuality surrounding her with the fountain and the other female birds which it attracts and the aggressive invitation of the nightingale, sinfully indifferent to the purity of the turtledove.

The address of the nightingale raises another level of meaning for the ballad, that of the courtly love of medieval society and its relationship to higher religious values.[20] The words of the exchange between the two birds recall the formulas of the courtly game, particularly when the nightingale expresses his willingness to be a "servant [of love]" and when the turtledove, understanding the direction of his words, angrily rejects any chance of her being his "friend" (i.e., the mistress of the male servant of love; *amiga* is still used in modern Spanish as a euphemism for "mistress" in the current debased sense of the word.) Although courtly love was generally accepted in the Middle Ages, and indeed survived in a modified form for several centuries thereafter, it has generally been called a sinful, extramarital alternative—and diversion from— Christian virtue, resolved either by marriage and its appropriate fidelity or by renunciation and repentance of one's sinful if nevertheless delightful ways. While many apologists were anxious to reconcile courtly and more canonically Christian concepts of love, the general attitude that they were irreconcilable remained, the principal stumbling block being that courtly love exalted the position of the woman, whereas the man was to be the dominant member of a Christian marriage. The bleakest vision in Spanish literature of the evils of courtly love is to be found in the *Celestina,* first printed in 1499, where it constitutes a motivating theme of the work.

In our ballad, courtly love is basically presented negatively. The advances of the nightingale, advances that would have the turtledove abandon the path of virtue which she has chosen symbolically by avoiding the fountain's waters, are in terms of the invitation to the game of love. The invitation, however, is given short shrift, as the turtledove launches into a reply seven times longer than her would-be servant's greeting. Her words not only make clear her decision to observe the expected continence of the faithful widow, but suggest the degree of her grief and sense of discord with erotic nature. The negatives of lines 15–22 are meant to emphasize both her anguish as well as the distaste occasioned by the "consolation" she sees offered in the male's invitation. In addition, they stand in antithetical relationship to the abandoned sexuality suggested by the four opening lines of the ballad. Greenness, flowers in bloom, clear water, all are May symbols of spring fertility and sexuality that can no longer attract the woman sustained only by her grief and her sense of virtue. The last is perhaps the least obvious reference: the turtledove's agitation of the water before drinking it expresses both her own spiritual agitation as well as a refusal to partake of the clear waters associated with the vigorous and erotic cold running fountain.

The final lines of the ballad are mutually complementary to the extent that the turtledove rejects the only two possibilities for acceptance of the nightingale's advances: she will be neither his mistress in courtly love—clearly sinful—nor will she be his wife in proper marriage—an equally odious choice since it will violate the higher virtue of marital fidelity in death. The strength of the ballad's statement concerning the praiseworthy femininity of the turtledove derives from this dual refusal. The virtue of angrily denouncing the sensuous and sinful game of courtly love is compounded by the equally explicit refusal to accept the option of a virtuous liaison. Although the ballad lies outside the orbit of the extensive medieval poetry dealing with the nuances of courtly love, the anonymous poet has employed references to the phenomenon, as well as references to the semipagan eroticism evoked by the cold fountain, in order to emphasize the extent to which the faithful turtledove has risen beyond them to represent a purity and a virtuousness of the highest order for the Christian soul.

IV *Amorous Ballads*

In contrast to "Fontefrida," marital infidelity is the topic of "Blancaniña" ("White Child"), a perennial favorite of collections and a ballad whose traditional popularity must owe something to the unmistakable theme of sexual mischief and punishment. Unlike the first four ballads examined in this chaper, "Blancaniña" is more strictly narrative in the basic sense of the word as we have used it in reference to the historical ballads. It may thus be set aside from those novelesque ballads which evince more of an interest in the lyrical imagination and in a symbolism of a nondramatic nature. Although "Fontefrida" deals with love—and the "Ballad of the Prisoner" also in a remoter and more abstract sense— "Blancaniña" projects love as a fundamental denominator of human conflict. To this extent, this ballad is closer in structure and orientation to those recurring characteristics of the *Romancero viejo* to which we referred in Chapter 3. It is a ballad that not only establishes a context in which human beings are seen to come into emotional, if not violent, conflict, but we see as well that that conflict concerns values that must be considered basic to a society. In this case, those values are the comforts of love as opposed to the marital responsibility of the wife toward her absent husband.

In the case of "Fontefrida," it should be obvious that there is no conflict implied: the entire focal point of sympathy is directed toward the turtledove, and the eroticism represented by the fountain and by the nightingale is given no support whatever. Therefore, although both ballads deal with feminine fidelity to their mates, the orientation is different enough between the two compositions to justify our separation of them into two quite distinct groupings of novelesque ballads. In addition, the division of "Blancaniña" into two juxtaposed segments and the abrupt conclusion of narrative suggest general ballad features that we have had much occasion to point out, features which are not particularly important in the case of the first three ballads of this chapter. The best-known text of "Blancaniña" follows:[21]

'Blanca sois, señora mía,	("You are white, my lady,
más que el rayo del sol;	more so than the sun's rays.
¿si la dormiré esta noche	Shall I sleep this night
desarmado y sin pavor?	unarmed and without fear?
5 Que siete años había, siete,	For seven years, seven,

que no me desarmo, no;
más negras tengo mis carnes
que un tiznado carbón.'
'Dormidla, señor, dormidla
10 desarmado sin temor,
que el conde es ido a la caza
a los montes de León.'
'¡Rabia le mate los perros
y águilas el su halcón,
15 y del monte hasta casa
a él arrastre el morón!'

Ellos en aquesto estando
su marido que llegó:
'¿Qué hacéis, la Blancaniña,
20 hija de padre traidor?'
'Señor, peino mis cabellos,
péinolos con gran dolor,
que me dejéis a mí sola
y a los montes os vais vos.'
25 'Esa palabra, la niña,
no era sino traición:
¿cúyo es aquel caballo
que allá abajo relinchó?'
'Señor, era de mi padre,
30 y envióoslo para vos.'
'¿Cúyas son aquellas armas
que están en el corredor?'
'Señor, eran de mi hermano,
y hoy os las envió.'
35 '¿Cúya es aquella lanza,
desde aquí la veo yo?'
'¡Tomadla, conde, tomadla,
matadme con ella vos,
que aquesta muerte, buen conde,
40 bien os la merezco yo!'

I've not disarmed at all,
and my skin is blacker
than coal-black coal."
"Sleep, sir, sleep,
unarmed and without fear,
for the Count is off hunting
in the mountains of Leon."
"May his dogs die of rabies,
may the eagles get his falcon,
and may he be dragged all the
way home from the mountain by his
horse!"
With them engaged in this,
her husband arrived:
"What are you doing, Blancaniña,
daughter of a traitorous father?"
"Sire, I'm combing my hair,
combing it with great anxiety,
for you leave me all alone
and off to the mountains you go."
"That, child,
is nothing but treachery.
Whose horse is that
that neighed down below?"
"Sire, it was my father's
and he sent it for you."
"Whose arms are those
that are in the hall?"
"Sire, they were my brother's
and today he sent them to you."
"Whose lance is that
that I can see from here?"
"Take it, Count, take it,
kill me with it,
for this death, good Count,
I do richly deserve!")

The initial segment of the ballad contains the exchange between
the woman and the unknown suitor returned from seven years of
combat (lines 1–16). Many features of this exchange are somewhat
enigmatic or ill defined at best. What is the central issue, however,
is the courtly nature of the dialogue. Each of the two speakers is
given the same amount of space—eight lines—and there are two

basic verbal correlations between what they say to each other. The first correlation is antithetical: she is of startling whiteness of appearance, while his blackness is that of the night whose onset he refers to in his courteous request for comfort. The second correlation is between the question in lines 3–4 and the echoing response of lines 9–10. The two phrasings are not identical, but their closeness of wording, more emphatic than a simple "yes" on the part of the woman, serves to suggest her eagerness at the prospect put before her.

The enigmatic aspects of these opening lines concern the identity of the man involved. Actually, identity is less important to the extent that few would worry about such biographical questions. More to the point is what the man is in relation to the woman and what are the circumstances of his appearance. Their coming together may be intended to be understood as casual, and the soldier is simply taking advantage of a fortunate circumstance. By the same token, the wife's violent denunciation of her husband, who is absent on the hunt, that exclusively male venture in which women are quite forgotten, implies a smoldering rancor of resentfulness at having been abandoned by the man who may legally relieve the tedium of her solitude. To the modern reader the setting is far too familiar from the repertoire of the traveling salesman and from the less humorous folklore of modern suburbia to require much effort at comprehension. As far as medieval literature is concerned, the ascendent role of woman in the art and literature of courtly life is usually attributed in part to the frequent absences of the husband in his preoccupation with the obligations of feudal society. The woman, left to her own devices, encouraged and participated eagerly in the new game of courtly, and adulterous, love. The soldier's address to Blancaniña and her reply may not be particularly indicative of courtly love beyond the servility of the former's polite question; but the fact that it is a soldier, and therefore presumably of winning masculinity, and the resentful solitude of the woman suggest a circumstance readily understandable.

The color contrast between the neglected wife and the aggressive warrior bespeaks, in turn, some attempt on the minstrel's part to clue our sympathies for the principals involved. The woman's whiteness may be only a synecdoche for her dazzling beauty, but it may also point up some sense of virtue and innocence. Although not virginal, the woman, were it not for the heartless cruelty of her husband's abandonment, might be expected to be exemplary in her wifely role. However, given her resentment and presented as she is with the opportunity to mitigate her loneliness, she yields quickly to the advances of the soldier, characterized by the sinful blackness of passion. While the ballad may be less than desirably explicit on the meaning of the contrast used, to the extent that we expect literature to have a reason for what it does, we are justified in seeking an initial meaning for white versus black in terms of the circumstances presented. From another point of view, the blackness of the returned soldier may be only a hyperbolic way of presenting the forced continance of his seven years of combat which matches well the enforced continance of the beautiful but abandoned wife; both are understandably anxious to remedy that unfortunate problem. The words used between the two are not without some irony: "unarmed and without fear" refers somewhat cleverly to his status as a soldier as well as to the threat of an enraged and righteous husband. The woman's reply is both an invitation to the man to disarm as a soldier—to put behind the seven years of continance— as well as to forget any worry as far as her husband is concerned. It is at this point that she indulges in her spiteful tirade against the one who should be her rightful bedtime companion.

The second segment of the ballad begins with line 17. Blancaniña is at the moment berating her husband's greater interest in hunting and expressing her wish that his absence will be properly punished (a more "sophisticated" poem might invoke Diana here), when the husband arrives to interrupt the violent speech. It is worth noting that the formula "being engaged in that" is used. It is a formula associated closely with the historical ballads, where it is frequently used to provide a transition from one scene to another, often when the two are in conflict in some way (cf. our comments on the last of the Cid ballads, where the formula is used to introduce the momentous arrival of the warrior at court). In this ballad, the formula functions to underline the surprise and the suspense involved with the man's appearance and the discovery which we assume he is to make.

As is to be expected, the subsequent exchange between husband and wife exploits appropriately the suspense generated by the former's sudden and unheralded arrival. The man's address to his wife (lines 19–20) is in sharp contrast to the servility of the soldier's praise and question in lines 1–4. It is difficult to know exactly how to understand them, for again the ballad is a bit inexplicit. We might suppose that the husband suspects treachery on Blancaniña's part and speaks to her accordingly. Or we might be expected to see in his words a lack of respect on his part toward her that explains his greater interest in the hunt and further reinforces the resentfulness of the wife's words in her answer to the man who is able to appreciate her as a woman. Blancaniña's tame reply to her husband's bitter interrogation must be seen in the foregoing context. It is probable that the alternation between harsh query from the husband and solicitous answer from the wife in lines 19–36 is intended to strengthen our sympathy for the woman and our acceptance of the justice of her words of resentment. This is particularly so in her first reply (lines 21–24), where she gently, not violently, reproaches her spouse for his absence. Of course, the latter only continues the unpleasantness of his interrogation.

While it is possible that some historical incident lies behind the composition of the ballad, an incident concerning the man's reference to his father-in-law's character and the wife's reply that the things which her husband suspects are an indication of infidelity are only gifts to him from her family, as far as the audience is concerned, that the woman attributes the horse and the arms to her vilified family is only sweet sarcasm on her part. The result is to charge her words with an irony obvious to us but of which the man is at first unaware. We know the source of these things and know that they do indeed indict the woman for infidelity. But at the same time, the man's unkind absence and his even unkinder references to her family urge us to appreciate her point of view and to enjoy with her the sarcasm of the ironic reference to her family's generosity to the man who has spoken so ill of them.

There is a certain rhetorical formality to the exchange between husband and wife. The last three of the four questions put to Blancaniña refer to what the husband has found outside his door (the first refers in general to his wife's activities). Each of these three queries begins with "whose is/are" and thus accord a tone of formalized interrogation to the encounter. The formality is sustained by the wife, who appears to acknowledge her husband's superior role by politely addressing him as "sire." As the questioning proceeds, the audience hangs on the development of the interrogation, which sets out formally to proceed from item to item of the soldier's abandoned equipment. The stylized format of the husband's question and of the wife's reply is necessary to establish one fixed tone for the narrative. It is a tone which is sustained for almost twenty lines (half of the total lines of the ballad) and is used, not for any intrinsic value, but solely in order that it may be broken by the abrupt change in the concluding four lines of the composition. When her husband puts his third question concerning the objects that he has found, Blancaniña does not respond as we would expect her to on the basis of her previous replies. Rather, she abruptly changes the entire tone of the exchange to demand that her husband use the lance—the third item about which he inquires—to execute her for her infidelity.

This change in tone accomplishes several things. First of all, it presents the audience with a tremendous shock. Up this point, if anything, we have been led to accept the premise that there is some justification for Blancaniña's dalliance with the soldier who so conveniently arrives to mitigate the anxiety of her solitude. Both her own words in lines 11–16 and 21–24 and the unpleasantness of her husband's angry return are intended to convince us that, while she may not be morally virtuous, humanly she is to be pitied. Our shock when it comes is occasioned not only by the violence (again) of her words, but also by the harsh self-denunciation which they contain. By creating first one tone for the narrative and then proceeding to rupture it with the woman's hysterical cry for her own death, the minstrel has underlined that much more the intensity of emotion which Blancaniña has struggled to suppress. That she is in the end unsuccessful derives as much from her awareness that her husband cannot be persuaded to believe her attempts to mask her infidelity as from the general emotional pitch of her feelings that comes through in the exchange with the soldier. Blancaniña is overwrought, one assumes, from the cruelty of her husband's actions and this state leads both to her infidelity toward him as well as her own hysterical betrayal.

The reader may decide to maintain his sympathy for Blancaniña: she is up to the end the victim of an unkind husband. Or one may decide that the abrupt shift in tone and the sense of overriding guilt that wells up in the woman to bring about her acknowledgment of sin are designed to suggest the stark irony of her name and the purity of virtue associated with it. The woman is a sinner and as such deserves the retribution which she herself demands in her anguished cry of shame. It would not be difficult to see in this last scene some unconscious symbology made more obvious to the modern reader familiar with contemporary psychological analysis. The sexual significance of the soldier's lance, a significance not necessarily consciously grasped by either the characters of the ballad or by the latter's audience, is strongly implicated in whatever triggers Blancaniña's final words of guilt. We need not overly emphasize this point, for the problem of sexual desire is patent enough in the narrative from the opening encounter between the soldier and the woman, and it is the conflict between this desire and the righteous indignation of a husband who, no matter how indifferent and heartless, nevertheless has the moral advantage which constitutes the fundamental interest of the poem. Most readers incline toward sympathy for Blancaniña, and our comments have tended to single out those aspects of the ballad's structure that engage audience sympathy for her. In the light of such an analysis, the violence of the woman's own self-denunciation can only be seen as the final attempt by the minstrel to impress upon us deeply the nature of the woman's sin and the violent human emotions which, while they may not justify it, lie behind that sin and explain with compelling vividness the circumstance that brought it into being. In this sense, "Blancaniña" is a ballad of no mean human understanding, a ballad which in its narrative explores with striking intensity an aspect of human suffering.

V *"Madruga don Alonso"*

Love scorned and punished with calculating vengeance is a theme of perhaps too much dramatic intensity to find welcome reception in the early Renaissance courtly poetry, more comfortable with motives that explore the inner psychological mechanisms of the amorous experience. Thus, the following ballad, although dealing with a topic of love, is closer in spirit to the violence of Blancaniña's emotions—and closer to the interest of high Renaissance drama— than it is to fifteenth-century courtly love poetry. This fact may explain why texts are absent from the early Renaissance collections and why versions are only known to survive in the modern popular oral tradition.[22] Nevertheless, the black arts deployed by the protagonist Moriana to take revenge against her lover's scorn recall the undercurrents of sorcery so frequently found in medieval and Renaissance culture:

Madruga don Alonso
a poco del Sol salido;
convidando va a su boda
a los parientes y amigos;
5 *a las puertas de Morïana*
sofrenaba su rocino:
—Buenos días, Morïana.
—Don Alonso, bien venido.
—Vengo a brindarte, Morïana,
10 *para mi boda el domingo.*
—Esas bodas, don Alonso,
debieran ser conmigo;
pero ya que no lo sean,
igual el convite estimo,
15 *y en prueba de la amistad*
beberás del fresco vino,
el que solías beber
dentro de mi cuarto florido.
Morïana, muy ligera,
20 *en su cuarto se ha metido;*
tres onzas de solimán
con el acero ha molido,
de la víbora los ojos,
sangre de un alacrán vivo:
25 *—Bebe, bebe, don Alonso,*
bebe de este fresco vino.
—Bebe primero, Morïana,
que así está puesto en estilo.
Levantó el vaso Morïana,
30 *lo puso en sus labios finos;*
los dientes tiene menudos,
gota dentro no ha vertido.
Don Alonso, como es mozo,
maldita gota ha perdido.
35 *—¿Qué me diste, Morïana,*
qué me diste en este vino?
¡Las riendas tengo en la mano
y no veo a mi rocino!
—Vuelve a casa, don Alonso,
40 *que el día va ya corrido*
y se celará tu esposa
si quedas acá conmigo.
—¿Qué me diste, Morïana,
que pierdo todo el sentido?

(Don Alonso gets up at dawn
when the Sun has just come up
and goes around inviting to his
wedding friends and relatives.
In front of Moriana's door
he suddenly draws up his horse:
"Good day, Moriana."
"Welcome, Don Alonso."
"I come to invite you, Moriana,
to my wedding on Sunday."
"That marriage, Don Alonso,
was to have been with me.
But since it is not,
I appreciate the invitation anyway.
And in proof of friendship
you will drink the fresh wine,
the wine you used to drink
inside my flowered room."
Moriana very quickly
has gone into her room.
Three ounces of corrosive sublimate
she grinds up with steel,
viper eyes
and the blood of a living scorpion.
"Drink, drink, Don Alonso,
drink of this fresh wine."
"You drink first, Moriana,
for that is the custom."
Moriana raised the glass
up to her fine lips.
Her teeth are so small
that not a drop gets through.
Don Alonso, since he is young,
doesn't waste a drop.
"What did you give me, Moriana,
what did you give me in this wine?
I'm holding the reins in my hand,
but I can't see my horse!"
"Return home, Don Alonso;
the day is getting on
and your spouse will be jealous
if you stay here with me."
"What did you give me, Moriana,
for I'm losing consciousness?

45   *¡Sáname de este veneno:*   Cure me of this poison
      yo me he de casar contigo!   and I will marry you!"
      —No puede ser, don Alonso,   "That cannot be, Don Alonso,
      que el corazón te ha partido.   for your heart has broken."
      —¡Desdichada de mi madre   "Woe is my mother
50   *que ya no me verá vivo!*   who will not see me alive!"
      —Más desdichada la mía   "More so mine
      desque te hube conocido.   since the day I met you.")

(pp. 125–26)

This ballad is surprisingly amoral to the extent that no attempt is made to engage sympathy for either one of the two principals. That is to say, little interest is evident in suggesting that one or the other is justified in what is done or that the other is sinfully inferior and therefore deserving of suffering. The main focal point of interest appears, instead, to be directed exclusively toward portraying the steps to which Moriana goes in punishing Alonso's rejection of her and his engagement to another woman. Moriana, while she may not emerge superior to Alonso from a moral point of view, is undoubtedly his superior in wit. Indeed, the first major question raised by the ballad is why does Alonso unmindfully—and heartlessly— parade before Moriana on his way to be married to another woman. One facetious answer is that this action is necessary in order to occasion his former lover's unrepenting revenge. Although there is always an element of truth in such a statement—the stage must be set in one way or another—speaking more seriously we should find a justification within the development of the ballad for Alonso's unjudicious behavior.

The past relationship between Alonso and Moriana is presented exclusively from the point of view of the woman and is therefore extremely colored by her present feelings. Her greeting and subsequent actions toward Alonso, up to the latter's awareness that he has been poisoned, are ironic to such a degree that we cannot fail to understand Moriana's sentiments and appreciate her cleverness in punishing Alonso for his treachery in love. Her apparent charity in offering to toast his wedding happiness with him despite the reminder that she was to have been the bride is both a device to inform the audience as to the relationship between the two—or, better, how this relationship has been drastically changed—as well as to give an indication of the slyness of the woman and the relative unawareness of the man (lines 11–18). This ballad depends almost exclusively on dialogue to introduce the conflict at issue and to underline the manner in which that conflict will achieve resolution. The only passages that are not dialogue introduce Alonso's visit to Moriana (lines 1–6) and the description of the potion which the wronged woman prepares (lines 19–24 and 29–34). Otherwise, exploiting the dramatic potential of skillfully presented oral literature, the minstrel relies on the characters to reveal in their own words the narrative action. Such a revelation depends to a great extent on the audience's ability to grasp the intense irony and sarcasm of Moriana's speeches, given as they are without editorial comment from the minstrel himself. The heaviness of the irony obvious in the woman's words may be due in large measure to the necessity to make her feelings unmistakably evident.

Lines 16–18 constitute probably the most important part of the ballad in the sense that here we see the central conflict given formulation against the background of the foregoing ironic and deceptive friendliness of the woman. The antithesis between "you will drink the fresh wine" and "[the fresh wine] which you *used* to drink" (lines 16 and 17 respectively) evoke the tension in the woman's memory between what was and what is no longer. The wine which Alonso used to drink was a wine served under the aegis of love and feelings of true friendship (i.e., the literal meaning of line 15). The wine which is to be served to him now is borne by a hand moved by deep and resentful hatred, a hatred that cannot be concealed from us by the superficial expression of friendship in Moriana's invitation. Of course, Alonso is unable to perceive this tension and this antithesis. We assume that he is unable to see a conflict between himself and the rejected woman. Indeed, that he can see no conflict bespeaks, we suggest, the motivation behind not only his unmindful visit on his wedding day to the woman who was to be but is not now to be his wife, but as well most likely behind his rejection of Moriana in the first place. Alonso, aside from just possibly not being too bright, is more certainly a man of appalling insensitivity and indiscretion, a flaw in his personality which grievously hurts Moriana as well as bringing down upon him his own hideous death.

In this sense, Moriana's poisoning of Alonso may be seen to serve a dual purpose. The potion is on one level her revenge, but on another level it is the means by which Alonso is made aware of the extent of his own stupidity. The artistry of the ballad is particularly evident in the closing lines of the poem, in which the final exchange between the two persons transcends personal feelings and projects the repercussions of their actions in terms of the effects on their respective mothers: if Alonso's mother is about to suffer the grief and humiliation of her son's murder, it cannot compare with the anguish which Moriana's mother has *already* experienced because of the reproachful behavior of her daughter's one-time suitor. This is Moriana's final attempt to force Alonso to appreciate the disaster that he has wrought, a disaster that he pays for with life itself. We do not know if Alonso comprehends. His only words that are meaningful are his frantic question of the woman as to what she has served him, repeated in growing pain (lines 35 and 43), his injunction that she cure him and his tardy promise to marry her after all if she does.

The poison that Moriana prepares in lines 19–24 is an objective correlative of her grief and recalls the ancient tradition of love brews. Of direct appeal to the imagination of the audience, the mixture that she prepares in the room where the couple had passed happy hours that are now only a bitter memory, invokes folk knowledge of the efficacious if nefarious qualities of the ingredients mentioned. A modern reader can only be sensitive to the general gist of the scene, but there is little doubt as to what effect the drink is intended to have. The only clear symbol is the viper's eyes. The viper in the Western tradition points to man's sinful involvement with love and passion, an involvement that is at the heart of Moriana's present hatred of Alonso. The eyes, which in the lover are the windows of his soul, now become a basic ingredient in this inverted philter that is destined to cause the death, rather than to stimulate the passion, of the man. Of course it does cause a twisted manifestation of passion. When he has drunk the potion and it has begun to work its deadly effect, Alonso makes the promise of marriage to Moriana which, we assume, he has denied her in contracting to marry another. Such a detail is, for one familiar with the role of love potions mixed either out of true love or out of love turned to hatred, indicative of the blackest of humor.

The concluding half of the ballad represents the dialogue between the two former loved ones after the one has partaken of the hideous draught. The growing sense of death in Alonso's voice is given counterpoint by Moriana's calm and somewhat coquettish words. Of particularly mordant effect is her charming advice to him to be off, that it is unseemly for him to keep his bride waiting while he dallies with her. The coolness of her response to his plea that she administer the antidote to the poison before it is too late is an equally galling note. For hatred such as he has engendered in her there is no antidote, and for the poison which she has offered him and of which he has drunk in his own ignorance there cannot likewise be a remedy. The poison, one notes, "breaks his heart," a rather unusual effect that serves, however, to correlate with how Alonso has broken the heart of the woman in his cruel indifference to her love. The general dullness of Alonso is made that much more striking in that the one note of courtly courtesy on his part in the composition is his insistence that Moriana drink first from the "wine of friendship" which she has prepared, "for that is the custom." This note provides the ballad with the opportunity to describe how Moriana carefully pretends to sip her share, while Alonso in his foolhardy manner drinks the potion down to the last drop. Moriana's invitation to Alonso to drink (lines 25–26), with its three-fold imperative, rings out as almost an incantation for its occurrence just after the description of the mixing of the poison and the introduction which it represents to the morbid resolution of the conflict which the drink itself will effect.

Seen in the perspective of the other novelesque ballads that we have examined in this chapter, the composition detailing what might be titled "The Poison of Moriana" (or "Madruga don Alonso") is far from delightful and comforting. Its greatest departure from the spirit of the majority of the early Spanish ballads arises, not from the intensity of emotion or violence of behavior which it depicts, for these are common staples of the very best of the *romances viejos*. Its forcefulness derives, rather, from the amorality with which the central conflict and its vengeful resolution are portrayed. Whereas in most ballads, as indeed in most of the literature of the pragmatic Western tradition, some attempt is made to engage our emotions and our sympathies for one or another side in the conflict, in the case of Moriana's tale what we have is an appeal to our less than noble fascination with unredeemable violence, with vengeance whose only justification is its own intensity and its successful appeal to the unmistakable and inescapable nefarious nature of man. The only saving transcendency in Moriana's murder of her heartless lover is perhaps the emphasis on the revelation to Alonso of his damning indifference to the strength of Moriana's past love that must lie behind the intensity of her present hatred. This in

itself cannot constitute for the society of the ballad a moral justification for her revenge, but it does give meaning and human significance to the violence of her actions. That the background of
religious devotion given for medieval society by the traditions of
clerical literature are only in part a reality is indicated strongly
by a ballad of immense popular acceptance that bespeaks in its
amoral violence a fundamental understanding of the nature and
consequences of the unmitigated hatred that love can inspire in
the human soul. The success of this ballad is due principally to the
skillful devices of irony and correlation for bringing out and underlining that emotional fact. [23]

VI *"Herido está don Tristán"*

One of the most characteristic segments of the *Romancero viejo*
is made up of those ballads inspired, not by Hispanic affairs, but
by the Matter of France: the deeds and personages of the Court
of Charlemagne at the end of the Low Middle Ages. The following
chapter is devoted to the study of these widely diffused works,
peculiar for the lack of "native" identification one associates with
popular and semipopular literature. There is one other French
influence in Spanish literature aside from the Carolingian ballads.
The Matter of Brittany had some influence, seen in the handful
of texts deriving from fourteenth- and fifteenth-century translations of *Tristan and Isolde,* one of the most important works of
the medieval literature of France. Much has been written concerning the mythic and Freudian dimensions of the work: Wagner's
version of the legend, and recent stagings of that Romantic opera
even more so, emphasize the presence of motives and conflicts
that well up, not from the domain of social and feudal values, but
from obscure corners of human emotion. Thus, for many, both
the original story and the opera reveal inescapable Freudian motifs.
The most indicative manifestation of this more intensely psychic
orientation is to be seen, superficially, in the famous magical and
supernatural elements of the original work and derivate traditions.
In the ballad text which we offer for analysis, the foregoing features
emerge in the almost incantatory tone of the narrative, in the
complete submergence of any real personalization of the two
lovers—atypically, there is no dialogue—and in the magico-sym-
bolic function of the essentially elliptic facts mentioned: [24]

Herido está don Tristán	(Don Tristán has been seriously
de una mala lanzada;	wounded by a lance.
diérasela el rey su tío	His uncle the King did it
por celos que dél cataba.	out of jealousy.
5 *El hierro tiene en el cuerpo,*	The iron is in his body,
de fuera le tiembla el asta.	and the shaft sticks out, quivering.
Valo a ver la reina Iseo	Queen Iseo goes to see him
por la su desdicha mala;	for her own misfortune.
júntanse boca con boca	They join their mouths
10 *cuanto una misa rezada,*	for as long as it takes to say a Mass.
llora el uno, llora el otro,	One cries, the other cries,
la cama bañan en agua;	and the bed is bathed in water.
allí nace un arboledo	There a plant blooms
que azucena se llamaba,	that is called a lily.
15 *cualquier mujer que la come*	Any woman who eats it
luego se siente preñada;	will later feel pregnant.
comiérala reina Iseo	Queen Iseo ate it
por la su desdicha mala.	for her own misfortune.)

One's first reaction to this text is that an extensive amount of traditionalization must have taken place to account for the lack of any context that might orient a reader unfamiliar with the source legend and its various versions. Although it is likely that the reader is able to ascertain the general lines of development in the ballad, there is little other than the names to recall the grief and intense sentiment occasioned by Tristán's desire, which is mutual, toward Isolde (Iseo) the bride of his uncle Mark and the man who is a father-figure to Tristán. It is a passion awakened by a potent philter of which the two have partaken by error. Although both struggle to overcome the spell which the potion has cast upon their souls, in the end they have no choice but to accept the role and its consequences that chance has thrust upon them. It is this preoccupation with desire and passion that cannot be dominated by awareness, by law, or by will and implicitly rejects the freedom of the soul attributed to it by Christianity, which has evoked the emotions of tragedy on the one hand and the fascination of students with the amoral powers exerted by man's unconscious on the other. That the latter interest has been largely appropriate attests to the quality of a work which, like the fourteenth-century Spanish *Libro de buen amor (Book of Good Love)*, makes it painfully clear within the medieval context that grace and the subjection of the sinful soul was more than the matter of a few prayers and a strong will. From the point of view of the ballad and its success in Spain, both among sophisticated poets and the popular audience, it is more than probable that the focus on the strength of emotions which were acknowledgedly sinful and socially unacceptable is more at issue than references to the supernatural, which only provide further artistic highlighting.

The most striking feature of the ballad is the matter-of-fact tone with which the three principal incidents are related. For example, the first six lines—the eighteen-line ballad is composed of three equal segments—relate how Tristán has been wounded by his uncle out of jealousy. Although familiarity with the legend will make clear that it is a wounding born of justified sentiments, the ballad's schematic presentation suppresses any comment on or reference to a justification for the uncle's actions. The first four lines are given stylistic emphasis by virtue of the verse-initial verb phrase, accompanied by an inversion of syntactical elements. Both line 1 and line 3 begin with the verb rather than the subject, a usage not uncommon in Spanish but which is worth noting here for the emphasis which any element that comes at the beginning of the poetic line receives. Moreover, the inversion of participle and verb in line 1 (rather uncommon) and the inversion of verb and objects in line 3 (far more frequent) are sufficiently "poetic" in nature to call attention. The asyndeton between the complete sentence of lines 1–2 and that of lines 3–4 plus the parallelism created between the first and third lines by the pattern of verb phrase plus subject and between the second and fourth lines by two prepositional phrases combine to give an unusually formulaic aspect to the opening statement of circumstance. The unemotional comment of lines 5–6 provides, furthermore, a jarring note: the tension between the drastic nature of the attack, still so recent that the shaft of the lance is described as still quivering, and the syntactic chiasmus of the two lines (noun-verb-locative phrase [line 5] vs. locative phrase-verb-noun [line 6]) provide a statement of dramatic event of a nonchalance infrequently found in the early ballads.[25] Direct or implied editorial comment by the narrative voice is a frequent procedure in the immediate establishment of a rhetorical or attitudinal point of view, as analysis of many texts in this study has shown. After one-third of the total lines of the ballad, we know that Tristán has been grievously wounded as punishment for transgressions; but, unless we rely on sympathies created by the nonballad versions, we do not know how to react to Tristán. Audience identification with the personages of the ballad is an important ingredient of the compositions which explains to a large extent their structures: the ballad is presented in such a manner as to evoke immediate and specific reactions. However, in the case of this Tristán text, lack of response cues serves only to evoke surprise over the horror of the man's wound and a bewilderment as to the justice of his uncle's reasons.

The second six-line segment of the ballad presents a problem as to chronology. Although the present tense of the verb begins line 7 (and note the recurrence of the syntax of line 3), the "misfortune" mentioned in line eight is in reality the cause of Tristán's cruel wound. It is when Mark discovers that there have been relations between Isolde and his nephew that revenge becomes unavoidably necessary. The remaining lines on the encounter between the two lovers make clear the extent of their relationship and, unless verisimilitude is to be suspended for dramatic effect, depict a passion not likely to be facilitated by the quivering shaft of the protruding lance. Given the vacillating and ambiguous usage of tenses in the *Romancero viejo*, Szertics' study[26] makes it clear that such a shift from a past tense verb to a present tense verb is not an unusual stylistic phenomenon. The result is the vividness that attends the illusion of presenting something as occurring this very moment of telling. Thus, if we substitute the logical past-tense verbs in lines 7, 9, 11, 12, what we have is a context that explains with ample justification the uncle's vengeful attack. It may be a justification born more of moral rectitude as a wronged husband than of a sympathetic understanding of human weaknesses, but the scene between the two lovers does nevertheless place the terrible lancination in some sort of cause-and-effect perspective. The sorrow which Iseo and Tristán feel for themselves and for their love may be assumed to be transmitted to the audience. That is, we now have a point of view with regard to our attitude toward the lovers. One notes the use again of formulaic diction in line 11, an element that is part of the larger asyndeton of the entire six lines that depict the fateful meeting of the two.

It is never too wise critically to speculate on the motives underlying particular stylistic procedures or on the effects which they produce or may be meant to produce. Our grasp of what constitutes style and how it works in a literary text is still too deplorably

primitive and impressionistic to permit statements that can with-
stand close and skeptical scrutiny. Although the formalized effect
created by the parallelism of lines and its subsequent restraining
of emotional outpouring on the narrator's part may be characteristics
that are aptly evaluated in terms of style, to assign with security
any function or affective value to this asyndeton is more difficult.
While we can say that a modification to polysyndeton would
probably create a comic effect in lines 7–12, the absence of conjunctions does not necessarily enhance the mood of somberness
and sorrow seemingly indicated by the meaning of the lines. If
anything, asyndeton does at least, by suppressing the overt linking
function of conjunctions, force us to see the underlying relationship
between the five verbal actions presented so elliptically. We suggest,
reiterating what has been said so far, that these six lines are meant
to characterize the love between Tristán and Iseo, both its strength
and its dominion over them, and the tearful sorrow which it awakens
in their hearts as a prefiguration of their even greater suffering
with Mark's revenge. This middle part of the ballad appears to
precede the first segment logically in the chain of events and to
provide a motivation for the wounding of Tristán presented in
lines 1–6.

The third and final portion of the ballad describes the symbolic
reification, not only of Tristán's death at his uncle's avenging hands,
but of the tragic quality of the love borne by the lovers for each
other. The lily is an old Christian symbol of purity and chastity.
Perhaps its use here is ironic; perhaps we are to understand that
Mark's revenge is for unrequited desire rather than sinful passion
fulfilled. Or perhaps the purity symbolized by the lily bespeaks
the quality of the love that did exist between the two, a love which
they did not seek but which was inevitable. Interpretation is not
easy here, for although the latter possibility is the most inviting,
given the touching description of the meeting in lines 7–12, we must
rely on external knowledge of the meaning of the legend in order
to assess the nature of Tristán and Iseo's love. In order to avoid
recourse to the legend, we must be willing to assert that the ballad
intends us to believe that the love between the two was of a nobility
that transcended social and moral codes, an assertion probably
too exaggerated or presumptuous for most readers. Matters can
be facilitated by begging the question of the symbolism of the
blooming lily and treating it as a phenomenon more indicative of

the strength of sorrow between the lovers and the fertility of the tears shed in that sorrow. The last four lines of the ballad make it obvious that the lily given life by the tears is a direct and lasting manifestation of their love. Both the fertility of the tears themselves and the efficaciousness of fertility of the lily seem to point to an unmistakable sexual allusion on the part of the relationship between the man and woman. The lily may be a symbol of purity and such a symbolism may be implied on a higher level, but on the more literal level of the effect of the lily on a woman, the uncle's reasons for revenge appear not to have been illfounded.

The lily produced by tears shed on the lovers' bed, the lance by which Tristán is punished, the intensity of love between the latter and Iseo, and the qualities of the lily all combine to suggest a symbolism of sexuality not normally found in the early ballad. We have mentioned in passing for other compositions the possibility of Freudian interpretations for an analysis so inclined. However, the presence of elements easily seen in terms of the fateful passion between Tristán and Iseo that in themselves represent common symbols of sexuality argues for a more direct approach to such a level of meaning in this ballad. The indication and discussion of these elements do not modify significantly our interpretation of the poem, unless it is to establish firmly the sinful passion of their love. Rather, any accuracy of description, either in terms of the minstrel's conscious selection, in terms of mythic comprehension, or in terms of an unconscious understanding of symbolic potential, only serves to strengthen the presentation of the ballad's pre-occupation with sinful love punished yet not obliterated. That that love endures in the form of a flower of sexual connotation, born of a sexual relationship and the fertile tears and punishing lance occasioned by that relationship, is meant to speak emphatically of the profound and tragic power of a blinding passion which, albeit sinful, became the inescapable fate of two human beings.

VII   *"El conde Niño"*

With a tune reminiscent of "Oh My Darling Clementine," the ballad of Count Olinos—or Count Niño (Child) in our text—is a far more elaborate representation of the symbolic reification of a forbidden love, this time of the most noble purity. One suspects that an actual historical circumstance underlies the feeling of the woman's family toward the pretentions of the Count, but all that remains in the ballad, of immense modern popularity, is their cruel and unyielding comprehension of the young love which can only find true realization beyond the grave:

Conde Niño por amores	(Count Niño out of love
es niño y pasó la mar;	is a child and crossed the sea.
va a dar agua a su caballo	He goes to water his horse
la mañana de San Juan.	the morning of St. John's Day.
5 *Mientras el caballo bebe,*	While the horse is drinking,
él canta dulce cantar;	he sings a sweet song.
todas las aves del cielo	All the birds of the sky
se paraban a escuchar,	stopped to listen,
caminante que camina	a traveler that was traveling
10 *olvida su caminar,*	forgot his travel,
navegante que navega	a sailor that was sailing
la nave vuelve hacia allá.	turns his ship in that direction.
La reina estaba labrando,	The Queen is embroidering
la hija durmiendo está:	and her daughter sleeps.
15 *—Levantos, Albaniña,*	"Wake up, Albaniña,
de vuestro dulce folgar,	from your sweet rest
sentiréis cantar hermoso	and you will hear the pretty song
la sirenita del mar.	of the little sea siren."
—No es la sirenita, madre,	"That's not the little siren, mother,
20 *la de tan bello cantar,*	the one whose song is pretty,
si no es el conde Niño	but Count Niño
que por mí quiere finar.	who is pining away for me.
¡Quién le pudiese valer	Would that I could help him
en su tan triste penar!	in his sad suffering!"
25 *—Si por tus amores pena,*	"If he's suffering for your love,
¡oh, mal haya su cantar!,	damned be his song!
y por que nunca los goce,	So that he will never enjoy your love,
yo le mandaré matar.	I will have him killed."
—Si le manda matar, madre,	"If you have him killed, mother,
30 *juntos nos han de enterrar.*	they will have to bury us both."
Él murió a la medianoche,	He died at midnight,
ella a los gallos cantar;	she at the cock's crow.
a ella, como hija de reyes,	She, as the daughter of Kings,
la entierran en el altar;	they bury at the altar.
35 *a él, como hijo de conde,*	He, as the son of a Count,
unos pasos más atrás.	a few paces behind.
De ella nació un rosal blanco,	From her a white rosebush was born,
dél nació un espino albar;	from him was born a dawn-like haw-
	thorne.

	crece el uno, crece el otro,	The one grows, the other grows,
40	*los dos se van a juntar;*	and they both join.
	las ramitas que se alcanzan	The branches that touch
	fuertes abrazos se dan,	are locked in strong embraces,
	y las que no se alcanzaban	and those that do not touch
	no dejan de suspirar.	never stop sighing.
45	*La reina, llena de envidia,*	The Queen, full of envy,
	ambos los mandó cortar;	ordered both cut down,
	el galán que los cortaba	and the man that cut them
	no cesaba de llorar.	could not stop crying.
	De ella naciera una garza,	From her a heron was born,
50	*de él un fuerte gavilán,*	from him a strong sparrow hawk.
	juntos vuelan por el cielo,	And together they fly through the sky,
	juntos vuelan par a par.	together side by side.)

(pp. 127–28)

Clearly, the overwhelming interest of this ballad, aside from the unfortunate difficulties of the lovers in life, is the employment of the device of metamorphosis to give an emphatic and symbolic value to the death-through-love relationship of the two. Metamorphosis is a concept known from Antiquity, and Ovid gave perhaps the best literary realization to the idea of dramatic change imposed upon an individual by virtue of his character. In the Roman poet's work, such change is more indicative of personality flaws and transgressions against morals, ethics, or the will of the Gods. The individual to be punished is given a form that bespeaks his condemnation, an ironic formula underlying the *contrapassi* ("turnabouts") of Dante's Christian *Divine Comedy* and Kafka's absurd and surrealistic *Metamorphosis*. Note that change in this context is associated with sin and damnation, rather than with virtue and its reward. Human failings, of course, always have attracted man's greatest interest, perhaps justifiably. However, the Christian tradition, with its emphasis on Divine salvation, can be said to account for those instances where nobility of soul receives the outward manifestation of conversion into a positive symbol, as is the case in this ballad. To be sure, the origins of the specific legend of Olinos/Niño may owe much to folklore and the Oriental tradition (one only need recall the recurrence of transformation in the Germanic folk tales), and a certain amount of research has been devoted to the question.[27] Whatever its precise origins and literary antecedents may be, this is the one ballad which makes greatest use of the metamorphosis which transcends quotidian reality to give a supernatural embodiment to an abstract ideal hidden from the world in the souls of the two lovers. As is the case with all symbology, the intent is to give impressive and comprehensible form in art to what we cannot experience, or perhaps even know, in the world of daily reality.

The development of meaning in the first segment of the ballad (lines 1–12) is not clear. It would seem that greater attention is to be focused on the stylistic exercise of adnominatio than on any "logical meaning" of these opening lines. What only emerges comprehensibly is that the Count has crossed the waters to arrive where he will be heard by the woman he loves. As Menéndez Pidal has observed,[28] some contamination from the ballad of Infante Arnaldos appears likely. The entire setting is immediately given the heightened color of wondrous events by the simple mention of the morning of St. John's Day, a reference so charged with meaning in medieval literature as to make allusion to it sufficient to establish a mood of mystery and the prefigurement of the marvelous. Perhaps the insistence on adnominatio—it occurs in lines 6, 9, and 11–12, and in lines 1 and 2 if we count the relationship between the man's name and his qualification as a child—is meant to contribute to the mood by its noncolloquial and therefore potentially poetic or lyrical nature. Such a procedure as that involving a play on morphologically related words contributes less to meaning than it does to the purely affective function of much poetry. In the case of the opening of this ballad, the reference to Midsummer and the repeated stylistic feature combine to suggest something of an unreal mood for the initial narrative action. In addition, the quality of the man's song, probably the surest sign of contamination from the Arnaldos ballad, contributes a further note of the unusual. Nevertheless, since no real context of the supernatural is established in these opening twelve lines, the charm of the Count's singing must be taken more as an indication of his sentimental distraction. It is a distraction that expresses itself in the song that has such an impact upon the birds, which presumably can appreciate the feelings that it signifies, as well as leading him in his wanderings to within earshot of the girl's mother. Niño's love is thus given an initial substantiation by the entire context, designed to appeal to our imagination and wonderment, with which the ballad opens.

Adnominatio is again present in the second segment of the ballad as a device for linking the two lovers. Albaniña (literally, "Dawn-child") recalls both the name and description of the Count as well as the morningtide in which his approach takes place. The dialogue between Albaniña and her mother reveals a fundamental irony in terms of the relationship between the two lovers. The mother's initial impression is that the lovely song of the Count is that of the siren, and she enjoins her daughter to marvel with her at its beauty. The daughter, however, recognizes the voice of her beloved and rashly corrects her mother's error. The meaning of this interchange derives from the significance of both the sea and the song. The sea in the opening verses is part of the context established for Niño's arrival. How much mystery is to be associated with its presence is impossible to determine. However, its expanse and Niño's necessity to traverse it in order to reach Albaniña represent at least the breach between the two given verbalization by the mother's threats in lines 25–28.

The song in turn, while bespeaking both Niño's love as well as his sorrow, comes also to prefigure the death of the lovers. Although Albaniña makes clear that the Count is singing and not a siren of the sea, the mother's first identification is not completely inappropriate. The song is a catalyst for subsequent suffering and as such is indeed a call to destruction originating unknowingly with one who has indeed come from the sea. Albaniña's impossible wish in lines 23–24, rhetorically an adynaton, is even more ironic in her emotional betrayal of affection for the Count: she does not realize that, far from alleviating his sorrow, the song is to lead to the death of the two. Also pregnant with double meaning is her interpretation of the significance of the song earlier in lines 21–22. She uses the verb "die" less literally than in terms of its meaning in courtly love, where the frustrated lover declares that the intensity of his pangs of love will surely lead to his demise. Both are soon to find that the rhetoric of their emotions is to become cruel reality.

The masculine rhyme of parts of the ballad, particularly in this segment (lines 13–30), reinforces the principal points made concerning the relationship between Niño and Albaniña. Special attention is due to the occurrence of rhyming infinitives in lines 16, 20, 22, 24, 26, 28, and 30. The girl's "sweet resting" of line sixteen is placed in violent contrast to the references in the subsequent lines to the fateful song, to suffering and dying in love, and to the death which the mother promises for the Count in order, for what reason we are not told, to protect her daughter from him. The latter reasserts the bond between her and Niño, finally, by her own reference to death and to the interment which she seems to sense will be the only union possible between them. This segment is the only dialogue of the somewhat longer-than-usual ballad and serves to show in the vivid terms of casual conversation turned bitterly emotional the degree of tragic conflict created by the forbidden love.

The remaining half of the ballad is probably the most important and memorable. The function of the introduction and mother-daughter dialogue is only to establish a context in which the minstrel can develop his depiction of the phenomena that attend the death of Niño and Albaniña and give objective meaning to the strength and the nobility of love between them. This last and longest part of the poem is divided into subsegments. The first covers lines 31–44 and is given parallelistic unity by three sets of references. The second subsegment, lines 45–52, is the final apotheosis of the two dead lovers. If we examine closely the verses describing the death of Niño and Albaniña, we find that the minstrel has chosen to present alternating references to the two in which he establishes a physical and symbolic relationship between them in death. For example, in lines 31–32, the temporal context of their actual death is described (although it is not clear if the girl, as did the Count most surely, died by her parents' hand or out of mortal sorrow). The exactitude of the temporal references and their role as portentous times of the day are affective colorings of the fact of death that are designed to draw out the audience's sense of the heinous crime that has taken place. In addition, the reference to the girl's death at dawn with the cock's song must remind us of Niño's song at dawn which set in motion the tragic denouement of their love. Less obvious is the reference to the cock itself. While it might be simply part of the allusion to the early morning when the girl dies, there is also the strong possibility, given the subsequent avian symbolization of the lovers, that the minstrel is recalling the common medieval use of the cock to indicate resurrection and rebirth.[29] In this context, where we are told of the death of Niño and Albaniña, we are also provided with a prefigurement of their transmutation into symbols of eternal and pure love joined in holy unity.

The second set of parallel references, in lines 33–36, refers to the physical union of the two, not in love, but in the proximity of their graves in death. It is significant that the poem makes clear the locale of their interment, for the altar is probably meant to remind us of the nobility of their love. Certainly, from the point of view of verisimilitude, the two would not likely have been buried together, given the implied animosity that underlies the impossibility of their love. The ballad's statement to the effect that it is death that has brought them together, so to speak, can only be taken in a basically symbolic sense. The last correlation between the two, lines 37–44, is the longest, and involves a final fusion of their two souls in a physical floral union denied their persons in life. The white rosebush that springs from the girl's grave is readily recognizable as the sign of the purity which we understand to have characterized her sentiments toward Niño (cf. the "charity" of her statements to her mother concerning the Count). Although the hawthorne, the plant propagated by Niño's grave, has no accepted symbolic value in Western literature, the adjective used to modify it, based on the root meaning "dawn," makes clear a similar purity for the man and also recalls the woman's name, Albaniña, as well as the time of day involved in the opening circumstances of the ballad and the death of the beloved. The fusion of the two signs when they intertwine as they grow is described in terms of a "strong embrace" that bespeaks the physical union of the two in death, who were but united in spirit in life.

As if the foregoing tripartite symbolic portrayal of the everlasting strength of young and innocent love were not enough, the ballad summarizes in an eight-line concluding segment the injustice and hatred that constituted the unrelenting framework of their noble but forbidden love. The strength of the queen's envy at seeing her separation of the two in life frustrated by their union in death correlates with the strength of sentiment between the two lovers that manifests itself even more strongly in death. The spiteful destruction of the rosebush and the hawthorne is but a reenactment of the mother's earlier threat and its fulfillment to destroy the relationship between the Count and her daughter.

From an artistic point of view, this final segment permits the minstrel to reemphasize the context of the tragic conflict of pure emotions with uncomprehending hatred, as well as to provide one last objective representation of the eternal purity of those emotions in a second and definitive metamorphosis of the two souls. The male sparrow hawk and the female heron which arise from the denuded graves and ascend in union to heaven are one last emphatic portrayal of the bond between Niño and Albaniña, a bond which the queen has been unable to dissolve even with death, and of the transcendent sanctity of a love which seeks its ultimate consolation and resolution in the flight of the bird from the baseness of an evil and spiteful world. In addition to any concluding striking image afforded by the closing transmutation, the minstrel's procedure, in its essential reaffirmation of the symbolically achieved union between Niño and Albaniña, underlines the parallelistic organization of the poem throughout. The physical separation between the two lovers in the opening half of the poem, which contrasts with the oneness of sentiment given form by the song which he sings and which she comprehends all too well, is correlated with the physical union in death betokened by interment, by the flowering and entwined bushes, and by the joined flight of the two birds, the two souls of the lovers released at last from the separation imposed upon them by earthly restraint.

As is the case with any work of literature which uses juxtaposition and parallel organization, this ballad aims at underscoring the intensity of human emotion involved in the story of the Count and the Princess and serves in the insistence of the representation of the same issue from several different points of view to evoke in the audience an appropriately intense awareness of that emotion and identification with it. Young and innocent love that is strengthened by the hatred and cruelty that would, and often does, impose death as its penalty is an easy subject for the poet who wants our sympathetic reaction. The ballad of Count Niño's tragic love attempts to give an even greater dignification to its narrative through the use of an extensive and elaborate series of symbols that in the last analysis reinforce our appreciation of the conflict and feelings involved as well as constitute an element of artistic strength.

VIII *Summing Up*

Our analysis of the novelesque ballads has attempted to indicate the ways in which many of the characteristics of the historical ballads are evident in these works of a somewhat different origin: the abrupt beginnings and endings, the elliptic fashion of expression, the devices for intense appeal to audience involvement with the conflicts at issue, the interest in the individual as a personalized representation of ethical and moral values. Nevertheless, as attention to the organization and themes of the novelesque ballads indicates, the range of interests extends understandably beyond the more institutional values in which the feudal protagonists of the historical ballads find themselves caught up. The best of the *romances novelescos* still retain an immense attraction for the modern reader for the profundity of their interest in the fundamental conflicts of human nature, even though those conflicts may be essentially immoral and socially unacceptable, as well as for the intensity of portrayal of those conflicts through the minstrel's mature and competent understanding of the affective potential of a well-wrought literary structure.

CHAPTER 6

The Carolingian Ballads

PERHAPS the most unusual yet indicative segments of the *Romancero viejo* is made up of the ballads inspired in one way or another by the body of medieval Carolingian lore, based on the court of Charlemagne and the exploits of Roland, France's great epic hero. It is a group of ballads unusual in that it represents the extensive influence on and development by a supposedly basically popular, unlettered minstrelsy of a foreign tradition of little direct pertinence to Peninsular reality. Yet on the other hand, the Carolingian compositions are indicative of the creative spirit of the Spanish ballad in a more profound sense. If the medieval Spanish ballads, despite their diffusion, modification, and preservation by groups not directly associated with "sophisticated" literature, do indeed represent a corpus of poetry striking for their artistry and their fundamental concern with human nature, then the ability to develop an extensive group of traditional texts based on "foreign" literature bespeaks the ways in which the Spanish ballad is far more than just a mythic and folkloric expression of the people. Although the ballad based on literature of French origin bears little resemblance to the more direct imitations of the material which begins to reach the Peninsula from across the Pyrenees in the twelfth century, the very fact that this material could be of any interest at all to the individuals involved in the development of the *romances* argues well for seeing the Spanish ballad as essentially a creative literary phenomenon that sought inspiration in widely divergent sources.

As is to be expected with a genre that has attracted as much critical attention as the early ballads have, the origins and sources of the Carolingian works have been amply investigated, both with relation to the parent works of French literature and to the manifestations of the latter that became known in the Peninsula and served as the basis for the many subsequent ballads.[1] As is now widely accepted, the influence of the far more feudally developed French court began around the first period of political stabilization in Spain, the twelfth century. Indeed, many of the French works dealt with the struggle on or near Spanish soil against the Moors, a circumstance of content which may have played some role in the interest shown by the first literate groups to translate the French materials into Spanish or to imitate them in semioriginal Spanish compositions.

This is an interest, obviously, that must have flourished over a long period of time, from the early introduction of the French works into Spain up to the fifteenth century, when we find the full development of the early ballads. Of course, by this time the French had long ceased to have any interest in this feudally inspired literature, the nascent Renaissance and antimedieval Humanism having rejected it definitively. In Spain, however, despite an equally strong strain of Humanism and an emerging Renaissance, those levels of society which found interest in the ballads clearly did not have any intense antipathy toward medieval topics, and the ballads, historical, Carolingian, etc., flourished alongside the sophisticated courtly literature of the time. Nevertheless, the catholicity of interest of the balladeers, enjoying the French and Arabic themes as much as the historical Spanish ones, is indicative of a certain weakening of bonds with the original meanings of those themes, a fact which must also be taken into account when attempting to explain the works' lack of precision in geographical and historical references. Emphasis fell undoubtedly on the creative treatment to be given the *materia prima* rather than on faithfully reflecting any documentary circumstances of origin. In turn, the ballads acquired enough of the stature of creative and imaginative literature to have some influence on that fantastic genre of fifteenth-century Spain, also of French heritage, the books of chivalry.[2]

Indeed, the influences of French materials, particularly those dealing with conflicts between French heroes and the Moors, became so strong that the creation of the one truly fictional Spanish epic hero, Bernardo del Carpio, is credited to a reaction in the Peninsula against French treatment of the "affairs" of the former and the need to supplant a figure of the stature of Roland with an equally powerful national model. Although we were unable to discuss the ballads on Bernardo del Carpio in Chapter 3 for want of space, the creation of the figure, the composition of the epic materials, and the subsequent development of a body of ballads add further testimony to this one manifestation of French literary influence.

With regard to the nature of the Carolingian ballads, Entwistle reminds us that the Carolingian cycle is only vaguely related to the Charlemagne materials.[3] The group formed by these ballads in reality is a catchall for ballads that do derive more or less directly from French sources, as, for example, those deriving from the thirteenth-century *Roncesvalles,* based on late Roland literature,[4] those ballads which have faint traces of French influence in personal names and place references, and those where, as far as internal narrative is concerned, non-Castilian affiliation is discernible. As we shall point out in our examination of representative texts, distortion is great enough to alarm anyone looking for documentary fact; it underlines once again the creative process of the early Spanish ballad. When one examines the characteristics of the Carolingian ballads that give them any recognizable autonomy from the other ballads that we have examined, he is struck by their relative superficiality. Horace S. Craig summarizes as follows:

There are, nevertheless, some general traits common to the Carolingian *romances*. One is the formation of the [Past Perfect] with the auxiliary *fué* and the infinitive [i.e., "He went to speak" = "He had spoken"] (assonance can be prolonged indefinitely this way). There is a regular use of certain out of the way words, such as *sacramento* for *juramento* ["oath"], and *lexar* for *dejar* ["to permit"]. The partitive is frequently employed, "tantos matan de los moros [so many are killed of the Moors]. . . ." Proper names terminate in "s" as Oliveros, Gaiferos, Carlos, Calainos; this is a survival of the Old French nominatives in -s. Repetitions are of course numerous—this characteristic is found in the French epic. Maledictions and omens of one sort or another are found in the Carolingian *romances* in Spain as well as in the French epics. Concern with articles of dress is another trait found in many of these *romances*.[5]

Unless we distinguish broadly between Roland and non-Roland materials, or base ourselves on putative French parent works, no real classification of the Carolingian ballads is possible. Despite the fact that the ballads themselves are considered fragments of longer works, either Spanish translations of French originals or French works themselves surviving among the French living in Spain, and that these medieval ballads underwent the same process of traditionalization as the historical compositions, no neat categorization is forthcoming. Indeed, the miscellaneous nature of some of the works at issue has led to a certain blurring of lines between the Carolingian and the novelesque ballads, and the grouping from one collection to another may reveal several significant differences of opinion. Craig, in the article which we have already cited, includes the ballad of the vengeful Moriana in his broad listing of fifteen Carolingian categories, although we have placed that ballad in a different category in a preceding chapter. At the same time, perhaps it is inaccurate from a historical point of view to distinguish between Carolingian materials and other French sources, as we and others have done by treating the ballads derived from the story of Tristan and Isolde under the heading of novelesque ballads. What underlies such a division is, one will recall, the fact that France during the Middle Ages does not present a unified literary tradition (as Spain does not either), and a distinction is generally made between the Breton Matter of which *Tristan* is exemplary and the Francien Carolingian material—the French Matter— exemplified by the far more diverse and influential Roland epic(s). Taxonomy is, in the end, only a minor function of literary scholarship: it certainly influences often our understanding of a work (as our comments on the extremely elliptic Tristan ballad make clear), but we cannot allow the vagaries that remain to delay our discussion of the texts themselves, important and aesthetically valuable despite the uncertainties surrounding their parentage and classification. We now turn our attention to three compositions which we believe are indicative of the Carolingian ballads.

I Ballads Based on the Roland Material

The ballad of "Doña Alda" has been one of the most widely commented of the Spanish texts, mostly because of its clear link with the Roland material (Alda is Roland's betrothed; Aude is her name in French) and because of its nevertheless highly original elaboration.[6] Alda is given the briefest of mention in the *Song of Roland,* where she appears only to suffer mortal collapse upon learning of the hero's death in combat. In the Spanish ballad, on the other hand, we find that the central interest is in creating an interpretation of the woman and the events leading up to the arrival of the disastrous news. The product is a ballad of unusual artistic accomplishment:[7]

En París está doña Alda	(Doña Alda is in Paris,
la esposa de don Roldán,	the wife of Don Roldán,
trescientas damas con ella	with three hundred ladies

para la acompañar;	to keep her company.
5 *todas visten un vestido,*	All are dressed the same.
todas calzan un calzar,	All are shod the same.
todas comen a una mesa,	All eat at one table.
todas comían de un pan,	All ate from one loaf.
si no era doña Alda	All except Doña Alda,
10 *que era la mayoral.*	who was the overseer.
Las ciento hilaban oro,	One hundred spun gold,
las ciento tejen cendal,	one hundred weave gauze.
las ciento tañen instrumentos	One hundred strum instruments
para doña Alda holgar.	to give Doña Alda pleasure.
15 *Al son de los instrumentos*	With the sound of the instruments
doña Alda adormido se ha;	Doña Alda has fallen asleep.
ensoñado había un sueño,	She dreams a dream,
un sueño de gran pesar.	a dream of terrible weight.
Recordó despavorida	She woke up in a fright,
20 *y con un pavor muy grande,*	with a terrible fright,
los gritos daba tan grandes	and her cries were so terrible
que se oían en la ciudad.	that they were heard in the city.
Allí hablaron sus doncellas,	There her ladies spoke,
bien oiréis lo que dirán:	you will hear well what they say:
25 *'¿Qué es aquesto, mi señora?*	"What is this, my lady,
¿Quién es el que os hizo mal?'	who has done you ill?"
'Un sueño soñé, doncellas,	"I dreamt a dream, ladies,
que me ha dado gran pesar:	which has given me great anxiety:
que me veía en un monte	I saw myself atop a mountain
30 *en un desierto lugar;*	in a deserted place.
de so los montes muy altos	From under the highest mountains
un azor vide volar,	I saw a goshawk flying,
tras dél viene una aguililla	and behind him a little eagle
que lo ahinca muy mal.	that pursues him
35 *El azor con grande cuita*	The goshawk, quite scared,
metióse so mi brial;	gets under my tunic,
al aguililla con grande ira	but the eagle furiously
de allí lo iba a sacar:	goes in after him
con las uñas lo despluma,	and plucks his feathers off with his claws
40 *con el pico lo deshace.'*	and tears him apart with his beak."
Allí habló su camarera,	There spoke up a chambermaid;
bien oiréis lo que dirá:	you will hear well what she says:
'Aquese sueño, señora,	"That dream, madam,
bien os lo entiendo soltar:	I can interpret for you well:
45 *el azor es vuestro esposo*	the goshawk is your husband
que viene de allén la mar;	who comes from beyond the sea

el águila sodes vos	and the little eagle is you
con la cual ha de casar,	whom he is to marry,
y aquel monte es la iglesia	and that mountain is the church
50 *donde os han de velar.'*	where they are to watch over you."
'Si así es, mi camarera,	"If that is so, my chambermaid,
bien te lo entiendo pagar.'	I know how to pay you well."
Otro día de mañana	The next morning
cartas de fuera le traen;	letters are brought to her from afar,
55 *tintas venían de dentro,*	stained on the inside,
de fuera escritas con sangre,	written on the outside in blood,
que su Roldán era muerto	telling her that Roldán had died
en la caza de Roncesvalles.	in the rout at Roncesvalles.)

(pp. 150–51)

Like the overwhelming majority of the traditional ballads, "Doña Alda" is basically the elaboration of a narrative circumstance in a longer source-text. In this case, it is the *Song of Roland,* or, more accurately, some later version and the Spanish reworking, *Roncesvalles* (the Roncevaux of French literature). Nevertheless, as Menéndez Pidal has pointed out in his previously cited study, the relationship between French original and Spanish ballad is so scant as to be really nonexistent beyond the use of the name of Roland's betrothed (converted in the *romance* into his wife) and the announcement of the death of the warrior at Roncesvalles. The whole fabric of the ballad, the elaboration of setting, the creation of a sense of pathos for Alda's innocence, the portentous dream—all are unique to the ballad and any other now lost Spanish version of the event. In fact, as a moment's consideration of the artistic quality of the composition will reveal, its literary interest and value derive from the imaginative material completely extraneous to the supposed sources. To enter into the discussion of whether these all-important elements are the work of an expert individual creative consciousness or the "accidental" but felicitious result of the process of traditionalization is essentially, we suggest, to miss the most important point. A Spanish ballad related via fragmentation to more extensive epic materials manifests itself in versions impressive for their distance from the putative originals and for the poetic unity of highly original form which they have come to assume. This is even true in the case of the so-called minstrel ballads *(romances juglarescos).* As we pointed out in the beginning of this chapter, and as commentators have frequently observed, the Carolingian ballads are, from the point of view of internal characteristics, often only vaguely and superficially related to any assumed parent French originals.

What is to be our reaction in the face of such a unique elaboration of the primary narrative material? As was suggested repeatedly in our close analysis of the historical ballads, which can be compared to surviving non-ballad sources, the sometimes drastic modifications which a "story line" undergoes in its evolution as a ballad are indicative of a desire—individual or collective—to bring out a specific view of history or of man or of his circumstance. This is of course what the literary historian has long recognized as the force underlying the reworking of inherited literary influences: the important writer of a later generation always makes his own in some outstanding way the thematic and rhetorical formulas that he borrows from an earlier tradition, with the result that the influential and the influenced works may demonstrate entirely different interpretations of the subject matter. (Witness what happens to the late-medieval Cid material, the basis for the historical ballads we have examined, when it is reworked by Corneille in his sixteenth-century drama.) In the case of the ballad of "Doña Alda," therefore, the most pertinent question is not what are the relations with the French epic, but rather what has happened to the person of Alda as she is taken over into the ballad and why such radical changes are effected.

Turning to the text of the ballad, we find a tripartite division. In lines 1–14, we are given a setting, a way of life, so to speak, for the woman. In contrast to the audience's knowledge that Roldán (mentioned in line 2) is supposedly engaged in mortal and dramatic conflict with the heathen Moors in the Pyrenees on the edge of civilization, doña Alda is portrayed as surrounded by a luxury indicative of the best of courtly grandeur. Three hundred ladies attend her—a number of no particular relevance except for giving a hyperbolic dimension to the description. The extensive anaphora of lines 5–8 serves to emphasize this hyperbole and to impress upon us the undiminished magnificence of Alda's court. The latter is introduced in lines 9–10, after the careful attention to the establishment of a sumptuous context, as she is presented as the most impressive of them all. The effect of Alda being surrounded by care-free elegance is reinforced by the second anaphora, lines 11–13, where the three hundred attendants are presented in terms of groups of one hundred, engaged in the activities appropriate to a woman of wealth and leisure. Spinning, weaving, the playing of musical instruments: these are occupations suitable to a woman of the most exquisite refinement. Line 14 makes clear this function with its assurance that the activities described have only one purpose: to give pleasure to doña Alda.

To what end does the ballad make such an issue out of the setting for Alda's subsequent grief? Certainly, line 14 turns out to be ironic when seen in terms of what is about to transpire: all of the perfection of setting and environment cannot in the end protect the woman from the tragedy which is about to befall her (this is the Humpty-Dumpty motif, of course). We suggest that this is the principal goal which the introductory verses fulfill, that of setting a dream-like stage of elegance far removed from reality and in essence a highly striking context when seen against the horror of combat to which the woman's husband is at that very moment exposed. Indeed, the sleep induced by the courtly leisure of her existence is more than just a casual event. Alda may be physically lulled into her deep slumber by the well-tuned music of her attendants. But hers is also an emotional numbness, as the entire environment of her existence, presented so insistently through the hyperbole of number and the emphasis of anaphora, serves to isolate her from the reality of the unpleasant danger to which her husband is exposed.

Thus, when Alda dreams, it is a dream which on one level extends the drowsy pleasure induced by the pleasing music of her women. But on another level, the dream that results from the elegant, courtly *otium* of her existence is to reveal to her prophetically what she is unable to sense while awake. The dream is indeed prophetic; it represents a frequent device, as we have indicated, in medieval poetry in general. In this case, it is allegorical to the extent that the prophecy is expressed in terms of hidden symbols which require interpretation in order to be understood. The dream is, in short, a vision that demands a skillful awareness on the part of the dream if it is to be understood, an important point when we consider the denouement of the ballad. Why the dream should be allegorical must be approached from the point of view of literary design, although the medieval poet must surely have been aware to some degree of real dreams that occur to man in a symbolic and not immediately intelligible form. But the psychiatric knowledge of the role that dreams play in the human subconscious cannot be projected to any extent upon medieval literature, and we must be content with seeing the dream more as a literary device for betokening something about Alda than as any attempt to exploit the fact that man often does dream in terms of subconscious symbols. In other words, a psychoanalytic interpretation of Alda's dream is less appropriate than simply an acceptance of it as an expression of what does, in fact, become obvious: the tragic and violent death of her husband, a death which she is totally unprepared to envision (consciously) and to accept. The description of the dream, lines 15–52, is relatively unrevealing as far as the dream itself is concerned.

Rather, the purpose of the dream, which Alda herself relates in vivid detail, is to establish a reaction on the part of the audience toward her own person. This is done in two stages. First, when Alda relates her dream to her three hundred women—the suggestion of whose presence again reminds us of the privileged existence which the young woman leads—it should be obvious that she is unprepared to comprehend its meaning. Although her waking remembrance of the somnial event is apparently quite complete, it does not hide the fact that the attack on the goshawk by the small eagle is beyond her ability to understand, particularly when she relates that the dream has a very clear pertinence to her own person. The violence of the conclusion of the dream and the role which Alda herself plays in it are, on the other hand, designed to make clear to the audience that the dream is a prophecy of impending disaster. It is in the nature of literary works that what happens should have an automatic relationship with what has been presented as the background setting. In this case, it is Roldán and the circumstances of his wife's life. In other words, given the introductory material, although Alda in her drowsiness and alarm may be unable to make any sense of the dream, we would normally understand a meaning for it anyway on the basis of the more restricted and unmistakable context that has been given us: Alda is about to be the focal point of a mortal disaster that she is powerless to prevent. Such a disaster —and few readers would err here—is to involve her beloved husband. What we are trying to say is that literary works are often characterized by the clues which they leave for their audience, clues which are nevertheless unavailable to the principals around whom turn the fateful actions of the work. This type of irony, so observable in the early Spanish ballads—we have pointed it out at least with reference to the Infantes of Lara, "Abenámar," Moriana, the Alhama ballad—permits the reader to understand what is going on as well as to appreciate the extent to which, for their own greater misfortune and eventual dismay, the main characters do not. The result of such a procedure can be either scorn (as in the case of King Juan in "Abenámar") or pity. The latter is most likely the emotion meant to be evoked by Alda's confusion and uncomprehending agitation when she awakens from the dream.

Lines 41–52 are probably the most important segment of the composition. It is at this point that an astute chambermaid comes forth to offer an interpretation of the dream: it is to be interpreted as the forthcoming marriage of Roldán and Alda. (The confusion created by the use of the word "wife" in line 2 and the implication here that the marriage has not yet been consecrated may be either an inattention to accuracy on the part of the ballad or an indication that *esposa* is to be understood in an older meaning of "fiancée," a meaning shared with the English cognate, "spouse.") The chambermaid's interpretation is patently false. It is so wide of the mark, failing, for example, to take into account the violent destruction of the goshawk by the eagle, that the audience has little difficulty in rejecting it as inappropriate. Whether the chambermaid is fawning or merely stupid is not brought out, and it is not an important detail. More central is Alda's ready acceptance of a "happy" interpretation of the dream (lines 51–52). Intentionally or otherwise, the chambermaid has provided a meaning for the allegorical prophecy in keeping with Alda's own disposition.

What is significant about all this is simply the fact that Alda *is* disposed to overlook the inadequacy of her attendant's interpretation and to console herself from the dread caused by her dream with the first tranquilizing suggestion to be offered. In the tradition of medieval allegorical literature, the ballad is exemplary in detailing the symbolic vision and then following it with what is (at first glance) meant to be a useful and revealing gloss. Such a practice is to be found in the famous Introduction to Gonzalo de Berceo's thirteenth-century *Milagros de Nuestra Señora (Miracles of Our Lady)*, where we find an allegory using manifestations of nature, as in the ballad of doña Alda. (The other most frequent allegorical procedure is that of abstract personification, as in the French thirteenth-century *Roman de la Rose* [*Romance of the Rose*].) Thus, any audience familiar with this common literary procedure in medieval literature will greet the words of the chambermaid with an accustomed attention to the gloss that usually follows the allegory and provides an explanation for it. That the gloss is so obviously inaccurate is an irony that depends as much on our anticipation of revelation as it does on Alda's all-too-hasty acceptance of the woman's false words. Both through the delineation of a confused and bewildered Alda and the irony of a glaringly inadequate gloss on a prophetic dream of an alarming nature, the ballad seeks to present the pathetic figure of a woman effectively isolated from reality. If Alda is intended to be viewed as a "victim" of anything, it is of an existence, surrounded by courtly opulence, that ill prepares her to comprehend with sensitivity the harsh realities of life as they symbolically reveal themselves to her in the dream. That not only life and death are involved, but love as well, emphasizes even more Alda's pathetic innocence.

One may safely assume that the concluding segment of the ballad, lines 53–58, is anticlimactic for the audience, if not for Alda. We know more or less that the prophetic dream *must*, in the fashion of such experiences, become cruel reality, and it is therefore not a surprise to witness the arrival of the messenger and learn of Roldán's death in the mountains at Roncesvalles. These concluding lines are not for our information, despite their accurate reference to the Roland legend. Their function is to allow us to see Alda's dream correctly interpreted for her and the false if not condescending gloss tragically proven wrong. Alda's innocent belief in her chambermaid's words are but the foreshadowing context for the recitation of the true meaning. Both her innocence and the clear inadequacy of the maid's words prefigure with certainty the message of an irrevocable disaster.

In turn, the abrupt ending with which the ballad is most known, aside from being indicative of the Spanish ballad as a whole, suppresses any portrayal of Alda's own reaction to the news. Indeed, this is of particular importance, for the only real role of Alda in the *Song of Roland* is to fall in a mortal swoon when the news of the defeat at Roncevaux is announced, thereby manifesting in quintessence the grief of the French people. That this detail is omitted in the ballad demonstrates the greater attention of early Hispanic minstrelsy to effective poetic rhetoric than to documentary accuracy. "Knowing when to fall quiet," as Menéndez Pidal has put it, is an outstanding artistic quality of the balladeers. In this instance, the result is to tell us, in effect, that we should know all too well how Alda will react: the sudden realization of the full meaning of her dream and of the nonsense of the chambermaid's interpretation will produce the expected mortal grief. Irony and foreshadowing in the ballad have been too intense to require the explanation of Alda's reaction, and the abrupt ending is a tribute to audience understanding of the circumstance created in the work and to the poet for his skill in executing his creation.

If E. M. Wilson is accurate in assessing the tragic note of the early Spanish ballads,[8] our analysis of Alda's innocence and the context of her vision and its meaning underline the interest of a large number of works in how fundamental human suffering befalls even the most mighty. The "Fall of the Princes" ("La caída de los príncipes") is a commonplace of Spanish culture and bespeaks an awareness of how Adverse Fortune, while it may come to him with greater frequency, is not the exclusive experience of the humble man. The strongest and the richest, as the Dances of Death were wont to articulate with ill-concealed glee, believe at their own foolhardy risk in a privileged protection from suffering. In the case of Alda, the Spanish ballad is recognized for its brilliance, not for any routine reconstruction of the "spirit" or the "meaning" of the French epic, but for its outstanding elaboration of one rather marginal incident as a commentary on how harsh is the cruel fact of life and death and how even harsher it is when it intrudes upon the comfortable existence of one whose whole way of life is an attempt to mask and to "give exalted pleasure" as a substitute for that harshness.

II *"Durandarte"*

One of the most peculiar ballads, when examined alongside French originals, is "Durandarte," a ballad in which Roland's sword appears transformed into a knight. It is a metamorphosis that demonstrates all too vividly the usually superficial influence on Hispanic materials found in the Carolingian ballads. In all fairness we must note however that there is some evidence that such a "personalization" of the sword is already to be found in late French *chansons de geste* and is probably just as indicative of the weakening of the epic material on native soil before its penetration into the Peninsula. The major difference is, of course, that the "inaccuracies" of the

Spanish ballads vis-à-vis French sources are rendered inconsequential by the artistry of the compositions themselves. Moreover, the further transformation of Durandarte into an exemplary figure of amorous constancy is unquestionably foreign to any epic context and reinforces our earlier observations about the lack of clear lines between the pseudo-epic and historical Carolingian ballads and the novelesque ballads, where lyrically treated symbols of love are frequent. It is not surprising to find that "Durandarte" remained a favorite throughout the Renaissance and The Baroque period, a time when poets were engaged in replacing the vast majority of medieval compositions with newer and supposedly more "artistic" ballads. "Durandarte" is, in addition, an unusually short example of the *romances carolingios:*

'Durandarte, Durandarte,	("Durandarte, Durandarte,
buen caballero probado,	good proven knight,
yo te ruego que hablemos	I beg you for us to talk
en aquel tiempo pasado,	about that time gone by
5 *y dime si se te acuerda*	and tell me if you recall
cuando fuiste enamorado,	when you were in love,
cuando en galas e invenciones	when in celebrations and tourneys
publicabas tu cuidado,	you published your intention,
cuando venciste a los moros	when you defeated Moors
10 *en campo por mí aplazado;*	on the field that I stipulated.
agora, desconocido,	Now, stranger,
di ¿ por qué me has olvidado?'	do tell, why have you forgotten me?"
'Palabras son lisonjeras,	"Those are flattering words,
señora, de vuestro grado,	madam, of your desire,
15 *que si yo mudanza hice*	for if I made any change
vos lo habéis todo causado,	you caused it all
pues amaste a Gaiferos	because you loved Gaiferos
cuando yo fui desterrado;	while I was in exile.
que si amor queréis conmigo	If you want to have love from me
20 *tenéislo muy mal pensado,*	you are badly mistaken,
que por no sufrir ultraje	for rather than suffer insult
moriré desesperado.'	I will die out of desperation.")

(pp. 167–68)

Tied in with another well-known Carolingian ballad, in which Durandarte's death in battle is the central action ("¡Oh Belerma!, ¡Oh Belerma!"), the present text is outstanding for the parallelism and anaphora of the exchange between the warrior and the woman

whom he once served faithfully. The context of the poem is unmistakably courtly. The woman refers to the practices of courtly
love, such as the service of the woman and feats of valor in her
honor, the knight's publication of his amatory allegiance, and so
on. Durandarte, in his courteous reply to the woman's pouting
accusations, speaks of the sort of rejection and ill-treatment that
served as the common fare of the ardent love liege. Indeed, her
scorn has been so injurious to that love that it has resulted in the
all-important *mudanza* ("change") to which Durandarte alludes
and of which the woman is aware. *Mudanza* is a cliché of love poetry
and is used to speak of the vicissitudes of fortune that plague the
lover, of the transformations in spirit and flesh wrought by the
devastating experience of unrequited passion, of the counterforces
of constancy which the lover must struggle frantically and freneti-
cally to keep under control, lest the very fabric of the relationship
be rent by distraction. All of these are commonplaces of the love
literature contemporary to the references of the ballad and suggest
that, despite differing origins and development, the minstrels involved in the traditional formation of this ballad were not unaware of the more aristocratic culture that was enjoying its own
highly productive expansion during the late fourteenth and early
fifteenth centuries.

What is different about the ballad when we examine it in terms of
the fifteenth-century *Cancioneros,* the extensive "songbooks" that
served as anthologies of the early courtly poetry, is the rhetoric
in favor of Durandarte and against the woman. Perhaps it would
be more accurate to place emphasis on the manner in which we are
meant to react negatively to the woman who harangues Durandarte
so forcefully in the first half of the composition. For, to a great
extent, the poetry of late courtly love is naturally enough a rhetoric
in defense of the servant of the woman. Only men write of their
amorous experiences at this time (although during the high Middle
Ages there is a tradition in Galaico-Portuguese of the *cantiga de
amigo,* the "song of the [male] friend," in which the woman relates
her amorous suffering), and thus their poetry is an implicit defense
of their own noble but ill-received service to the woman. While
the latter may be gently criticized for her insensitivity to the man's
constancy and respect, he is too much of a gentleman to openly
speak against the woman, as this would destroy the very basis on
which he means to attract ultimately her attention. Thus the poetry

in which the love liege speaks is more a hymn of praise to the man's unblemished soul, and the poem is often addressed to the woman in the attempt to weaken her cruel resistence.

In the ballad, on the other hand, we have no narrative voice, only the dialogue of the two individuals as if it were being overheard. Neither speaks directly "toward" us or to anyone beyond each other, and consequently does not pretend to convince an audience of the righteousness of his (her) behavior. Where the usual poem of courtly love is a public confession addressed nevertheless by the man to his woman, the ballad is a private exchange, so to speak, between Durandarte and a woman toward whom he has shown the utmost respect. Their exchange, in the nature of private conversations, betrays a frankness appropriate to the supposedly unwitnessed encounter between two persons who enjoyed in the past an exclusive relationship. The ballad, therefore, approaches the characterization of the exemplary constancy of Durandarte through an effectively negative portrayal of a woman who would impugn the quality of his behavior toward her person.

The woman's speech, which is somewhat longer than Durandarte's reply, is given first. This is necessary since she is the attacker and her pouting accusations establish a context in which Durandarte's rejoinder will strengthen his own position but will effectively dissipate any audience sympathy for hers. The unidentified damsel does not speak with noticeable restraint. Indeed, the anaphora in lines 6, 7, and 9 of the temporal conjunction not only underlines the forceful attack of her words but as well makes clear that what is at painful issue between the two persons is a relationship which has ceased to obtain. At the same time, the woman is not reticent in alluding to her role, now quite past, as the mistress of the relationship, as she very definitely relates Durandarte's past service to her own will (line 10, especially). Still feeling herself the dominant partner in the relationship, as a woman experienced in the strict ways of courtly love, it is she who raises the subject and it is she who attempts to humiliate the man by her forceful approach, reinforced as she must feel by almost sarcastic references to how Durandarte is known as a "proven gentleman" (line 2). Sarcasm is evident also in her snide qualification, "if you remember" (line 5) and in the epithet by which she addresses him, "stranger" (line 11). Her closing question is as direct as it can be and constitutes an unmitigated challenge to Durandarte's honor as the man who has supposedly been her faithful servant in love: "Tell me," she demands, "why have you forgotten me?" To forget the woman, to manifest the contempt of nonrecognition, is an insult that turns upon the man and damns him as a gentleman. In one sense, with some modifications the woman's speech could be isolated and examined on its own as representative of the *man's* frequent complaint against the woman, whose snub is a calculated procedure for increasing the ardent passion and suffering service of the man. But this is not a composition from the songbooks of courtly love; it is the woman speaking and she is demanding with the ill-concealed pique accorded her by the right to know why Durandarte, the paragon of courtly virtue, has scorned her.

Durandarte's reply (lines 13–22) is, as we have suggested, meant both to redeem him from the woman's insulting accusations and to turn the charge of courtly error against her own person. The ironic fact, as it soon becomes apparent, is that the accusations of inconstancy leveled against Durandarte should have been uttered with greater emphasis first by the man himself. The noble warrior's measured reply, a reply carefully structured on the basis of unemotional parallel phrasing ("for if . . . then . . ."), makes it clear that the woman herself has been more blatantly unfaithful to Durandarte and furthermore she has been unfaithful to him during a period of harsh exile (presumably in battle) when he should have been most able to trust her loyalty. Gaiferos, a figure in his own right in several Carolingian ballads, and a figure inherited from French literature, supplanted Durandarte in the affections of the woman as her loyal love liege during the warrior's absence. If his present inattention to the woman is insulting, her past treachery which cannot have been a secret is irrevocably damning. In this way the ballad stresses forcefully the superiority of Durandarte. In terms of literary rhetoric—how we are made to accept what is presented to us—by having Durandarte first accused and then by showing him respond with his own charge that not only adequately answers the woman's accusing questions but shows her as more the guilty party for her heinous treachery, the minstrel realizes his intent to evoke our sympathy for the betrayed constancy of the warrior.

At the same time, there is no attempt to depict Durandante as pitiful. If he bears his emotional wounds in silence, when he is challenged he responds with a quiet but determined intensity that provides another level of contrast between the two protagonists.

His subdued emotion is all the more dignified for the unchecked haughtiness of the challenge articulated by his former mistress in the service of love. The juxtaposition of their former speech and of its content provides a context which is highly inappropriate to courtly love and which betokens the deception and reversal of feeling—the *mudanza*—that have taken place.

There is a certain paired relationship between the three-fold anaphora of the woman's accusation and the three-fold anaphora of the knight's cool reply. If the two speeches are meant to reveal an ironic situation for accusation and justification, such a pairing can only serve to strengthen the propriety of Durandarte's behavior and the cruel duplicity of the woman. For example, her challenge is emphasized by the three anaphoric occurrences of the temporal conjunction, and she refers to three past circumstances: when Durandarte (1) loved her (line 6), (2) when he proclaimed that love in good courtly fashion (lines 7–8), (3) when he did combat in her name (lines 9–10). When Durandarte answers the accusations, in both the implied and the direct replies, he formulates his justification in the indirect terms of a three-fold causal relationship: (1) her treachery has resulted in a justifiable change of love (lines 15–18), (2) she lacks perspective in wishing that the old relationship still be maintained (lines 19–20), (3) he would rather suffer a death of desperation than subject himself to (her) outrage (lines 21–22). It is clear that in both series, the first and the third elements bear a close resemblance: being in love vs. having fallen out of love, doing humble service vs. spurning the way in which it has become a humiliating outrage. In the case of the second elements, announcing one's love vs. rejecting its offer, any approximation must be based on "recognition." The servant of love announces his loyalty for the recognition of both the woman and her society; toward this end the man "publishes" his commitment openly in tourneys and other contests.

This has been indeed the past nature of Durandarte's relationship to the woman. On the other hand, the principal manner in which she now accuses him is by demanding to know why he does not accord her recognition: why is he a "stranger" (line 11), can he "remember" how it used to be (lines 4–5), why has he "forgotten" her (line 12). His reply is not to pretend that there can be love between them; i.e., that he can accept or "recognize" any commitment toward the woman (lines 19–20). Thus, where he formerly recognized in public and acknowledged his commitment to her, in private he now rejects any possible feeling for her. It is the subtle shift between his earlier open declaration of allegiance and his present inability to pay the woman any heed which approximates the middle elements in their formulaic speeches to one another and which best underlines the irretrievable loss of courtly sentiment that has occurred as a result of her own cruel treachery.

The concluding lines of the ballad are calculated to evoke maximum audience sympathy. It is significant that the woman is not allowed to reply to Durandarte's self-justification, a fact that implies that we are to accept it at face value: his response is of such overwhelming validity that there is nothing that the woman can do but silently withdraw in well-deserved humiliation. Durandarte's pathetic statement that he will die of desperation, presumably out of true love heartlessly betrayed, is meant on one level to correlate with the woman's accusations. This is the juxtaposition of combat in the woman's name vs. refusal to suffer offense any longer because of her. On the other hand, it is an affirmation charged with sufficient pathos to focus attention exclusively on itself. In this last way the poem shifts emphasis from the juxtaposition between the woman's harsh words and the knight's noble defense, to conclude with a final evocation of feeling for the man, a feeling that excludes with unmistakable emphasis the woman who earlier was so confident in her assumed dominance. As we have pointed out, Durandarte bears some noticeable relationships to the late-medieval versions of courtly love as we find them in the songbooks of the court poets. Nevertheless, where these versions most frequently manifest themselves as lachrymose defenses of the faithful but rejected lover, the ballad, lacking any commitment to the by now tired clichés of the aristocratic game of love, is unhesitant to structure its presentation of the confrontation between the man and the woman in order to underline with unsubtle emphasis the perfidy of the "pure" mistress and the constancy of one who emerges as the symbol of knightly devotion betrayed but given dignity by its own righteousness.

III *"Gerineldos"*

Our next ballad text survives in its best version in the modern popular tradition, first discovered in the last century; like many a large number of the Carolingian ballads, it is rather long, so that quoting it in its entirety in a study such as this is inadvisable. Many studies have traced the impressive diffusion of versions of Gerineldos' story throughout the Peninsula.[9] The fact that modern versions that have been discovered are better than those recorded in the early Renaissance collections may or may not be of great importance for ballad theories. The relative weakness of the early versions, when seen alongside the undeniable superiority of more recent texts, may indeed be the result of the ameliorating process of traditionalization. But it may also indicate only that the early collections were unfortunate in having access to inadequate variants, despite the possibility that better ones may have been in existence, or that the collections made unfelicitous choices of available texts.[10] Whatever the case may be, little question remains that modern traditional texts merit the analytic attention that cannot be provided for what medieval versions survive in printed form.

The ballad deals with a common enough circumstance. Gerineldos, a page in the service of the King, is tendered a most attractive invitation by the Monarch's daughter to render her "three hours of service" that night. After some hesitation, Gerineldos accepts, is received warmly by the woman, and remains to pass the night with her. The King, after an unsettling dream, awakens to find his page missing, and, guessing some sort of treachery because of the dream he has had, goes in search of the youth, finds him in bed with his daughter, and leaves his sword between the sleeping couple as witness of their indiscretion (cf. a similar circumstance in the Breton *Tristan* material). Although Gerineldos later attempts tactfully to calm the King, the latter accuses him of the treachery of which his sword has been a witness and vows that the page will die by its edge. Although the suggestion has been made that the Carolingian affiliation of this ballad is the story of the illicit relationship between Eginhard, Charlemagne's tutor and secretary, and Emma, the latter's daughter, any real demonstration of this contact with historical fact has been eliminated entirely from the ballad. While the Tristán ballad which we examined above, although sketchy, retained at least the accuracy of the names, this ballad bears no useful resemblance to the events of Charlemagne's court. (The putative identity between the names "Gerineldos" and "Eginhard" surely cannot be more than *ad hoc* philology, so garbled are the necessary sound changes that would have to be involved.) Thus we see that in the

case of "Gerineldos," if one proceeds on the basis of the text itself,
rather than any relationship which it "must" have had with Carolingian material, classification here is only of the vaguest sort and
contributes little to understanding the nature of the composition.
Whether or not it is indeed Carolingian becomes an issue of little
consequence given the superficiality of any overt relationship to
the materials dealing with the reign of Charlemagne. As Entwistle
has pointed out, [11] any historical allusions to the court of the French
monarch have been suppressed and what we have as a result is a
ballad which deals with a common enough situation, the "squire
of low degree," or more accurately, the illicit amorous relationship
between the King's daughter and his own trusted page.

One of the major questions surrounding an understanding of
the ballad is whether or not Gerineldos is drawn innocently into
the affair with the princess, or whether his hesitation is only a
shrewd attempt to protect himself in a potentially dangerous situation (cf. the timely "discretion" of Cava in the Rodrigo ballads).
The ballad begins thus: [12]

	'Gerineldos, Gerineldos,	("Gerineldos, Gerineldos,
	mi camarero pulido,	my handsome chamberlain,
	¡quién te tuviera esta noche	would that I had tonight
	tres horas a mi servicio!'	three hours of service from you!"
5	*'Como soy vuestro criado,*	"Since I am your servant,
	señora, burláis conmigo.'	madam, you make fun of me."
	'No me burlo, Gerineldos,	"No I don't, Gerineldos,
	que de veras te lo digo.'	I'm speaking to you sincerely."
	'¿A cuál hora, bella infanta,	"What time, pretty Infanta,
10	*cumpliréis lo prometido?'*	will you make good your promise?"
	'Entre la una y las dos	"Between one and two
	cuando el rey esté dormido'	when the King has gone to sleep.")

There is nothing unusual about the abrupt opening; enough
early Spanish ballads employ it so as to make it one basic structural
denominator. As in many other examples, it serves here to suppress
any preestablished position on the part of the audience. We barely
know who are involved, let alone what the relationship is of one to
the other and what our attitude toward that relationship is to be.
All we have are the words of the woman addressing the man in
what appears to be especially bold terms. We assume, to be sure,
that such boldness is due to the woman's superior station. When

she addresses Gerineldos as "my attractive chamberlain," we are provided both with an identification of the man and an indication of his position of inferiority that permits both the boldness of the princess's words and the nature of her invitation. Line 2 presents something of a textual problem. Later portions of the ballad make it clear that Gerineldos is the valet of the King (line 34). The woman's address could either be the result of confusion in the process of transmission and elaboration, where line 34 has been substituted incorrectly for some "original" line 2, or it could be an attempt on the part of the minstrel to provide a correlation between Gerineldos' "service" to the princess and his betrayal of confidence and loyalty in his service to the King. The phrase contained in line 2 may be seen as a term of endearment on the woman's part, meant to attract Gerineldos' attention and meant to provide the context for the request for "service" enunciated in line 4.

The "service" of which the woman speaks is reminiscent of the formulas of courtly love. However, as we have pointed out, courtly love entails the emotional involvement of the gentleman in glorifying the person of his beloved before the world, not in providing her with physical satisfaction. Indeed, courtly love implies the aloofness of the woman, who rarely condescends to permit the servant of love to gaze upon her, let alone touch the hem of her garment, and not the boldness of an unmistakable sexual invitation. Any audience familiar with the concepts of courtly love—and previous ballads have tended to indicate that despite its restriction to the highborn the more popular listeners had some awareness of its meaning—will grasp the double meaning of the woman's declaration. Using a phrase from a game of predominantly "pure" love, she unceremoniously invites Gerineldos to engage in physical love. At the same time, her words remind Gerineldos, and us as well, that the man of her choice is, after all, only a servant in the social sense and obliged to heed his mistress's bidding.

When Gerineldos speaks, he exploits the woman's words, using the shield of his lowly station to ascertain if she does in fact wish to "command his services" as she has seemingly indicated. Whether Gerineldos does indeed hesitate out of timidity or whether he is only attempting to strengthen his position offers the principal interest of his opening statement. The degree to which the King may be justified in his anger at Gerineldos' actions and the degree to which we accept his promise of vengeance depends on whether or not the page is in fact the more clever of the two sinners in taking advantage of his feeling for the girl. His ready acceptance of the princess's offer when he ascertains that she is not joking is now unhesitating, as he inquires in lines 9–10 about the arrangements of the event. When the two part, there can be little question that Gerineldos is quite willing to "serve" his mistress appropriately. The irony of the reference to a context of courtly love both increases our appreciation of the direct approach taken by the two and the basically illicit nature of the relationship which they have accepted. In lines 13–18, which we do not quote, the ballad relates a detail meant to impress upon us Gerineldos' adeptness at that sort of thing as shown by his preparations to make his way to the woman's chambers. He circles the palace thrice, he circles the castle thrice (lines 16–17), an affirmation designed less to provide meaningful information than to create a mood of stealth and concerted care in excecuting a delicate adventure. Now before the woman's door, Gerineldos addresses her:

	'Abráisme', dijo, 'señora,	("Open up, madam," he said,
20	*abráisme, cuerpo garrido.'*	"open up, beautiful body."
	'¿Quién sois vos, el caballero,	"Who are you, knight,
	que llamáis así al postigo?'	come calling at my postern gate?"
	'Gerineldos soy, señora,	"I'm Gerineldos, madam,
	vuestro tan querido amigo.'	your beloved friend.")

In contrast to the initial exchange between the two individuals, the roles are now reversed. It is Gerineldos who has assumed the initiative and it is the princess whose hesitancy underlines the step which they are about to take. The parallel between line 2 (the princess's epithet for Gerineldos and the indication of her attraction to him) and line 20 (Gerineldos' epithet for the woman and the indication in turn of his physical attraction toward his mistress) serves to bring out the interrelationship of their desires. Their will has become one and through the device of showing them as addressing each other in similar terms, the minstrel has us see that neither is after all more dominant than the other in the affair which is now reaching its conclusion.

The interrelationship between Gerineldos and the princess is reinforced by the depiction at this point of her hesitation in opening the door to the man. Each has been aggressive in speaking to the other, but both have hesitated out of some sort of caution, if only momentarily. Their respective moments of hesitation may best be interpreted as the suggestion of an awareness that their actions are illicit and therefore deserving of a second thought. In this way the ballad, without the necessity for the narrative voice to intervene and state matters directly, organizes its narrative presentation so that we are aware of the events which are taking place and also of having some idea of the "psychological" reaction of the protagonists to those events which they are experiencing or shaping before our eyes. The dual aggressiveness and the dual demurral are more than simply narrative elaboration on the part of the minstrel(s). The two circumstances (lines 1–12 and lines 18–24) demonstrate one way in which a ballad may attempt to make us aware of the principals' own conscious involvement in their actions. In this ballad, such an indication is of some importance to the extent that the appearance of the King and his anger over what he discovers will demand from the audience a position vis-à-vis the two lovers. We suggest that the poem has, in the development of the tryst between the two young people and its fulfillment (cf. the explicit details of lines 25–28), made it clear that both are fully conscious of their actions and both have proceeded with a frankness uncharacteristic of the restraint of courtly love. Gerineldos' use in lines 23–24 of "mistress" and "friend" are only further ironic variations on the forthright agreement between the two to satisfy their physical desires. Meanwhile, the girl's father has been dreaming:

	Recordado había el rey	(The King had awakened
30	*del sueño despavorido,*	frightened from a dream.
	tres veces lo había llamado,	Three times had he called
	ninguna le ha respondido.	and not once was he answered.
	'Gerineldos, Gerineldos,	"Gerineldos, Gerineldos,
	mi camarero pulido,	my handsome valet,
35	*¿si me andas en traición,*	are you betraying me,
	trátasme como a enemigo?	treating me like an enemy?
	O con la infanta dormías	Either you are sleeping with the Infanta
	o el alcázar me has vendido.'	or you have sold my castle.")

The King's dream (and note that the ballad avoids identifying him as Charlemagne) is technically less a prophecy than a vision, a dream in which events that are in fact taking place or which have taken place are revealed to the sleeper in true or in allegorical form. Here, the latter appears to be the case, for the King awakens with only a vague idea of what has occurred. He only knows that some act of treachery involving Gerineldos is at issue. With reference to the dream, the composition has shifted from the relationship between the two adolescents to an investigation of how their illicit deed is discovered and how the situation will be resolved. To this extent, where the first half of the ballad has been more concerned with describing the coming together of Gerineldos and the princess, with any editorial comment being more implied than stated, the second portion of the poem is directly concerned with a moral position toward the sinful fulfillment of desire that has occurred. It is in this first characterization of the King and his dream that the phrase of lines 1–2 is repeated. In lines 33–34, the King unknowingly repeats his daughter's words concerning the page (does he hear her in his dream?). The repetition is ironic since it refers to completely different attitudes toward the man, as well as introducing at this point the King's discovery of his page's treachery, a treachery which was initiated by the woman's earlier use of the phrase. The repetition, therefore, functions to tie the two halves of the ballad together and to prefigure the significant—and logical—differences of attitude between father and daughter toward the behavior of the page. In terms of other dreams described in the *Romancero viejo,* it is worth noting that we are not told the nature of the King's dream, only his reaction. His own interpretation in lines 37–38 is intriguing: one would like to know which allegorical figures narrow down to the choice mentioned by the concerned monarch.

The last segment of the ballad describes the father's discovery that his first interpretation was indeed accurate. He prepares to avenge himself for his page's perfidy:

45 *Sacara luego la espada,*	(Then he took out his sword
entre entrambos la ha metido,	and placed it between the two,
para que al volver del sueño	so that when they awoke
catasen que el yerro ha visto.	they would know that he had seen their error.
Recordado hubo la infanta,	The Infanta had awakened,
50 *vio la espada y dio un suspiro:*	saw the sword and sighed.
'Recordar heis, Gerineldos,	"Wake up, Gerineldos,
que ya érades sentido;	for you have been heard.
que la espada de mi padre	My father's sword

de nuestro yerro es testigo.'	is witness to our error."
55 *Gerineldos va a su estancia,*	Gerineldos returns to his quarters
le sale el rey de improviso:	and the King suddenly comes up to him:
'¿Donde vienes, Gerineldos,	"Whence do you come, Gerineldos,
tan mustio, descolorido?'	so gloomy and pale?"
'Del jardín vengo, señor,	"I come from the garden, sire,
60 *de coger flores y lirios,*	from picking flowers and lilies,
y la rosa más fragante	and the most fragrant rose of all
mis colores ha comido.'	has sapped all my color."
'¡Mientes, mientes Gerineldos,	"You lie, you lie, Gerineldos,
que con la infanta has dormido;	you've slept with the Infanta.
65 *testigo de ella mi espada,*	My sword is her witness
en su filo está el castigo.'	and its blade is your punishment.")

The most significant aspect of these closing lines is the comportment of Gerineldos. Now completely satisfied with his handling
of the affair with the princess, he appears before her father with
an impertinence which, we must assume, is disconsonant with his
former loyal service. The girl's words to him when they awaken
and discover the father's sword between them is a frank admission
of error. The use of the latter word tends, one notes, to indicate
that a point of honor is involved rather than any issue of morality
and sin. In turn, when the King confronts him, Gerineldos strikes
an attitude of nonchalance that contrasts with the obvious intensity
of the King's emotions, wronged by his page both as a father and
as a lord.

Perhaps the best part of the ballad is Gerineldos' response to
the monarch's rhetorical demand to know whence he comes.
Gerineldos replies that he comes from the garden, where he has
been plucking flowers, notably the most fragrant rose of all (lines
59–62). The King calls him a liar and promises him the just punishment by the sword that has been a witness to his treachery. On
one level the exchange between the two men is to be taken at face
value. Gerineldos attempts to hide his earlier whereabouts, but
the King's angry knowledge makes his attempted deceit that much
more impertinent, precipitating accusations and revenge. On another level, however, Gerineldos' words are symbolically correct.
One of the most frequent commonplaces of medieval literature is
that of the rose.[13] *Collige rosas* ("Gather ye rosebuds [while ye
may]") is the injunction to man to take advantage of his youth

and of the abandoned sensuality symbolized by the rites of May. Thus, when Gerineldos assures his master that he has been in the garden plucking flowers and that he has plucked the most fragrant rose of all, he is speaking with a cheeky frankness that the King is, however, unable to grasp, supposedly because he does not catch the figurative sexual allusion of the page's words. Indeed, the effect of these lines—and it cannot be construed as any accident that Gerineldos speaks of his recent activities in terms of the "garden of love"—depends on the audience's ability to understand how his answer is in a figurative way really an open admission of his relations with the princess. Of course, the origin of Gerineldos' reply may be attributable to an unknown minstrel familiar with courtly symbologies. Despite audience ignorance, the allusion may have been retained in the diffusion of the ballad simply as one reasonably impertinent, irrelevant response to the infuriated master. For any reader, however, familiar with the commonplace of the rose, Gerineldos' words increase in meaning. Not only are they just simply impertinent, since he knows that the father has discovered the two sleeping together, but they are also a taunt thrown in the King's face. By admitting openly to his defloration of the princess, the page is that much more impertinent. The fact that he speaks symbolically in a manner that the King cannot understand is, from our point of view, the crowning insult and one which justifies for us the vengeful violence to which he is about to fall victim.

Although we realize it more than does the King, Gerineldos' behavior has been of the greatest treachery. Not only has he taken advantage of his mistress's awakened desires; he has thrown in her father's face his and her betrayal as well. In this way, the ballad makes certain that the audience will accept the righteous indignation shown by the wronged father and the wronged master, and we leave Gerineldos confident that he will receive the punishment that he has earned in his own reprehensible behavior, for which he must now be responsible before the *temporal* lord against whom he has erred most grievously. Regardless of any affiliation with Carolingian materials and their cultural backgrounds, the ballad "Gerineldos" is understandable enough within a feudal or Christian context that places a premium upon man's responsibility to his lord (and/or Lord) and the castigation which must befall him for any betrayal of that responsibility. That Gerineldos is in the end impenitent is for us the best justification of all for his lord's righteous vengeance. In this sense, the ballad exploits in stark terms the contrast between the sensual abandonment of the lovers in the first half of the composition and their discovery by the King and its consequences in the final portion of the work. It is a stark contrast that recalls for the audience the antithesis between licentious selfishness and harsh responsibility that underlies Western civilization in so many recurrent ways.

IV *Summing Up*

Our comments on three representative Carolingian ballads have followed the same procedure accorded other more "national" compositions examined in the three preceding chapters. By examining these texts derived in some vague sort of way from extra-Peninsular sources we have hoped to show that, while certain superficial characteristics do substantiate their classification as an autonomous group, the process of traditionalization responsible for their development in Spain and for the form(s) in which they survive has treated them as nothing more nor less than ballads. The result has been, therefore, that while superficially distinguishing characteristics remain, beyond their often unwieldy length, the rhetorical organization and the artistic quality of the Carolingian group do not differ in any major way from the three other groups that we have considered. In the last analysis, as ballads these texts lend themselves to the same type of approach and to the same sort of understanding as excellent and sophisticated poetry of popular appeal as do the more typically "Spanish" selections of the *Romancero viejo*.

CHAPTER 7

Concluding Remarks

THE foregoing analysis in depth of major examples of the early Spanish ballads is unmistakably indicative of a desire—and the implied affirmation of a necessity—to examine those ballads as examples of autonomous poetic art. In approaching them in such a manner so apparently antithetical to their customary treatment by Spanish literary historians, we have neither avoided the issue of a "poetry that lives in variants" nor have we affirmed the anonymous presence of single, individual authors. As has hopefully been made clear in Chapter 2, by shifting emphasis from the circumstances of poetic *genesis* to those of textual *existence,* it is possible to select an important and widely accepted variant and to discuss in a productive manner the meaning and value of an excellent artefact that may have, incidentally, been wrought by several competent hands. One other logical procedure, not employed in this study, would be to study as autonomous pieces all known variants of a given ballad toward establishing the aesthetic superiority of certain ones over the others.

Our extensive comments on the rhetorical and structural features that support meaning and result in poetic artistry may appear overly detailed to those critics who prefer a brief synthesis—an abstract— of a poem rather than a description in detail of the devices involved in the understanding and appreciation of a text. Nevertheless, the existence of numerous overviews of the Spanish ballad, whose importance in the literary heritage of Spain has favored it with generous critical attention, argues for a presentation of the works that will place greater emphasis on the ballad as poetry than has been forthcoming in even more recent research, which, if anything, has tended more toward the anthropological. Furthermore, the availability of Entwistle's superb study, all the more valuable for the contextualization of the Spanish ballad within the European tradition, renders less urgent a repetition in English of the well-established generalities of the subject.

Far from eschewing the importance of critical discussion within the framework of significant commentaries of literary history, the examination which we have presented of major ballad texts has relied on established opinion for the purpose of seeing the works themselves within the larger context of medieval traditions. Indeed our examination has in many instances pretended to provide, on the basis of an analysis of intrinsic features, a more solid validation of accepted interpretations. This was, indeed, the case with the ballad of the Infante Arnaldos. The study of literature which emphasizes and dwells on the characteristics of organization, audience appeal, and aesthetic procedures no more pretends to ignore the larger issues of literary heritage and tradition than does the poet pretend to ignore the universal problems of mankind when he addresses himself to the suffering of one man's soul. There is a synecdochical relationship that obtains inescapably in both instances and which provides a necessary basis for comprehension. Nevertheless, each manifestation of a universal pattern is obviously unique in many important ways, and therein lies the value and the attraction of the individual.

As is the case with any literary tradition, the early Spanish Ballad is constituted by an enormous bulk of works but remembered and prized for the brilliance and the profundity of a human vision given great artistic form in only a few of those works. If the present introduction to the early Spanish ballad has accomplished anything beyond the preliminary characterization of a singular literary phenomenon, it has been the attempt to give a careful representation of and validation to the artistic substance, the artistic organization, and the artistic realization of the most valuable and aesthetically sophisticated examples of that tradition. As Menéndez Pidal himself observed on more than one occasion, the ballads may have been passed from mouth to mouth as part of a rustic and popular tradition, but there is no doubt that the ballads in general and the best versions in particular are manifestations of a poetic artistry of no mean competence. The most that any critical commentary can hope to achieve is a convincing characterization of that undeniable competence. "Infante Arnaldos" may not be a poetics of the ballad. But the seaman's injunction is nevertheless applicable: it is only when we have committed ourselves fully to experience a composition in all of its multiple details that we may begin to understand the mystery of its song.

Appendix on Ballad Metrics

The Spanish ballad makes use of two basic metric phenomena: octosyllabic verse and assonantal rhyme.

1. *Octosyllabic Verse*

The basis of Spanish versification is the metric syllable, a poetic convention based on various accommodations of the syllabic unit of Spanish phonology. Although the linguistic analysis of the latter may reveal different criteria,[1] the syllable as it is used in Spanish poetry is defined by the following assumptions:

    a. Each unitary vowel is considered to constitute one syllable. This excludes combinations of vowels that occur when one word ends in a vowel and the next word begins with a vowel (see b. below).

Thus the line:

El / que / da/ba / dig/ni/da/des
1   2   3 4   5 6 7 8

    b. Any combination of vowels created when one word ends in a vowel and the next word begins with a vowel is usually treated metrically as one vowel (see, however, h. below), the running together being called *sinalefa* (synaloepha); thus syllable 4:

A / ca/za / va el / rey / don / Pe/dro
1   2 3   4   5   6   7 8

    c. Within words, "strong vowels" (*a-e-o*) that occur in combinations count metrically as one vowel apiece; "diphthongs"— combinations of weak vowels (*i-u*), or combinations of unstressed weak and strong vowels—count metrically as one vowel: thus syllables 3 and 4, and 2 and 7, respectively, in these lines:

de / la he/bre/a / san/gre in/gra/ta
1   2   3 4   5   6   7 8
po/nién/do/le / va / más / mie/do
1 2   3 4   5   6   7 8

    d. Combinations described in b. which do not count as one metric vowel—i.e., where the two adjacent vowels count as two separate syllables—rarely occur. When found, they exemplify *hiato* (hiatus); thus syllables 1 and 2:

yo / a / vos / o/tro / da/rí/a
1   2   3   4 5   6 7 8

e. A strong vowel and a stressed weak vowel count metrically as separate vowels; thus syllables 7 and 8:

yo / a / vos / o/tro / da/rí/a
1   2   3   4 5   6 7 8

f. Combinations of weak vowels or weak and strong vowels, described in c., which do not count as one syllable, are also infrequent. Where found, they constitute *diéresis* (diaeresis). Each vowel counts as one metric syllable; thus syllables 6 and 7:

por/que es / el mo/ro i/dï/o/ta
1   2   3   4   5 6 7 8

g. Combinations may be found of strong vowels, which usually would count as one metric syllable per vowel, that will count as one metric syllable per combination. This is *sinéresis* (syneresis), and also included is the circumstance where a stressed weak vowel and a strong vowel—which usually count separately—may count as one metric syllable; thus syllable 3:

co/mo hé/roe / lo / pro/cla/ma/ron
1   2   3   4   5   6   7   8

h. Combinations resulting from words that end in a vowel or a diphthong followed by a word beginning with a vowel or another diphthong usually count as one metric syllable, although *hiato* may occur; thus syllables 4 and 3 and 4, respectively:

el / prin /ci/pio y / fin / del / can/to
1   2   3   4   5   6   7 8

La / glo/ria / e/ra / com/ple/ta
1   2   3   4 5   6   7   8

i. The preceding sections cover the phenomena leading to octosyllabic count most likely to be found in the ballads. Note that orthographic combinations consisting of initial *h* followed by *u* plus another vowel or of initial *h* followed by *i* plus another vowel will usually be treated in Spanish poetry as a sequence of two vowels, while orthographic combinations consisting of *y* followed by a vowel will always be treated as a consonant/vowel sequence. Some dialectical variation renders this observation only partially true; nevertheless, it holds for most poetry.

j. Sections a. to h. all apply regardless of the ending of the last word in a line. Spanish poetry always assumes that a line ends in an unstressed syllable preceded immediately by a stressed one; thus *canto* of h. above. This is an assumption that usually does obtain in reality. However, if a line ends in a stressed vowel, the last vowel counts as two metric syllables (i.e., it is taken as consisting of the stressed syllable followed by a "dummy" unstressed syllable):

Ál/ce/se   /   lue/go   el   /   re/al
1   2   3   4   5   6 7 8

y   aun/que   /   va   /   de   /   San/ta/ Fe
1   2   3   4   5   6 7 8

cu/ya   /   cla/rí/fi/ca   /   luz
1   2   3 4 5 6   7 8

The *Romancero viejo* abounds in lines of this sort. The ideal "extra" syllable most frequently is the result of an *e* which may be present—for sound etymological reasons—in the medieval form of the word, but which has been dropped in modern Spanish. Thus, medieval *tomare* (i.e., the infinitive) alternates in texts with modern *tomar*, *vivide* with *vivid*, *reale* with *real*, etc. Note however the conservation of this *e* in plurals: modern *real* vs. *reales*, *luz* vs. *luces*, etc. Older texts may show the *e*, may insert a paragogic *e* that has no etymological justification, or simply alternate lines consisting of a stressed syllable followed by unstressed *e* with lines consisting of a stressed syllable alone that are supposed to match (see e. below). In every case, eight metric syllables must be derived from a line that, when principles a. to h. are taken into consideration, shows eight actual syllables or only seven.[2]

2. *Assonantal Rhyme*

Assonantal rhyme—feminine rhyme in English and French metrics—involves the last two metric syllables of a line of poetry.

a. Where the last two metric syllables are two actual syllables of one vowel each, the rhyme is based on a one-to-one correspondence between the respective vowels in each position; thus the final words of these assonanting lines:

     . . . la hubo entreg*ado*
     . . . hubo mostr*ado*
     . . . su cab*allo*
     . . . la m*ano*
     . . . iba rode*ado*

b. When one of the vowels consists of a diphthong, as in examples 2, 5, 7, 8 below, only the strong vowel segment or mora is involved in the rhyme:

     . . . su est*ado*
     . . . había cri*ado*
     . . . deshered*ado*

     . . . líquida pl*ata*
     . . . de Ar*abia*
     . . . se des*angra*

     . . . del r*eino*
     . . . como fi*ero*
     . . . con el d*edo*

c. Consonants, therefore, play no role whatever, and may or may not be present between the last two rhyming vowels of a line:

     . . . Muza pas*ea*
     . . . la gu*erra*

d. Accidental masculine or consonantal rhyme may occur, particularly when parts of speech tending to rhyme consonantally are involved, such as verb forms. For example, three past participles rhyme assonantally as well as consonantally in 2. a. above, lines 1, 2, and 5.

e. Where rhymed lines end in a stressed vowel that counts as two metric syllables, rhyme is on the basis of the stressed vowels alone (column one) or on the basis of the stressed vowel and the etymological or paragogic *e* (column two):

. . . oí toc*ar*	. . . oí toc*are*
. . . de Abid*ar*	. . . de Abid*are*
. . . fuerte capit*án*	. . . fuerte capit*áne*
. . . el C*id*	. . . el C*ide*
. . . de reñ*ir*	. . . de reñ*ire*
. . . que fu*ir*	. . . que fu*ire*

f. Assonantal rhyme is formally represented by giving the two vowels together, separated by a dash: "a ballad with *a-e* assonance." In the case of circumstance e., it is "a ballad with *a* assonance" or "with *a-e* assonance" when the text includes the added *e*.

g. In the Spanish ballads, assonantal rhyme involves the fifteenth and sixteenth syllables of every sixteen-syllabled sequence. Thus, if the text reproduces the ballad arranged as sixteen-syllable verses, with caesura between the two octosyllabic hemistichs forming each verse, the lines will all rhyme assonantally. On the other hand, if the text reproduces the ballad arranged in octosyllabic verses—as modern anthologies have tended to do and as we do in this study—then only the lines of even number will rhyme assonantally. As observed in Chapter 1, with the exception of some historical ballads, any given ballad tends to have only one assonantal rhyme throughout.

Notes to Appendix

1. For an analysis of the differences between the syllabic unit of Spanish poetry and of the modern colloquial language, see David W. Foster, "A Phonological Grammar of Spanish Metrics," *Boletín de filología* [Universidad de Chile], 20 (1968), 211–27.

2. Although it is literally absent from the *Romancero viejo,* the converse circumstance of j. can occur in Spanish poetry. This is where a line ends in a stressed syllable followed by two unstressed syllables *(verso esdrújulo).* The two unstressed syllables count as only one metric syllable, and either or both may be involved with the stressed syllable in the sequence of assonantal rhyme. This pattern is exemplified by the following line from a modern ballad by Federico García Lorca:

Yo / nun/ca / lle/ga/ré a / Cór/doba
1   2   3   4   5   6   7   8

Notes and References
Selected Bibliography
Index

Notes and References

Chapter One

1. Princeton, N.J.: Princeton University Press, 1965, pp. 62–63. See also the article on the Spanish ballad, "Romance," pp. 712–13. For an examination of the Spanish ballad within the context of European balladry, see W. J. Entwistle, *European Balladry* (Oxford: The Clarendon Press, 1939).

2. Ruth DeMar Weber, in her doctoral dissertation published as "Formulistic Diction in the Spanish Ballad," *University of California Publications in Modern Philology,* 34, No. 2 (1951), 175–277, stresses the relationships between formulistic diction in the ballad and research on similar phenomena in folk poetry. To the extent that the ballads have their origins in the epic, Edmund De Chasca's discussion of the problem of folk poetry and formulistic diction in the epic is pertinent: "La literatura oral ante la crítica," Chapter II of his *El arte juglaresco en el "Cantar de Mio Cid"* (Madrid: Gredos, 1967). De Chasca, whose study is one of the most important analyses of the Cid epic to date, is in essential agreement with the thesis developed later in this study that, whatever the origins of oral poetry, the result is equally "literary" and subject to literary analysis. Weber's monograph, basically statistical in nature, supports the anthropological, neo-Romantic view concerning the "primitive" nature of formulistic diction.

3. A full discussion of this term is provided by Ludwig Pfandl, "La palabra española *romance,*" *Investigaciones lingüisticas,* 2 (1934), 242–62.

4. Several basic studies present the development of the phenomena of Vulgar Latin; especially useful for the beginner is Charles Hall Grandgent's *An Introduction to Vulgar Latin* (New York: Hafner, 1962 [orig. 1934]).

5. The best synoptic presentation of the emergence of literatures in the Romance languages and the struggle of ascendency of the latter over Latin is given by Erich Auerbach, *Introduction to Romance Languages and Literature* (New York: Capricorn Books, 1961).

6. The best expression of this thesis is to be found in Ramón Menéndez Pidal, *El Romancero español* (New York: Hispanic Society of America, 1910).

7. Ramón Menéndez Pidal, in *Poesía juglaresca y juglares* (Madrid: Espasa-Calpe, 1956 [orig. 1924]), discusses in detail the problem and implications of popular reception of essentially nonpopular literature.

8. Santillana's fifteenth-century *Prologue* . . . is the first written recognition of the contemporary *romances.* An analysis of his comments is

provided by W. C. Atkinson, "The Interpretation of 'Romances e cantares' in Santillana," *Hispanic Review,* 4 (1936), 1–10; and Dorothy Clotelle Clarke, "Remarks on the Early 'romances' and 'cantares'," *Hispanic Review,* 17 (1949), 89–123.

9. There are several important elaborations of this point: Bruce A. Beatie, "Oral-Traditional Composition in the Spanish Romancero of the Sixteenth Century," *Journal of Folklore Institute,* 1 (1964), 92–113; Diego Catalán Menéndez Pidal, "El 'motivo' y la 'variación' en la transmisión tradicional del Romancero," *Bulletin hispanique,* 61 (1959), 149–82; Daniel Devoto, "Sobre el estudio folklórico del Romancero español. Proposición para un método de estudio de la transmisión tradicional," *Bulletin hispanique,* 57 (1955), 233–91; María Goyri, "Romances que deben buscarse en la tradición oral," *Revista de archivos, bibliotecas y museos,* 15 (1906), 374–86 and 16 (1907), 24–36; Ramón Menéndez Pidal, "Le 'Romancero' et l'état latent de la poésie épique," *La table ronde,* No. 133 (1959), 136–43.

10. This type of composition, to be sure, may survive in several widely divergent versions. Nevertheless, the assumption is that there is a definable chronology for the versions and that, although it may not be the best from an objective extrinsic point of view, the last version is the poet's finished product.

11. Concerning the ballad in Spanish America, see Merle E. Simmons, *A Bibliography of the Romance and Related Forms in Spanish America* (Bloomington: Indiana University Press, 1963). This is an extremely thorough annotated guide to the *Romancero* in Latin America in general and in individual countries.

12. An indication of the importance of the Sephardic tradition is given by Ramón Menéndez Pidal in his "Catálogo del Romancero judío-español," in *Los romances de América y otros estudios* (Buenos Aires: Espasa-Calpe Argentina, 1939), pp. 128–99.

13. Pedro Salinas gives a rundown on the interest by contemporary Spanish poets in the ballad metre in "El romancismo y el siglo XX," in *Estudios hispánicos, homenaje a Archer Milton Huntington* (Wellesley, Mass.: Wellesley College Spanish Department, 1952), pp. 499–527.

14. For a discussion of these relationships see the previously cited work by Ramón Menéndez Pidal, *Poesía juglaresca y juglares,* as well as his study on the Spanish epic, *La epopeya castellana a través de la literatura española* (Buenos Aires: Espasa-Calpe, 1945 [originally published in French in 1910]).

15. This perpetuation of the ballad is presented by Ramón Menéndez Pidal in his study *Cómo vivió y cómo vive el Romancero* (Valencia: López Mezquita, 1947), as well as in previously mentioned studies by the same scholar. Critical exception is taken to some segments of Menéndez Pidal's thesis by P. Rajna, "Osservazioni e dubbi concernenti la storia delle romanze spagnuole," *Romanic Review,* 6 (1915), 1–41. Rajna's article reflects the

inability of many reputable scholars to accept what was then a radical hypothesis. Such doubts were—and still are—valid to the extent that Menéndez Pidal's arguments are meant to be all-inclusive and therefore all-exclusive as far as other major theories of ballad origins are concerned.

16. See in this regard the previously mentioned study by Diego Catalán Menéndez Pidal, "El 'motivo' y la 'variación' . . ." (note 9).

17. A major example of this interest is the ballad poetry of Federico Garcia Lorca (1899–1936), whose *Romancero gitano* (*Gypsy Ballads*; 1927), is a major document of the period. See Daniel Devoto, "García Lorca y los Romanceros," *Quaderni ibero-americani*, 3 (1956), 249–51.

18. Ramón Menéndez Pidal discusses this point in the latter part of his series of articles, "Poesía popular y Romancero," *Revista de filología española,* 1 (1914), 357–77; 2 (1915), 1–20, 105–36, 329–38; 3 (1916), 233–89.

19. D. Bodmer traces the development of the frontier ballads dealing with Granada in *Die granadinischen Romanzen in der europäischen Literatur. Untersuchen und Texte* (Zurich: Jruis, 1955). Manuel Alvar Lopez also analyzes the ballads on Granada—clearly the most popular and traditional examples of *romances fronterizos*—in *Granada y el Romancero* (Granada: Universidad, 1956).

20. Luis Seco de Lucena Paredes, for example, argues for later composition during the sixteenth century in his monograph, . . . *Investigaciones sobre el Romancero. Estudio de tres romances fronterizos* (Granada: Universidad, 1958).

21. Concerning the Renaissance Moorish ballads, see Glenroy Emmons, "The Historical and Literary Perspective of the 'Romances moriscos novelescos,'" *Hispania,* 44 (1961), 254–59.

22. Américo Castro makes much of this cohabitation, which included also of course the Jews, in his famous *The Structure of Spanish History* (Princeton, N.J.: Princeton University Press, 1954 [originally published in Spanish in 1948]).

23. Ramón Menéndez Pidal made a major contribution to the extension of his theories on the Spanish epic and ballad to the French works with *La Chanson de Roland y el Neotradicionalismo. Orígenes de la épica románica* (Madrid: Espasa-Calpe, 1959).

24. Ernst Robert Curtius, *European Literature and the Latin Middle Ages* (New York: Pantheon Books, 1953 [originally published in German in 1948]), documents this assertion, a major thesis of his study of the relationship between European literature and the Latin literary tradition.

25. This group is discussed by Pedro Luis Barcia, *El mester de clerecía* (Buenos Aires: Centro Editor de América Latina, 1967).

26. Such an interpretation is developed in detail by Karl Heisig, "Die Geschichtsmetaphysik des Rolandsliedes und ihre Vorgeschichte," *Zeitschrift für romanische Philologie,* 55 (1935), 1–87.

27. *La Chanson de Roland dans les littératures française et espagnole* (Paris: Les Belles Lettres, 1951), "Les Romances," pp. 503–28.

28. Ramón Menéndez Pidal, " 'Roncesvalles.' Un nuevo cantar de gesta espanol del siglo XIII," *Revista de filologia española,* 4 (1917), 105–204. Reprinted in a drastically cut form in *Tres poemas primitivos* (Buenos Aires: Espasa-Calpe, 1948), pp. 45–79.

29. Ramón Menéndez Pidal gathers together the pertinent evidence in *Reliquias de la poesía épica española* (Madrid: Espasa-Calpe, 1951).

30. See the studies on the music of the *Romancero* listed in the Bibliography. One notes surprisingly little research on a very important aspect of the ballads.

31. Spanish ballads may appear printed with verses of eight syllables— representing the individual hemistichs—or with verses of sixteen syllables —representing the rhyming unit. S. G. Armistead and J. H. Silverman assert that the latter representation is currently favored; see their review of C. Colin Smith's *Spanish Ballads* (which uses the former representation) in *Hispanic Review,* 37 (1969), 407–12. Concerning the issues surrounding development of this format, consult G. Cirot, "Le mouvement quaternaire dans les romances," *Bulletin hispanique,* 21 (1919), 103–42; Dorothy Clotelle Clarke, "Metric Problems in the 'Cancionero de romances,'" *Hispanic Review,* 23 (1955), 188–99; S. Griswold Morley, "Are the Spanish Romances Written in Quatrains?—and Other Questions," *Romanic Review,* 7 (1916), 42–82.

32. A commonplace assertion, given statistical support by Oliver T. Myers, "Syntactic and Formal Correlatives with Rhythm in the Spanish Octosyllable," *Romance Philology,* 20 (1967), 478–88.

33. *A History of Literary Criticism, 1750–1950* (New Haven, Conn.: Yale University Press, 1955–), Vol II, "Romanticism."

34. Curtius' study, note 24 above, was conceived as a "correction" to the belief, still persistent and basically Romantic in origin, that European literature in the Romance vernaculars developed autonomously—and somehow "popularly"—with little indebtedness to the thriving medieval Latin tradition, the direct descendant of the literature of Classical Antiquity.

35. Ramón Menéndez Pidal summarizes this position in his refutation of the Romantic thesis in the previously cited *El Romancero español.*

36. *Über die Romanzen-Poesie der Spanier* (Wien: Gerold, 1847).

37. Ramón Menéndez Pidal reviews the French position in his article, "Origins of Spanish Literature Considered in Relation to the Origin of Romance Literature," *Cahiers d'histoire mondiale,* 1 (1961), 752–70. Published for a French academic audience, the article is important for the Spaniard's reasons for rejecting the individualistic thesis.

38. We have already referred to Menéndez Pidal's work on the French epic in note 23 above.

39. R. Foulché-Delbosc, an eminent French Hispanist, advances the

individualistic position in *Essai sur les origines du Romancero. Prélude* (Paris: F. Paillart, 1912 [published in Spanish in 1914]). Ramón Menéndez Pidal's expected rebuttal came in "Los orígenes del Romancero," in *Los romances de América y otros estudios* (Buenos Aires: Espasa-Calpe Argentina, 1939), pp. 95–115. (The rebuttal was originally published in 1914.) Rajna, in his article cited above in note 15, was also a proponent of individualism in epic and ballad origins.

40. Manuel Milá y Fontanals' pioneering work on the fragmentation of the epics, with the ballads as a direct result, was first published in 1874: *De la poesía heroico-popular castellana* (Barcelona: Consejo Superior de Investigaciones Científicas, 1959). Although followed by Marcelino Menéndez y Pelayo, the first modern comprehensive critic of Spanish literature, and given fullest elaboration by Menéndez Pidal, Milá's work is actually the starting point in Spanish ballad criticism for the anti-Romantic, fragmentation theory.

41. The enormous importance of Menéndez Pidal's work, evident in the preceding notes, is surveyed by Ruth House Weber, "Ramón Menéndez Pidal and the Romancero," *Romance Philology,* 5 (1951), 15–25.

42. G. J. Geers, "El problema de los romances," *Neophilologus,* 5 (1920), 193–99.

43. "The Folkloristic Prestage of the Spanish Romance 'Conde Arnaldos,'" *Hispanic Review,* 23 (1955), 173–87; 24 (1956), 64–66. This article was later published in Spanish; see entry in the Bibliography.

44. Already cited in note 9. See also Bruce A. Beatie's study cited in note 9.

45. Note must also be taken of the dissertation by Hugh Nelson Seay, Jr., "A Classification of Motifs in the Traditional Ballad of Spain," *Dissertation Abstracts,* 19 (1959), 2052 (North Carolina), an analysis based on the Stith Thompson master outline of folklore motifs.

46. We will quote from the later edition, still in print, by Espasa-Calpe Argentina (Buenos Aires, 1938, etc.).

Chapter Two

1. For example, Sir Walter Scott's important early collection, *Minstrelsy of the Scottish Border* (1802–1803).

2. This difficulty prevails for literary history oriented towards authors, national literatures, mutual influences, and interrelationships between works and traditions. Trends in literary analysis that deemphasize the "authorial" point of view to stress internal structure or the relationship between a work and its audience do not find treating folk literature particularly difficult. For a presentation of research on the ties between folk and "artistic" literature, see Augusto Raúl Cortázar, *Folklore y literatura* (Buenos Aires: Editorial Universitaria de Buenos Aires, 1964).

3. See Ramón Menéndez Pidal, "Sobre geografía folklórica. Ensayo de un método," *Revista de filología española,* 7 (1920), 229–338; and *Cómo vivió y cómo vive el Romancero* (Valencia: López Mezquita, 1947).

4. Such speculation is found in the remark by Ángel Ganivet (1862–1898) that "Our theological and philosophical *Summa* is to be found in our *Romancero*" *(Idearium español* [1896]).

5. See René Wellek and Austin Warren's summary of these tendencies in their *Theory of Literature,* 3rd ed. (New York: Harcourt, Brace and World, 1962), Chapter Four, "Literary Theory, Criticism, and History."

6. It is to be remembered, however, that the printing of ballad anthologies in the sixteenth century corresponds with the decline of interest among the educated in the *Romancero viejo* and the rise of the *Romancero nuevo,* the Renaissance ballad tradition inspired by, but radically different in form and content from the medieval *romances.* It is not until the nineteenth century that there is a renewed interest among the scholarly and educated upper class in the medieval ballad, both in its pre-Renaissance form and in its surviving popular manifestations.

7. For example in Daniel Devoto, "Sobre el estudio folklórico del Romancero español. Proposición para un método de estudio de la transmisión tradicional," *Bulletin hispanique,* 57 (1955), 233–91.

8. Concerning the mythic perspective of conscious art, see Richard Chase, *The Quest for Myth* (Baton Rouge, La.: Louisiana State University Press, 1949).

9. "El problema de los romances," *Neophilologus,* 5 (1920), 193–99.

10. This position is carried to rather absurd conclusions, we believe, by Manuel Álvar López, who maintains as the focus of his study, "Patología y terapéutica rapsódicas. Cómo una canción se convierte en romance," *Revista de filología española,* 42 (1958–59), 19–35, that the popular tradition embodies therapeutic correctives for the pathologically afflicted ballad, resulting in the latter's rhapsodic reconstitution as a new and presumably healthier variant. If López Álvar were not a distinguished scholar, it would be easier to brush aside such assertions. Coming from a respected student of the Spanish ballad, they are that much more indicative of prevailing attitudes. For the more normal traditionalist opinion, see Ramón Menéndez Pidal, "Poesía tradicional en el Romancero hispano-portugués," in *Castilla: la tradición, el idioma,* 3a ed. (Madrid: Espasa-Calpe, 1955), pp. 41–74.

11. Geers, *op. cit.,* p. 196; the quote is from an uncited text by Menéndez Pidal of an observation made by Menéndez y Pelayo in 1876.

12. For a summary of these trends in contemporary criticism, see René Wellek, "American Literary Scholarship" and "The Main Trends of Twentieth-Century Criticism," both in his *Concepts of Criticism* (New Haven: Yale University Press, 1963), pp. 296–315 and 344–64, respectively.

13. The seminal works of Claude Levi-Strauss have been influential in the acceptance of these ideas.

14. As maintained by Gerard Genette, *Estructuralismo y crítica literaria* (Córdoba, Argentina: Editorial Universitaria de Córdoba, 1967).

15. Bruce A. Beatie summarizes this work in his article, "Oral-Traditional Composition in the Spanish Romancero of the Sixteenth Century," *Journal of Folklore Institute,* 1 (1964), 92–113.

16. Recent research on the rhetorical sophistication of the supposedly "ingenuous" poetry of Gonzalo de Berceo (13th century) is revealing. See the monographs by Joaquín Artiles, *Los recursos literarios de Berceo* (Madrid: Gredos, 1964) and Carmelo Gariano, *Análisis estilístico de los "Milagros de Nuestra Señora" de Berceo* (Madrid: Gredos, 1965).

17. In a recent article, Robert Goldwater discusses the problems presented by indigenous African art: where the anthropologist is only willing to consider origins and functions, the artist and the art critic are concerned with intrinsic aesthetic qualities, qualities which a supposedly "primitive and pragmatic" art shares in common with major aesthetic tendencies of twentieth-century European art. Goldwater offers a convincing affirmative answer to the question as to whether, despite its "non-aesthetic" genesis, indigenous African art can be considered aesthetically excellent and discussed accordingly. See "Black is Beautiful," *New York Review of Books,* 13, No. 11 (December 18, 1969), 36–40.

18. "Formulistic Diction in the Spanish Ballad," *University of California Publications in Modern Philology,* 34, No. 2 (1951), 175–277. Bruce A. Beatie, *op. cit.,* expresses some serious reservations concerning Weber's study.

19. A synthetic statement of these principles is given by Fredson Bowers, "Textual Criticism," in James Thorpe, *The Aims and Methods of Scholarship in Modern Languages and Literatures* (New York: Modern Language Association of America, 1963), pp. 23–42.

20. "The Aesthetics of Textual Criticism," *PMLA,* 80 (1965), 465–82.

21. See the studies analyzed by Helmut Hatzfeld, "Esthetic Criticism Applied to Medieval Romance Literature," *Romance Philology,* 1 (1948), 305–27. Nevertheless, the overwhelming majority of references in the various sections of John H. Fisher, *The Medieval Literature of Western Europe, a Review of Research, Mainly 1930–1960* (New York: New York University Press, 1966), are to studies of the more "traditional" sort. The listings in Helmut Hatzfeld's two extensive bibliographies show that medieval studies remain the least affected by newer currents in literary analysis: *Critical Bibliography of the New Stylistics as Applied to the Romance Literatures, 1900–1952* (Chapel Hill, N.C.: University of North Carolina Press, 1953) and *Critical Bibliography . . . , 1953–1965* (Chapel Hill, N.C.: University of North Carolina Press, 1966).

22. Concerning modern shifts in emphasis on the relationship author-

work-audience, see M. H. Abrams, *The Mirror and the Lamp: Romantic Theory and the Critical Tradition* (New York: Oxford University Press, 1953), Chapter I, "Introduction: Orientation of Critical Theories."

23. Morley's comments are part of a review of a monographic article by Menéndez Pidal; the review is published in *Romanic Review*, 9 (1918), 347–51.

24. It is ironic to note that one of the conclusions of Beatie's article is that the medieval collections are of dubious value to the folklorist in determining the presence of a true oral creative tradition of ballad composition; *op. cit.*, p. 110.

Chapter Three

1. All known surviving epic materials are reviewed by Ramón Menéndez Pidal in *Reliquias de la poesía española* (Madrid: Espasa-Calpe, 1951).

2. This sort of relationship is reviewed by S. Griswold Morley, "Spanish Ballad Problems. The Native Historical Themes," *University of California Publications in Modern Philology*, 13 (1925), 207–28; and by Ramón Menéndez Pidal, *La epopeya castellana a través de la literatura española* (Buenos Aires: Espasa-Calpe, 1945).

3. See Ramón Menéndez Pidal's study of this problem in "Rodrigo el último godo," in his *Floresta de leyendas heroicas* (Madrid: Espasa-Calpe, 1926), II.

4. The details of this source for the ballads are given in Ramón Menéndez Pidal, *Romancero tradicional de las lenguas hispánicas* . . . (Madrid: Gredos, 1957), I, 3–12. This is the best existing source for historical ballads (other than those dealing with the Cid and the Siege of Zamora) and background materials.

5. Hugh Nelson Seay, Jr. gives objective support for this conclusion in his thesis. See "A Classification of Motifs in the Traditional Ballads of Spain," *Dissertation Abstracts*, 19 (1959), 2052.

6. Unusual usage of verbal tense is a recurring characteristic of the ballads. Leo Spitzer first dwells on it in "Stilisch-syntaktisches aus den spanisch-portugiesischen Romanzen," *Zeitschrift für romanische Philologie*, 35 (1911), 192–230, 258–308. José Szertics devotes an entire study to the problem, *Tiempo y verbo en el Romancero viejo* (Madrid: Gredos, 1967). Although some tense "irregularities" may be related to matters of style, as Szertics claims, in many cases archaic, dialectical, and simply careless usage is more at issue.

7. I have not been able to examine Mariano Vidal Tolosana's article on the "psychology" of Rodrigo: "El rey don Rodrigo, o un ensayo de psicología histórica," *La lectura*, 19 (1919), 269–80.

8. In his pamphlet, *Tragic Themes in Spanish Ballads* (London: Hispanic and Luso-Brazilian Councils, 1958).

9. See Ramón Menéndez Pidal's study, *La leyenda de los Infantes de Lara* (Madrid: Hernando, 1934).

10. Background materials to the known texts are provided in *Romancero tradicional . . . ,* II, 85–95.

11. See the version reproduced in C. Colin Smith's anthology, *Spanish Ballads* (Oxford: Pergamon, 1964), p. 78, line 100.

12. To the best of our knowledge, no one has ever attempted to examine the early Spanish ballad in terms of prevalent medieval rhetorical procedures. The great majority of these procedures dealing with organization and presentation derive from the influential *Rhetorica ad Herennium* (c. 86–82 B.C.; attributed to Cicero). It is worth noting that rhetoric was conceived during Antiquity as "the art of public speaking and debate" (cf. the oral nature of the ballads), and it is only during the late medieval period that rhetoric and poetic—the art of writing verse—became synonymous. See Charles Sears Baldwin, *Medieval Rhetoric and Poetic (to 1400) Interpreted from Representative Works* (New York: Macmillan, 1928).

13. Attention is called to the change in assonantal rhyme at line 52. Such change is frequent in a long ballad that may represent the running together of scattered passages from the source epic.

14. For an extensive examination of the ballads as a compendium of folk ideology, see Glenroy Emmons' dissertation, "The *Romancero* as an Expression of the Spanish People: an Analysis of Medieval Spanish Ideology as Seen in the Oldest Historical Ballads," *Dissertation Abstracts,* 16 (1956), 2456.

15. This ballad is analyzed in Chapter Two by Paul Bénichou, *Creación poética en el Romancero tradicional* (Madrid: Gredos, 1968).

16. See Ramón Menéndez Pidal's comments in *Romancero hispánico . . .* (Madrid: Espasa-Calpe, 1953), I, 229–34.

17. See H. A. Paludan's contrastive study of the subject, "La fille épouse le meurtrier de son père. Remarques sur quelques 'romances' danois et espagnols," *Revista de filología española,* 13 (1926), 262–78. Concerning the subsequent popularity of the story, see A. Hämel, *Der Cid im spanischen drama des XVI und XVII Jahrhunderts* (Halle: M. Niemeyer, 1910).

18. Ramón Menéndez Pidal examines the versions and sources of this ballad in his study "'En Santa Gadea de Burgos,'" *Revista de filogia española,* 1 (1915), 357–77.

19. This is one of the thrusts of Edmund De Chasca's study, *El arte juglaresco en el "Cantar de Mio Cid"* (Madrid: Gredos, 1967).

20. See David William Foster, "Nota sobre la 'Afrenta de Corpes' y la unidad expresiva del *Poema de Mio*," *Romance Notes,* 12 (1970), 219–24.

21. See Ernst Robert Curtius' comments in *European Literature and the Latin Middle Ages* (New York: Pantheon, 1953), p. 202. The references come at the end of Chapter 10, "The Ideal Landscape," which examines the pathetic fallacy of idealized landscapes used in medieval literature.

22. William Rose, "El número en el 'Romancero del Cid,'" *Hispania,* 44 (1961), 454–56. The frequency with which numbers are used with sacramental meaning in religious and parareligious writings of the Middle Ages can lead to an indiscriminate application of those meanings to secular literature. While such application may be revealing, other evidence must also be provided in support of an interpretation in order to avoid critical subjectivity. Concerning numerical symbolism, see Curtius, Excursuses XV and XVI.

23. In the ballad "Al cielo poden justicia" ("They demand Heaven's justice"), Ordoño counsels the battered daughters:

35	*Llorando les dice:—¡Primas,*	(Crying he says to them: "Cousins,
	secretos del cielo son!	these are Heaven's secrets!
	No tuvo la culpa el Cid,	The Cid was not at fault,
	que el rey fué quien os casó;	for the King was the one who married you.
	mas buen padre tenéis, primas,	But your father is good, cousins,
40	*que vuelva por vueso honor.*	let him return your honor.")

(p. 188)

Chapter Four

1. *The Literature of the Spanish People, from Roman Times to the Present Day* (New York: Meridian, 1957).

2. Glenroy Emmons, "The Historical and Literary Perspective of the 'Romances Moriscos Novelescos,'" *Hispania,* 44 (1961), 254–59, summarizes this relationship with particular reference to the late ballads.

3. See Ramón Menéndez Pidal, *Romancero hispánico* . . . (Madrid: Espasa-Calpe, 1953), I, 301–16; II, 6–12.

4. For example, Luis Seco de Lucena Paredes, *Investigaciones sobre el Romancero. Estudios de tres romances fronterizos* (Granada: Universidad, 1958), offers evidence in support of late, sixteenth-century composition.

5. D. Bodmer, *Die granadinischen Romanzen in der europäischen Literatur* . . . (Zürich: Jruis, 1955), investigates the relationship of the Granada ballads with Pérez de Hita's work and their subsequent European diffusion. See also Manuel Álvar López, *Granada y el Romancero* (Granada: Universidad, 1956).

6. Our text is from C. Colin Smith, *Spanish Ballads* (Oxford: Pergamon Press, 1964), pp. 125–26.

7. See, for example, Erasmo Buceta, "Un dato sobre la historicidad del romance de 'Abenámar,'" *Revista de filología española,* 6 (1919), 57–59; and José María de Cossío, "Sobre Abenámar," *Boletín de la Biblioteca Menéndez Pelayo,* 11 (1929), 266–67.

8. Paul Bénichou, *Creación poética en el Romancero tradicional* (Madrid:

Gredos, 1968), "Abenámar," pp. 61–92. The quote is our translation of Bénichou's comments in Spanish.

9. As does Bénichou, pp. 79–85.

10. Menéndez Pidal considers this an unfortunate aspect of the text, and eliminates it in his version in the anthology which we have been using.

11. It must be remembered that our ballad does *not* describe the confrontation between two military leaders. Abenámar, as far as the composition is concerned, is an unknown entity as Bénichou's statement hopes to point out. Thus, the ballad does not directly concern opposing military might. However, as a matter of fact, most introductions to the ballad identify Abenámar as a Moorish chieftain who enlists Juan's support in order to become subsequently Yuçuf IV, ruler of Granada (1431–1432). The general orientation of the ballad appears to maintain the notion that Abenámar, while he may not necessarily be the vassal of Juan, as some historical interpretations have insisted, is nevertheless not his military opponent either.

12. It is worth noting that there is one set of variants with a considerably different ending. The version quoted in Menéndez Pidal's anthology reflects this difference, which relates how Juan, after having been refused by Granada, gathers his troops and leads a successful expedition against the city. If she cannot be his by choice, she will be his by force. Such a conclusion represents a major type of variant and the texts which so end can only be considered, in the light of our comments in Chapter 2, two completely different poems. The principal reason for this assertion is that our understanding of the composition is significantly altered if Juan is to assert himself militarily in order to make Granada his. Rather than a subtle and ironic ballad that makes obvious the noble superiority of the city, we have instead a pathetic humiliation of her through the monarch's use of force. This may indeed increase our sympathy for Granada and generate outright loathing for Juan and what he represents, but it is a "meaning" for the ballad completely different in tone to the text which we have analyzed and as a consequence merits treatment as a similar but significantly different ballad on basically the same theme.

13. B. González de Escandón, "Notas estilísticas sobre los romances fronterizos," *Universidad* [Zaragoza], 22 (1945), 442–62.

14. In turn "emplea" and "empleara" constitute a chiasmus, a procedure whereby the sequence "A B" is repeated in the form "B A," presumably for clever stylistic effect. An incident of chiasmus may involve identical phrases (but in their opposing orders) or virtually identical ones, as is the case with lines 30–31.

15. The implication of this phrase is examined in detail in David William Foster, "La representación formal de la estructura poética," *Revista hispánica moderna* (to appear).

Chapter Five

1. An exchange on this point is to be found in P. Rajna, "Osservazioni e dubbi concernenti la storia delle romanze spagnuole," *Romanic Review,* 6 (1915), 1–41, who argues for an earlier dating than the rest of the *Romancero viejo,* and Ramón Menéndez Pidal, in particular in his answer to Rajna in "Poema y canción," *Revista de filología española,* 3 (1916), 239–54, where the claim is made that as traditional ballads the novelesque texts are contemporaneous with the historical ballads.

2. See Alfonso el Sabio's thirteenth-century poem on the interrelationship of pagan and Marian May, discussed in David William Foster, "Medieval Poetic Tradition in Two *Cantigas profanas* by Alfonso el Sabio," *Romance Notes,* 8 (1967), 297–304.

3. An excellent presentation of this type of poetry is by Eugenio Asensio, "La poética del paralelismo," in *Poética y realidad en el cancionero peninsular de la edad media* (Madrid: Gredos, 1957), 75–132.

4. G. J. Geers makes reference to the principal issues of the debate in "El problema de los romances," *Neophilogogus,* 5 (1920), 193–99.

5. The most comprehensive study of what might be called "patterned" poetic diction is to be found in Dámaso Alonso and Carlos Bousoño, *Seis calas en la expresión literaria española . . . ;* 2. ed. (Madrid: Gredos, 1956).

6. The nonspecialist should be reminded that medieval Romance love poetry in the Peninsula means Portuguese or Catalan, since there is virtually no surviving tradition in the dialects known today as Spanish.

7. As brought out in Johan Huizinga's important study, *The Waning of the Middle Ages . . .* (Garden City, N.Y.: Doubleday, 1954).

8. See the following studies that refer to the relationship between the shorter and longer versions of the ballads: Leo Spitzer, "The Folkloristic Prestage of the Spanish Romance 'Conde Arnaldos,'" *Hispanic Review,* 23 (1955), 173–87; 24 (1956), 64–66 (earlier observations are to be found in Leo Spitzer, "Notas sobre romances españoles," *Revista de filología española,* 22 (1955), 153–74, 290–91); and Ramón Menéndez Pidal, *Poesía popular y poesía tradicional en la literatura española* (Oxford: Oxford University Press, 1922), where this ballad is given as demonstrative of the process of traditionalization.

9. In fact, in many dialects of Spanish the phrase *una casa sobre el mar* means a "seaside home." See the second principal definition of *sobre* given by the *Diccionario de la Real Academia Española.*

10. Concerning Midsummer as a literary theme, see J. T. Reid, "St. John's Day in Spanish Literature," *Hispania,* 18 (1935), 401–12.

11. Leo Spitzer discusses the influence of sea legends in "The Folkloristic Prestage . . ." (note 8).

12. See in this regard J. R. R. Tolkien's scholarly essay "On Fairy-

stories," reprinted in *The Tolkien Reader* (New York: Ballantine Books, 1966), second pagination, pp. 3–84.

13. The only scholarly attempt with which we are familiar to place the scant examples of Spanish fantasy literature within an international context is that of Jorge Luis Borges, *Antología de la literatura fantástica,* 3a ed. (Buenos Aires: Sudamericana, 1967). Although the Argentines have cultivated impressively the fantasy story as a separate genre, other Hispanic examples are not outstanding.

14. T. R. Hart, "'El Conde Arnaldos' and the Medieval Scriptural Tradition," *Modern Language Notes,* 72 (1957), 281–85.

15. See the introduction to David William Foster, *Christian Allegory in Early Hispanic Poetry* (Lexington, Ky.: The University Press of Kentucky, 1971). See also the symposium papers on panallegorism reproduced as "Patristic Exegesis in the Criticism of Medieval Literature," in Dorothy Bethurum, *Critical Approaches to Medieval Literature* (New York: Columbia University Press, 1960), pp. 1–82.

16. One of the most readily available is *The Bestiary, a Book of Beasts, being a Translation from a Latin Bestiary of the Twelfth Century,* made and edited by T. H. White (New York: G. P. Putnam's Sons, 1954). The turtledove and her legendary fidelity are discussed on pp. 145–46.

17. See the following studies: Eugenio Asensio, "'Fonte frida,' o encuentro del romance con la canción de Mayo," in *Poética y realidad . . . ,* pp. 241–77; Marcel Bataillon, "La tortolica de 'Fontefrida' y del 'Cántico espiritual,'" in *Varia lección de clásicos españoles* (Madrid: Gredos, 1964), pp. 144–66; D. Gazdaru, "Antecedentes latinos del tema literario de 'Fonte frida,'" *Anales de filología clásica,* 6 (1953–1954), 81–91; D. Gazdaru, "La suerte en Provenza y Cataluña del tema literario de Fontefrida," *Filología,* 7 (1961), 51–59.

18. Indeed the second part of the few surviving Castilian lyric texts of the twelfth century, the "Razón de amor" ("The Gloss on Love"), reveals a strong resemblance to "Fontefrida" in its use of birds and symbolic water. See Alfred B. Jacob, "The *Razón* as Christian Symbolism," *Hispanic Review,* 20 (1952), 282–301.

19. The only close biblical support is in St. Paul, 1 Corinthians 7: 8–9, where the author argues for the nonremarriage of widows, although his context is more one of being against marriage to begin with rather than the fidelity of widows.

20. The best discussion of courtly love for Spanish literature is to be found in Volume I of Otis H. Green, *Spain and the Western Tradition . . .* (Madison, Wisc.: University of Wisconsin Press, 1963–1966).

21. We quote from C. Colin Smith, *Spanish Ballads* (Oxford: Pergamon Press, 1964), pp. 197–98. W. J. Entwistle traces the development of the theme in "Blancaniña," *Revista de filología hispánica,* 1 (1939), 159–64.

22. Ramiro Ortiz, "Il 'Romance de Moriana,'" *Zeitschrift für romani-*

sche Philologie, 51 (1931), 707–21, presents a brief explication of the text.

23. We might mention at this point a ballad which is far too extensive— unusually so—to be included in this discussion. The "Ballad of Count Alarcos" is one of the most important of the novelesque ballads for its development of themes of courtly love in terms of a central conflict of broken marriage contract and the treachery, murder, and tragedy detailed with great artistic maturity. See the exhaustive study by Guido Mancini, *La romanza del Conde Alarcos. Note per una interpretazione* (Pisa: Goliardica, 1959), and the note by Vernon A. Chamberlin, "Origin and Significance of the Name 'Alarcos,'" *Symposium,* 13 (1959), 117–20.

24. Our text is from Smith, *op. cit.,* p. 182. We have not been able to examine Dámaso Alonso, "La leyenda de Tristán e Iseo y su influjo en España," In André Mary, *Tristán* (Barcelona, 1947), pp. 189–204.

25. Chiasmus is one of the recurring devices examined by Leo Spitzer, "Stilisch-syntakisches aus den spanischen-portugiesischen Romanzen," *Zeitschrift für romanische Philologie,* 35 (1911), 192–230, 258–308.

26. José Szertics, *Tiempo y verbo en el Romancero viejo* (Madrid: Gredos, 1967).

27. See José María Chacón y Calvo, "Conde Olinos," in his *Ensayos de literatura española* (Madrid: Hernando, 1928), pp. 123–51; W. J. Entwistle, "El Conde Olinos," *Revista de filología española,* 35 (1951), 237–48; and "Second Thoughts Concerning 'El Conde Olinos,'" *Romance Philology,* 7 (1953), 10–18.

28. In his *Flor nueva . . . ,* p. 129.

29. See the entry for "Cock" in J. E. Cirlot, *A Dictionary of Symbols* (New York: The Philosophical Library, 1962 [orig. published in Spanish in 1958]), p. 49.

Chapter Six

1. See the detailed studies by Jules Horrent, "Les Romances," in his *La Chanson de Roland dans les littératures française et espagnole* (Paris: Les Belles Lettres, 1951), pp. 503–28; and "Sur les romances carolingiens de Roncevaux," *Lettres romanes,* 9 (1955), 161–76. Horace S. Craig's presentation is more superficial: "A Study in 'Los romances del ciclo carolingio,'" *Modern Language Forum,* 25 (1940), 117–24.

2. See J. de Perott's comments on the relationships between ballads and books of chivalry in "Reminiscencias de romances en libros de caballerías," *Revista de filología española,* 2 (1915), 289–92.

3. See W. J. Entwistle, *European Balladry* (Oxford: The Clarendon Press, 1939), pp. 175ff.

4. Ramón Menéndez Pidal has two important studies on this group: "'Roncesvalles.' Un nuevo cantar de gesta español del siglo XIII," *Revista de filología española,* 4 (1917), 105–204; and "Sobre 'Roncesvalles' y la

crítica de los romances carolingios," *Revista de filología española*, 5 (1918), 396–98. The latter is a response to S. Griswold Morley's review of the first study, published in *Romanic Review*, 9 (1918), 347–51.

5. Craig, *op. cit.*, p. 122.

6. This ballad has been studied in terms of its French sources in Menéndez Pidal's articles cited in note 4 and by Ángelo Monteverdi, "Der Traum der schönen Alda," *Archiv für das Studium der neueren Sprachen und Literaturen*, 128 (1912), 202–4. See also Monteverdi's study of Alda in the French epic: "Alda la bella," *Studi medievali*, n.s., 1 (1928), 362–79.

7. All ballads quoted in this chapter are from C. Colin Smith's collection, *Spanish Ballads* (Oxford: Pergamon Press, 1964).

8. *Tragic Themes in Spanish Ballads* (London: Hispanic and Luso-Brazilian Councils, 1958).

9. See Ramón Menéndez Pidal, "Sobre geografía folklórica. Ensayo de un método," *Revista de filología española*, 7 (1920), 229–338; revised and published with other studies on this ballad (among others) in Ramon Menéndez Pidal, *et al.*, *Cómo vive un romançe. Dos ensayos sobre tradicionalidad* (Madrid: Consejo Superior de Investigaciones Científicas, 1954). For a presentation of one of the modern versions, see A. González Palencia, "Romance de Gerineldo en Albarracín," in his *Moros y cristianos en España medieval* (Madrid: Consejo Superior de Investigaciones Científicas, 1945), pp. 337–44.

10. There is, in addition, a third possibility. We know that some editors were not hesitant to alter the texts which they were collecting, and what was printed may often have been only an editor's own contribution to the process of modification that was so natural to the development of the ballads.

11. *Op. cit.*, p. 103.

12. The complete text of "Gerineldos" is to be found in Smith, *op. cit.*, pp. 183–84.

13. The theme is studied in Spanish literature by B. González de Escandón, *Los temas del "Carpe diem" y la brevedad de la rosa en la poesía española* (Barcelona: Clarasó, 1943).

Selected Bibliography

(Particularly important works have been marked with an asterisk)

PRIMARY SOURCES

1. Bibliography

SIMÓN DÍAZ, JOSÉ. "... Romanceros (ediciones ...)," in his *Bibliografía de la literatura hispánica* (Madrid: Consejo Superior de Investigaciones Científicas, 1960), III/2, 2–108, 527–28. A listing is provided of all known ballad collections from the sixteenth century on, along with notices of modern editions. Important not only for the completeness of coverage, but also for the detailed listing of contents of the major collections.

2. Modern Collections

DURÁN, AGUSTÍN. *Romancero general, o colección de romances castellanos anteriores al siglo XVIII* (Madrid: Rivadeneira, 1849–1851). (Biblioteca de Autores Españoles, vv. 10, 16.)

GARCÍA SOLALINDE, ANTONIO. *Cien romances escogidos* (Madrid: M. Jiménez-Fraud, 1919).

*MENÉNDEZ PIDAL, RAMÓN. *Flor nueva de romances viejos* (Madrid: La Lectura, 1928, and numerous subsequent editions).

*———, et al. *Romancero tradicional de las lenguas hispánicas (español, portugués, catalán, sefardí)* (Madrid: Gredos, 1957–). The intent is to present a detailed study along with texts of the traditional ballads. Several major scholars are involved in the compilation, and the product is an important contribution. Accompanies Menéndez Pidal (1953; 2 vols; q.v.).

MORLEY, S. GRISWOLD. *Spanish Ballads (romances escogidos)* (New York: Henry Holt, 1911).

SANTULLO, LUIS. *Romancero español* (Madrid: Aguilar, 1935).

SMITH, C. COLIN. *Spanish Ballads* (Oxford: Pergamon Press, 1964). The texts of this excellent anthology were taken principally from the Wolf and Hofmann collection.

*WOLF, FERDINAND JOSEPH, and C. HOFMANN. *Primavera y flor de romances* (Berlin: G. Lange, 1856). Reprinted with additions by Marcelino Menéndez y Pelayo, *Antología de poetas líricos castellanos* (Madrid:

Hernando, 1890–1908), vv. 8–9. It is this collection from which scholarly studies have tended to quote.

SECONDARY SOURCES

1. *General Ballad Criticism*

(a) Introduction, Histories, Problems

ÁLVAR LÓPEZ, MANUEL. "Patología y terapéutica rapsódicas. Cómo una canción se convierte en romance," *Revista de filología española,* 42 (1958–1959), 19–35. Promotes thesis that part of the development of variants is due to the "corrective therapy" applied by anonymous tradition to "pathologically defective" compositions. This highly animistic thesis is demonstrated in terms of some known textual variants.

ATKINSON, W. C. "The Interpretation of 'Romances e cantares' in Santillana," *Hispanic Review,* 4 (1936), 1–10. Discusses Santillana's vague use of the phrase to mean probably "poetic songs in Spanish."

———. "The Chronology of Spanish Ballad Origins," *Modern Language Review,* 32 (1937), 44–61. By use of chronological data, some weaknesses of the fragmentation theory are indicated.

*BEATIE, BRUCE A. "Oral-Traditional Composition in the Spanish Romancero of the Sixteenth Century," *Journal of Folklore Institute,* 1 (1964), 92–113. A valuable examination of the Spanish ballad within the framework of non-Hispanic research on the creative process of oral transmission. This research offers some support for the traditionalist view. Also dealt with is the view that the Carolingian ballads may be the most traditional/"folkloric" rather than the most literary.

*BÉNICHOU, PAUL. *Creación poética en el Romancero tradicional* (Madrid: Gredos, 1968). Studies three examples of traditional "composition" in the medieval ballad and three examples of modern descendent versions of medieval texts. Focuses on the creative, "poetic" working of the traditional process.

*CATALÁN MENÉNDEZ PIDAL, DIEGO. "El 'motivo' y la 'variación' en la transmisión tradicional del Romancero," *Bulletin hispanique,* 61 (1959), 149–82. Treats various versions of a ballad toward establishing controlling principles of the collective change and development of the ballad tradition.

CIROT, G. "Le mouvement quaternaire dans les romances," *Bulletin hispanique,* 21 (1919), 103–42. Response to Morley (1916; q.v.). Provides evidence for thesis that the organization of the ballads is on the basis of quatrain units, suggesting relationship with nonpopular poetry but admitting that content "overwhelms" any original strophic format.

————. "Deux notes sur les rapports entre romances et chroniques," *Bulletin hispanique*, 30 (1928), 250–55. Although general line of influence may be that of ballads on chronicles, Cirot offers some examples of ballads derived from the latter.

CLARKE, DOROTHY CLOTELLE. "Metric Problems in the 'Cancionero de romances,'" *Hispanic Review*, 23 (1955), 188–99. A descriptive and analytic study of the metric problems posed by medieval ballad texts.

*DEVOTO, DANIEL. "Sobre el estudio folklórico del Romancero español. Proposición para un método de estudio de la transmisión tradicional," *Bulletin hispanique*, 57 (1955), 233–91. After reviewing historical and literary work on the Romancero, Devoto defends vigorously the importance of admitting the role of folkloric sources in the study of ballad origins, development, and diffusion of specific works. There is abundant reference to Jungian and other theories of archetypal patterns.

*ENTWISTLE, WILLIAM JAMES. *European Balladry* (Oxford: The Clarendon Press, 1939 [available in a 1969 reprint]). A thorough and definitive study of European balladry from social, anthropological and historical points of view. Although there is little emphasis on artistic issues, it is important for placing the Hispanic ballad within the context of other European traditions.

FOULCHÉ-DELBOSC, R. *Essai sur les origines du Romancero. Prélude* (Paris: F. Paillart, 1912). Also published as *Ensayo sobre los orígenes del Romancero* . . . (Madrid: P. Pérez de Velasco, 1914). A trenchant critique of Ménendez Pidal's early opinions on the Romancero. Foulché adheres to the belief of individual—professional or amateur —authorship, without denying that *some* ballads may contain epic fragments. See Menéndez Pidal, "Los orígenes . . ." for a reply. A study not of the quality of the French Hispanist's other work.

*GARCÍA BLANCO, M. "El Romancero," in Guillermo Diaz-Plaja, *Historia general de las literaturas hispánicas* (Barcelona: Barna, 1949–1958), II, 3–51. An excellent introduction to the subject, with good documentation.

GEERS, G. J. "El problema de los romances," *Neophilologus*, 5 (1920), 193–99. A major statement of doubt in the all-encompassing validity of traditionalist views. In the face of the lack of documentary evidence, Geers suggests that to consider as coeval ballads and other medieval lyric poetry is equally valid.

MEJÍA, LEONOR M. "An Investigation of Spanish Ballad Originals," *Stanford University Abstracts of Dissertations*, 12 (1936–1937), 52–54. Abstract of an unpublished Ph.D. dissertation, Stanford University, 1937. An exhaustive attempt to validate further the fragmentation theory of Spanish ballad origins. Discusses major epic theories before treating in detail the question of ballad origins.

*MENÉNDEZ PIDAL, RAMÓN. *El Romancero español* (New York: Hispanic

Society of America, 1910). A series of lectures given at Columbia University, 5–7 April 1909. This early work sketches the author's basic position concerning the origins of the ballads in epic fragmentation and discusses the modern interest of both poets and critics in the ballad. Still a valuable introduction after more than sixty years.

————. "Los orígenes del Romancero," in *Los romances de América y otros estudios* (Buenos Aires: Espasa-Calpe Argentina, 1939), pp. 95–115 [orig. 1914]. Review of Foulché-Delbosc, *Essai,* q.v.

*————. "Poesía popular y Romancero," *Revista de filología española,* 1 (1914), 357–77; 2 (1915), 1–20, 105–36, 329–38; 3 (1916), 233–89. A series of ten essays, five dealing with texts and five with various important aspects of the ballads. One of Pidal's first extensive formulations of his theories.

————. "Sobre geografía folklórica. Ensayo de un método," *Revista de filología española,* 7 (1920), 229–338. Examines types of popular diffusion of ballad texts.

*————. *Poesía popular y poesía tradicional en la literatura española* (Oxford: Oxford University Press, 1922). Also published in *Los romances de América y otros estudios* (Buenos Aires: Espasa-Calpe Argentina, 1939), pp. 52–95. A general restatement, valuable particularly for the analysis of the ballad "Conde Arnaldos" in the light of traditionalist theories.

————. *El Romancero. Teorías e investigaciones* (Madrid: Páez, 1928). The nucleus of the reprint *Los romances de América,* q.v., whose pertinent contents are listed separately here.

————. "Poesía tradicional en el Romancero hispano-portugués," in *Castilla: la tradición, el idioma* (Madrid: Espasa-Calpe, 1945), pp. 41–74. Surveys theories on the nature of popular poetry, contrasting the latter with "individual art," which is rejected for the ballad. The latter must be given separate treatment for its unique development.

————. *Cómo vivió y cómo vive el Romancero* (Valencia: López Mezquita, 1947). A series of essays discussing with detailed examples the temporal and geographic distribution of traditional ballads.

————. *Romancero hispánico (hispano-portugués, americano y sefardí). Teoría e historia* (Madrid: Espasa-Calpe, 1953). 2 vols. In 23 chapters, each devoted to a major topic on the traditional ballad, this study represents the most detailed and exhaustive presentation of the subject. Particularly valuable for comments on important texts.

*————, et al. *Cómo vive un romance. Dos ensayos sobre tradicionalidad* (Madrid: Consejo Superior de Investigaciones Científicas, 1954). This is an extensive revision of the author's 1920 study, "Sobre geografía . . ." (q.v.), followed by further research done by Diego Catalán and Álvaro Galmes de Fuentes.

*MENÉNDEZ Y PELAYO, MARCELINO. "Tratado de los romances viejos," in *Antología de poetas líricos castellanos* (Madrid: Hernando, 1890–1908), vv. 11–12. An extensive analysis of the ballads within the context of the first major history of Spanish poetry. An early adherence to the fragmentation theory of ballad origins.

*MILÁ Y FONTANALS, MANUEL. *De la poesía heroico-popular castellana* (Barcelona: Consejo Superior de Investigaciones Científicas, 1959 [orig. 1874]). The first major statement against Romantic theories on the epic and the ballad. Both genres are studied in detail and the basic outlines of the fragmentation theory are established with the evidence that the ballads result from the late medieval breakup of the epics.

MORLEY, S. GRISWOLD. "Are the Spanish Romances Written in Quatrains? —and Other Questions," *Romanic Review,* 7 (1916), 42–82. Basically an examination of metric problems of the ballads, with a discussion of possible strophic organization on the basis of quatrains. Dominant interest is in providing contra-traditionist evidence.

———. "Chronological List of Early Spanish Ballads," *Hispanic Review,* 13, (1945), 273–87. Some general lines are presented on the basis of known collections and dating.

PFANDL, LUDWIG. "La palabra española *romance,*" *Investigaciones lingüísticas,* 2 (1934), 242–62. Reviews the origins and uses of the word in Spanish.

*RAJNA, P. "Osservazioni e dubbi concernenti la storia delle romanze spagnuole," *Romanic Review,* 6 (1915), 1–41. An important review of theses concerning the supposed uniqueness of Spanish ballad development. Indicates a number of reasons for doubting the universal validity of fragmentation.

*SPITZER, LEO. "Stilisch-syntaktisches aus den spanisch-portugiesischen Romanzen," *Zeitschrift für romanische Philologie,* 35 (1911), 192–230, 258–308. Basically an extensive catalog of five syntactic-stylistic phenomena: Tense (which emerges as quite a confusing problem), Assymetry (article, preposition, verb, etc.), Parallelism, Chiasmus, Disjointed Constructions. One of the first detailed attempts to single out recurring linguistic features.

*SZERTICS SZOMBATI, JOSÉ. *Tiempo y verbo en el Romancero viejo* (Madrid: Gredos, 1967). Going beyond the cataloging of indicative verbal forms used, the study aims at conclusions of an affective or stylistic nature, particularly where unusual or unexpected usage is encountered. Major weakness lies in ignoring more recent linguistic research.

*WEBER, RUTH DEMAR. "Formulistic Diction in the Spanish Ballad," *University of California Publications in Modern Philology,* 34, No. 2 (1951), 175–277. Originially a 1948 University of California dissertation under the name of Ruth DeMar House. A statistical study of types of formulistic diction in examples of various ballad types or groups in the attempt to demonstrate that the older and more popular a version, the more likely it is to employ such diction, which is assumed by definition to be essentially popular and unindicative of formal "artistic poetry." Ignores formulistic diction as a component of Western "professional" rhetoric.

WEBER, RUTH HOUSE. "Ramón Menéndez Pidal and the Romancero," *Romance Philology*, 5 (1951), 12–25. An annotated bibliography of Menéndez Pidal's important and seminal studies.

WOLF, FERDINAND JOSEPH. *Über die Romanzen-Poesie der Spanier* (Wien: Gerold, 1847). An extensive examination of Spanish ballads from the point of view of Romantic theories of *Volkspoesie*.

(b) Special Topics

BRAND, MARK. "Magic, Superstition, and Miracles in the Spanish Ballads," *University of Arizona Abstracts of Theses*, 36 (1943), 10 [Master's Thesis]. Investigates evidence of belief in the supernatural in the Spanish ballads. Although examples of such belief are abundant, ballads involved are generally of Spanish origin.

DOLLFUS, L. "Les femmes du Romancero," in *Études sur le Moyen Âge espagnol* (Paris: E. Leroux, 1894), pp. 84–146. Discusses three groups —wives, maidens, Moorish women—that are the staple of the ballads.

*EMMONS, GLENROY. "The *Romancero* as an Expression of the Ideology of the Spanish People. An Analysis of Medieval Spanish Ideology as Seen in the Oldest Historical Ballads," *Dissertation Abstracts*, 16 (1956), 2456. A University of New Mexico dissertation. Considers the ballads as ideological documents, with a stress on their antimonarchic sentiment, the secular nature of Castile, their attitude toward the Moors.

REID, J. T. "St. John's Day in Spanish Literature," *Hispania*, 18 (1935), 401–12. Discusses the references to the folk festival in Spanish literature, particularly where Christian accommodation is involved.

*SEAY, HUGH NELSON, JR. "A Classification of Motifs in the Traditional Ballads of Spain," *Dissertation Abstracts*, 19 (1959), 2052. A University of North Carolina dissertation. Classifies ballad motifs on the basis of the Stith Thompson index. Classification supports assertion concerning emphasis of traditional Spanish ballads on "realism," the lack of supernatural, humorous, and moral content, and the preference for sex, love, punishment motifs.

*WILSON, E. M. *Tragic Themes in Spanish Ballads* (London: Hispanic and Luso-Brazilian Councils, 1958). A general survey for the English reader, with an excellent discussion of the "tragic" aspects of ballads that juxtapose happiness and misery with the sense of Fortune's mutability.

Foreign Influences

ENTWISTLE, W. J. "La chanson populaire française en Espagne," *Bulletin hispanique,* 51 (1949), 255–68. After stressing national balladry as the authentic voice of a people, Entwistle discusses the nature of the approximately one hundred clear cases of "naturalization" by the traditional Spanish ballad of both themes and music of French songs.

MICHÄELIS DE VASCONCELOS, CAROLINA. *Estudos sobre o Romanceiro peninsular;* 2a ed. (Coimbra: Imprenta da Universidade, 1934 [orig. 1907?]). Discusses those segments of the Spanish ballad tradition that are Portuguese in origin.

VIQUEIRA BARREIRO, J. M. "El Romancero, vínculo hispanolusitano," *Biblos,* 30 (1954), 245–46; 31 (1955), 125–391. Also published as a book (Coimbra: Coimbra Editôra, 1956). Studies history and textual relations between Hispanic and Portuguese ballad traditions. Particularly useful for parallel texts, influences, and internal references.

Music

MARTÍNEZ TORNER, E. "Indicaciones prácticas sobre la notación musical de los romances," *Revista de filología española,* 10 (1923), 389–94. Problems of musical notation in the ballads.

————. "Ensayo de clasificación de las melodías de romance," in *Homenaje a Menéndez Pidal* (Madrid: Hernando, 1925), II, 391–402. Discusses types of ballad melodies.

2. Ballad Groups

(a) Historical Ballads (Our Chapter 3)

FRANKLIN, ALBERT B., III. *The Origins of the Legend and Romancero: "Bernardo del Carpio."* Unpublished Ph.D. dissertation, Harvard University, 1938.

*MENÉNDEZ PIDAL, RAMÓN. *La leyenda de los Infantes de Lara* (Madrid: Hernando, 1896). A meticulous examination of all materials related to the legend; the third chapter of the first part deals with the ballads.

————. "Notas para el Romancero del conde Fernán González," in *Homenaje á Menéndez y Pelayo* (Madrid: V. Suárez, 1899), I, 429–507. Detailed discussion of prose and poetic texts related to the historical ballads on Fernán González.

*————. *La epopeya castellana a través de literatura española* (Buenos Aires: Espasa-Calpe Argentina, 1945 [orig. published in French in 1910]). Originally a series of lectures; the fourth chapter defends the fragmentation theory in detail with support from the Cid ballads. The fifth chapter is a comprehensive history of the ballad.

————. "'En Santa Gadea de Burgos,'" *Revista de filología española,* 1 (1915), 357–77. Examines in detail the three major versions of this ballad in support of their deriving from the survival of epic materials rather than from later chronicles.

————. *Poesía juglaresca y juglares* (Madrid: Espasa-Calpe, 1956 [orig. 1924]). A discussion of the role of medieval minstrels in medieval society and the diffusion of epic and epic-related poetry.

*————. "Rodrigo el último godo," in *Floresta de leyendas heroicas* (Madrid: Espasa-Calpe, 1926), II. (Clásicos Castellanos, v. 7.) Extensive treatment, with a collection of texts, of the Rodrigo theme in medieval poetry.

MORLEY, S. GRISWOLD. "Spanish Ballad Problems. The Native Historical Themes," *University of California Publications in Modern Philology,* 13 (1925), 207–28. Summary of the general characteristics of the earliest Spanish ballads on national-historical themes. Morley in general is not too enthusiastic about Menéndez Pidal's theories.

PALUDAN, H. A. "La fille épouse le meurtrier de son père. Remarques sur quelques 'romances' danois et espagnols," *Revista de filología española,* 13 (1926), 262–78. Concerns the relationship between the Ximena ballads and Danish versions of the theme of the "daughter marries her father's murderer."

ROSE, WILLIAM. "El número en el 'Romancero del Cid,'" *Hispania,* 44 (1961), 454–56. Reviews recurring number patterns in the Cid ballads and proposes that the most important have a magical as well as artistic function.

(b) Frontier Ballads (Our Chapter 4)

ÁLVAR LÓPEZ, MANUEL. *Granada y el Romancero* (Granada: Universidad, 1956). Discussion of famous ballads on the Conquest of Granada.

BODMER, D. *Die granadinischen Romanzen in der europäischen Literatur. Untersuchung und Texte* (Zürich: Jruis, 1955). Discusses four of the most important ballads on Granada, their relationship to Pérez de Hita's prose history and other poetic works, as well as their diffusion in European literature.

BUCETA, ERASMO. "Un dato sobre la historicidad del romance de 'Abenámar,'" *Revista de filología española,* 6 (1919), 57–59. New evidence that the ballad "Abenámar" relates a historical incident.

COSSÍO, JOSÉ MARÍA DE. "Sobre Abenámar," *Boletín de la Biblioteca Menéndez Pelayo,* 11 (1929), 266–67. Reiterates the position that the composition is a historical anecdote on a fifteenth-century event.

EMMONS, GLENROY. "The Historical and Literary Perspective of the 'Romances moriscos novelescos,'" *Hispania,* 44 (1961), 254–59. Attempts to explain Christian respect for and sentimentalization of

Moorish and pseudo-Moorish themes. Title is somewhat misleading, as emphasis is on preseventeenth-century developments.

GONZÁLEZ DE ESCANDÓN, B. "Notas estilísticas sobre los romances fronterizos," *Universidad* [Zaragoza], 22 (1945), 442–62. Discusses a series of stylistic features associated with frontier ballads and exemplifying opposing forces of conciseness and expansiveness.

*SECO DE LUCENA PAREDES, LUIS. ... *Investigaciones sobre el Romancero. Estudio de tres romances fronterizos* (Granada: Universidad, 1958). Takes exception to the "news story theory" concerning the composition of the frontier ballads. Focusing on "Abenámar," attempts to substantiate a later, sixteenth-century composition, based on the chronicles and other sources.

*SPITZER, LEO. "Los romances españoles: el romance de Abenámar," *Asomante,* 1 (1945), 7–29. Also published in *Sobre antigua poesía española* (Buenos Aires: Universidad de Buenos Aires, Facultad de Filosofía y Letras, 1962), pp. 59–84. Application of the *explication de texte* method to the *Romancero.* The main discussion of the artistic effect of the poem is followed by historical considerations. The *romance* is seen as a tour de force: "each *romance* is a fatal moment, inherent in its temporal structure."

(c) Novelesque Ballads (Our Chapter 5)

*ASENSIO, E. "'Fonte frida,' o encuentro del romance con la canción de Mayo," *Nueva revista de filología hispánica,* 8 (1954), 365–88. Also published in *Poética y realidad en el cancionero peninsular de la edad media* (Madrid: Gredos, 1957), pp. 241–72. Addressed to the problem of sources for the novelesque ballad, with an examination of the one ballad as the result of the confluence of clerical culture and the popular, folkloric songs of May festivities, with emphasis on the latter.

BATAILLON, MARCEL. "La tortolica de 'Fontefrida' y del 'Cántico espiritual,'" *Nueva revista de filología hispánica,* 7 (1953), 291–306. Also published in *Varia lección de clásicos españoles* (Madrid: Gredos, 1964), pp. 144–66. Rejects idea that the theme of the turtledove in the ballad is necessarily copied from folklore and traces its widespread use in nonpopular Western literature.

CHACÓN Y CALVO, JOSÉ MARÍA. "El conde Olinos," in *Ensayos de literatura española* (Madrid: Hernando, 1928), pp. 123–51. Traces the development of the legend and notes versions found in Spain, Portugal, and Cuba.

ENTWISTLE, WILLIAM J. "'Blancaniña,'" *Revista de filología hispánica,* 1 (1939), 159–64. Refers to occurrence, often in a far cruder form than in Spain, in several other countries of poems concerning the theme of the "adulteress punished."

————. "El Conde Olinos," *Revista de filología española,* 35 (1951), 237–48. Discusses origins, stressing Byzantine and refuting Celtic sources.

————. "Second Thoughts Concerning 'El Conde Olinos,'" *Romance Philology,* 7 (1953), 10–18. Discusses Spanish and French influences.

GAZDARU, D. "Antecedentes latinos del tema literario de 'Fontefrida,'" *Anales de filología clásica,* 6 (1953–1954), 81–91. Traces Greek, Egyptian, and various Oriental sources for the theme of the "loyal turtledove," stressing transmission via the Bestiaries. Maintains mythico-religious origins.

*HART, T. R. "'El conde Arnaldos' and the Medieval Scriptural Tradition," *Modern Language Notes,* 72 (1957), 281–85. Applies exegetical interpretation in order to demonstrate an allegorical reference to Christianity.

*SPITZER, LEO. "The Folkloristic Prestage of the Spanish Romance 'Conde Arnaldos,'" *Hispanic Review,* 23 (1955), 173–87; 24 (1956), 64–66. Also published as "Período previo folklórico del romance de 'Conde Arnaldos,'" in *Sobre antigua poesía española* (Buenos Aires: Universidad de Buenos Aires, Facultad de Filosofía y Letras, 1962), pp. 85–103. Discusses the origins of this famous ballad, particularly with reference to the longer version and the folkloristic legends of the "sea spirits."

(d) Carolingian Ballads (Our Chapter 6)

CRAIG, H. S. "A Study in 'Los romances del ciclo carolingio,'" *Modern Language Forum,* 25 (1940), 117–24. This is "a general explanation of the appearance in Spain of legends connected with the French Carolingian lore . . ." No new material.

*HORRENT, JULES. "Les Romances," in *La Chanson de Roland dans les littératures française et espagnole* (Paris: Les Belles Lettres, 1951), pp. 503–28. Examines six ballads from the *Romancero viejo* based on French epic material; an excellent introduction.

————. "Sur les romances carolingiens de Roncevaux," *Lettres romanes,* 9 (1955), 161–76. A general commentary.

*MENÉNDEZ PIDAL, RAMÓN. "'Roncesvalles.' Un nuevo cantar de gesta español del siglo XIII," *Revista de filología española,* 4 (1917), 105–204. Also published in a briefer form in *Tres poetas primitivos* (Buenos Aires: Espasa-Calpe Argentina, 1948), pp. 45–79. Presentation of a major Carolingian epic fragment in Spanish that influenced several important ballads.

————. "Sobre 'Roncesvalles' y la crítica de los romances carolingios," *Revista de filología española,* 5 (1918), 396–98. Reaffirms French epic sources of Carolingian ballads in answer to Morley's 1918 article (q.v.).

MORLEY, S. GRISWOLD. "[Review of Menéndez Pidal's *RFE,* 4 article],"

Romanic Review, 9 (1918), 347–51. Supports thesis of ballad originality as opposed to epic fragmentation, particularly on the principle that each ballad should be examined separately as an autonomous text.

OCHRYMOWYCZ, OREST R. "Aspects of Oral Style in the *Romances juglarescos* of the Carolinguian Cycle," *Dissertation Abstracts,* 29 (1969), 2222A. A University of Iowa doctoral dissertation. Using Parry-Lord theories, attempts to "determine the poetic function of devices characteristic of oral composition . . ." Includes some basic conclusions regarding esthetic effects of technical aspects discussed and defends the ballads involved as mature, conscious art.

Index